BLOOD
AND OIL

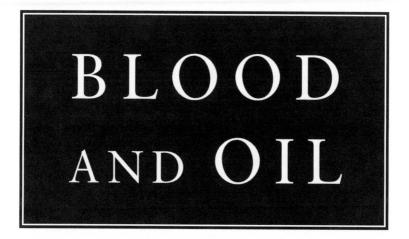

BLOOD AND OIL

The Dangers and Consequences of America's

Growing Petroleum Dependency

MICHAEL T. KLARE

METROPOLITAN BOOKS

HENRY HOLT AND COMPANY

NEW YORK

Metropolitan Books
Henry Holt and Company, LLC
Publishers since 1866
115 West 18th Street
New York, New York 10011

Metropolitan Books™ is a registered
trademark of Henry Holt and Company, LLC.

Copyright © 2004 by Michael T. Klare
All rights reserved.
Distributed in Canada by H. B. Fenn and Company Ltd.

Library of Congress Cataloging-in-Publication Data

Klare, Michael T., 1942–
    Blood and oil : the dangers and consequences of America's growing petroleum
dependency / Michael T. Klare.—1st ed.
        p. cm.
    Includes index.
    ISBN 0-8050-7313-2
        1. Petroleum industry and trade—United States. 2. Energy policy—United States. 3.
National security—United States. I. Title.
HD9566.K58 2004
333.8'232'0973—dc22   2004040278

Henry Holt books are available for special promotions and
premiums. For details contact: Director, Special Markets.

First Edition 2004
Designed by Fritz Metsch
Maps by Glenn Ruga
Printed in the United States of America
1   3   5   7   9   10   8   6   4   2

For my brother and sister,
Karl Ernest Klare and Jane Elizabeth Klare,
with eternal gratitude for their steadfast
loyalty and support

CONTENTS

PREFACE

There was a time, not so very long ago, when we thought that the end of the cold war would bring forth a world of greater peace and stability. Because so much of the strife of the cold-war era—in Korea, Vietnam, Afghanistan, and Central America, for example—was tied to the hostility between the United States and the Soviet Union, it was natural to assume that global violence would abate once the two superpowers ended their enmity. President George H. W. Bush even envisioned a "new world order," in which international disputes would be resolved through diplomacy and multilateral peacekeeping. But, of course, the new world order never materialized. We have seen as much armed conflict in the post-cold-war era as we saw earlier, and in some respects—notably the rise of terrorism—the world has become even more dangerous. Trying to explain this upsurge of violence in an era of diminished rivalry between the great powers is the most difficult task facing conflict analysts today.

To many observers, the explanation lies in identity politics—the reassertion of ethnic, religious, clan, and tribal ties in the wake of vanished ideologies and global disequilibrium. The best-known expression of this assessment was Harvard professor Samuel P. Huntington's influential 1993 *Foreign Affairs* article, "A Clash of Civilizations?" Dividing the world

into broad "civilizational" groupings—Western/Christian, Slavic/Ortho-
dox, Muslim, Hindu, and Confucian—Huntington argued that hostility
between these groups amounted to "the latest phase in the evolution of
conflict in the modern world." And, indeed, some of the most deadly encounters of the post-cold-war period, in such places as Bosnia, Kashmir,
and Chechnya, appear to bear out his theory. But many other wars and alliances of the past fifteen years do not—witness, for example, America's
partnership with such uncompromisingly Muslim states as Saudi Arabia
and the United Arab Emirates in the 1991 war against Iraq. Clearly, we
need to look for another explanation.

After examining a number of recent wars in Africa and Asia, I came to
a conclusion radically different from Huntington's: that *resources,* not
differences in civilizations or identities, are at the root of most contemporary conflict. In Angola and Sierra Leone, it was control of the dia-
mond fields that sustained the bloodshed for so long; in the Congo, gold
and copper; in Borneo and Cambodia, timber. Ethnic and religious antagonisms certainly played a role in these clashes, but usually as a mobi-
lizing ploy by the chieftains, warlords, and demagogues who were out to
dominate those promising sources of wealth. Time and again, my search
for the cause of a protracted war turned up a struggle over scarce or valuable materials: diamonds, gold, copper, old-growth timber, arable land,
fisheries, water—and, in several notable cases, oil.

When I presented these findings in my 2001 book *Resource Wars: The
New Landscape of Global Conflict,* I viewed all resources roughly the same
way: as vital materials whose growing scarcity in the twenty-first century
would trigger an endless series of hostilities unless we did a better job of
allocating the world's precious bounty. As I saw it, oil, water, land, and
minerals were each important enough to provoke a conflict when quantities were limited or when two or more groups laid claim to the same
source of supply. Oil would be a significant cause of conflict, but no more
so than any other resource.

Since then, a series of events has forced me to reevaluate that conclu-
sion. *Resource Wars* was published on May 17, 2001—the same day that
President George W. Bush's administration released its *National Energy
Policy,* prompting angry debate over the implications of our growing de-

pendence on imported oil and the merits of drilling in Alaska's Arctic National Wildlife Refuge (ANWR). Four months later, Al Qaeda operatives struck the World Trade Center in New York and the Pentagon in Washington, D.C. Suddenly terrorism became the nation's number-one security concern, triggering a new phase of U.S. military involvement in the Middle East. That fifteen of the nineteen hijackers were Saudis and that Saudi charities were linked to Al Qaeda brought new attention to America's ties with Saudi Arabia, our leading foreign oil supplier. Then, before long, President Bush and his lieutenants began talking about war with Iraq, once again raising the issue of oil as a factor in American foreign policy. All these developments compelled me to conclude that petroleum is unique among the world's resources—that it has more potential than any of the others to provoke major crises and conflicts in the years ahead.

Why should this be so? The answer was not immediately obvious. Of course, petroleum had been an important source of conflict throughout the twentieth century—but so, too, had water, land, and minerals. Now, in the twenty-first century, oil seemed to have outpaced all the others in its potential for sparking armed violence. To explain why *this* particular resource had acquired such a pivotal and volatile role, it seemed necessary to probe its significance more deeply. And so I undertook an intensive study of oil, geopolitics, and American foreign policy.

To some extent, this effort meant revisiting territory I had traveled before, notably the evolution of our country's ties with the oil producers of the Persian Gulf. Nevertheless, this old territory yielded some surprising revelations. For example, while President Franklin D. Roosevelt's February 1945 meeting with King Abdul Aziz ibn Saud of Saudi Arabia is well documented, there has been little recognition of the significance of that encounter, which produced the unprecedented oil-for-protection arrangement that has governed American ties with Saudi Arabia ever since. Just as striking is the saga of the Petroleum Reserves Corporation, an ill-fated but extraordinary effort by the Roosevelt administration to place Saudi Arabia's most prolific oil reservoirs under U.S. government ownership.

But my most crucial findings had to do with the centrality of cheap and abundant petroleum to the vigor and growth of the American economy and to the preservation of a distinctly *American* way of life. Although oil extraction and refining accounts for a relatively small share—perhaps 5 percent—of the nation's gross domestic product, the availability of vast quantities of relatively inexpensive petroleum is indispensable to a whole host of other industries, including automobile manufacture, road and highway construction, airlines, petrochemicals, agriculture, tourism, and suburban commerce. Taken together, these sectors make up the heart of the American economy, and without cheap oil they—and the way of life they make possible—could hardly survive.

And since cheap oil is essential to the nation's economic vigor, American leaders—of whatever party affiliation—have felt compelled to do whatever was necessary to ensure that enough was available to satisfy our ever-expanding requirements. Until the 1940s, this effort was primarily a *domestic policy* matter, since the United States possessed adequate untapped supplies to meet the country's basic needs. By the end of World War II, however, it was apparent that we would someday start to exhaust our reserves and would need large amounts of imported petroleum to supplement declining domestic supplies. At this point, oil became a *foreign policy* issue, with the federal government assuming a direct role in the pursuit of imported energy. And while the government has sometimes relied on private U.S. oil firms to initiate links with foreign producers, it has borne full responsibility for ensuring the security of our overseas energy investments.

In the process, oil has come to be treated differently from other trade commodities. The United States has long been dependent on foreign suppliers for critical materials like copper and cobalt, but this dependence has rarely shaped government policy. Oil, however, has been treated far more seriously, as a resource so vital to American prosperity that access to it must be protected at any cost, including the use of military force. In formal political discourse, petroleum is considered a *national security* matter—that is, a matter falling under the purview of the Department of Defense and other bodies responsible for safeguarding America's vital interests. In the name of national security, military force has frequently been used over the past fifty years to guarantee access to foreign petroleum and to protect such key suppliers as Saudi Arabia and Kuwait from internal revolt and external attack.

For most of this period, the public largely tolerated the deployment of the U.S. military in securing the global flow of petroleum. So long as oil remained abundant and the number of Americans who lost their lives in ensuring its availability remained low, people were generally prepared to look the other way as the United States established close ties with corrupt and repressive oil regimes. The federal government—and its partners in the oil industry—contributed to this tolerance by concealing the extent of their connivance with the Saudi royal family and other despotic suppliers. But 9/11 and its aftermath changed all that; it is now all too clear that these alliances have exposed the United States and its citizens to far greater risk of terrorism and oil-related conflict than anyone ever acknowledged, and the danger is growing. With domestic reserves facing long-term decline, we are becoming ever more dependent on foreign sources—and thus increasingly vulnerable to the violence and disorder that accompanies oil extraction in politically unstable and often hostile oil-producing countries.

The United States is not, of course, the only nation that needs more and more petroleum from providers in troubled areas. Europe and Japan are even more dependent on Persian Gulf oil than we are. And now China, with the world's fastest-growing economy, also needs additional energy from the Middle East. As a consequence, international competition for the same unreliable sources of supply is bound to intensify. To further complicate the picture, there are indications that the global supply of oil may start to contract in the not too distant future. While energy officials go on insisting that supplies will keep expanding in the years to come, some experts argue that we will soon reach "peak" worldwide oil output and then begin an irreversible decline. If these predictions prove accurate, less oil will be available, competition for it will increase, and, inevitably, the struggle for its control will become more and more acute.

Most Americans comprehend, at some basic level, that growing dependence on imported petroleum will expose us to a greater risk of involvement in foreign oil conflicts—as the multitude of placards screaming NO BLOOD FOR OIL in the antiwar demonstrations preceding the 2003 invasion of Iraq testified. But politicians and pundits regularly deny that there is any connection between blood and oil. "The only interest the United States has in the [Gulf] region is furthering the cause of peace and stability, not [Iraq's] ability to generate oil," President Bush's spokesperson, Ari Fleischer, avowed in late 2002. As the drive to war accelerated, Secretary of Defense Donald Rumsfeld declared, "This is not about oil, and anyone who thinks that, is badly misunderstanding the situation." We *know* that such statements cannot be true—the entire history of U.S. intervention in the Persian Gulf discredits them—yet most of us lack the information to see our way through these contradictions.

The United States now relies on imported petroleum for more than half of its total supply. Unless fundamental policies are changed, it can only become more profoundly dependent, ANWR or no ANWR. This incontrovertible conclusion makes the need for clarity all the more urgent, and we cannot rely on our leaders to provide it; they are far too invested in the status quo to be capable of candor. Only by tracing the evolution of U.S. oil policy and weighing its consequences for the future can we acquire the knowledge to do what it takes to sever the links between blood and oil. It is to that end that I have written this book.

BLOOD

AND OIL

The Dependency Dilemma:
Imported Oil and National Security

Tampa, Florida, is not one of the places you usually think of as a hub for American relations with the oil kingdoms of the Persian Gulf. It does not, like Houston, play host to any of the giant U.S. oil companies; it does not, like Washington, D.C., house the State Department and foreign embassies; and it does not, like New York, lay claim to the United Nations and the international news media. But Tampa does have something that none of those other cities can claim: the headquarters of the U.S. Central Command (Centcom), the nerve center for all U.S. military operations in the Persian Gulf region, including those now under way in Afghanistan and Iraq. Centcom forces, operating as they do in the greater Middle East, occupy the front lines in the war against terrorism and play a critical role in efforts to prevent the spread of weapons of mass destruction. From its very inception, however, Centcom's principal task has been to protect the global flow of petroleum.

Situated at MacDill Air Force Base in south-central Tampa, Centcom is one of the five regional "unified commands" that govern American combat forces around the world. (The others are the Southern Command, based in Miami; the European Command, based in Stuttgart; the Pacific Command, based in Honolulu; and the Northern Command, based in

Colorado Springs.) It is headed by a four-star general—currently General John P. Abizaid of the U.S. Army—and exercises direct command authority over all U.S. Army, Navy, Air Force, and Marine Corps contingents deployed in its "area of responsibility" (AOR), covering twenty-five mostly Muslim nations in the Persian Gulf area, the Horn of Africa, the Caspian Sea basin, and Southwest Asia. This vital but turbulent region includes Egypt, Iran, Iraq, Kuwait, Saudi Arabia, Somalia, Sudan, and Yemen.[1]

As its recent operations in Iraq and Afghanistan indicate, Centcom has emerged as one of the Pentagon's most important unified commands. It is not, however, the largest or best endowed. The European Command, in Stuttgart, has numerous bases in Europe and incorporates all the American forces assigned to NATO; the Pacific Command, in Honolulu, oversees powerful combat fleets and hundreds of thousands of troops in Asia and the Pacific. Centcom, in contrast, has few permanent operating bases of its own (other than MacDill) and has to borrow troops from the other commands when assembling a force to deploy in its AOR. What makes Centcom distinctive is that its forces inhabit an active war zone where American soldiers are fighting and dying on a daily basis.

The Central Command was formally established only two decades ago, on January 1, 1983. Since then, Centcom forces have fought in four major engagements: the Iran-Iraq War of 1980–88, the Persian Gulf War of 1991, the Afghanistan War of 2001, and the Iraq War of 2003. Centcom was also responsible for enforcing the containment of Saddam Hussein's Iraqi regime after the completion of Operation Desert Storm. Almost all the American soldiers who have died in combat since 1985 were serving under its authority, including the victims of terrorist attacks at the Khobar Towers in Saudi Arabia in June 1996 and aboard the USS *Cole* in October 2000.

Although Centcom's AOR stretches more than three thousand miles, from Egypt in the east to Kyrgyzstan in the west, its geographic and strategic heart is the Persian Gulf basin, the home of approximately two-thirds of the earth's known petroleum reserves. This area contains the world's five leading producers of oil—Iran, Iraq, Kuwait, Saudi Arabia, and the United Arab Emirates—and many of its most important suppliers of natural gas. Every day, tankers carrying approximately 14 million barrels of petroleum traverse the Gulf proper and pass through the narrow Strait of Hormuz on their way to markets around the world. Keeping this channel open and defeating any and all threats to the steady production of Persian Gulf oil is the overriding responsibility of Centcom forces.

The Central Command's basic mission was originally enunciated in the Carter Doctrine of January 23, 1980, which designated the secure

U.S. Central Command Area of Responsibility

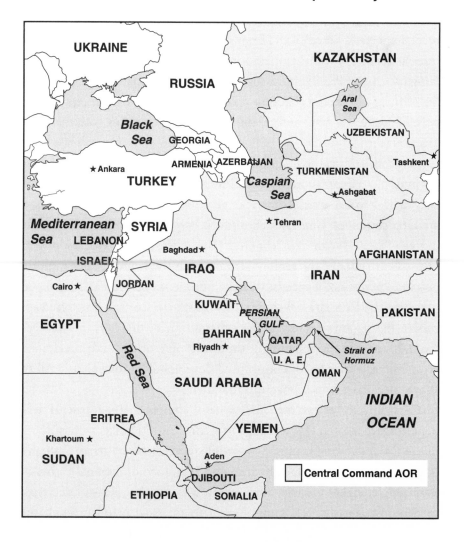

flow of Persian Gulf oil as a "vital interest" of the United States. Claiming that this key interest was threatened by the Soviet occupation of Afghanistan (which had begun in December 1979) and the near-simultaneous rise of a radical Islamic regime in Iran, President Jimmy Carter told Congress that Washington would use "any means necessary, including military force," to keep the oil flowing.[2] At that time, however, the United States had few forces in the Gulf and only a limited capacity to deploy additional troops in the region; moreover, authority over any American forces that might be deployed there was divided between the European and the Pacific commands, complicating coordination. In order to back up his proclamation, Carter established the Rapid Deployment Joint Task Force (RDJTF) at MacDill Air Force Base and gave it responsibility for combat operations in the Gulf. Three years later, on January 1, 1983, President Ronald Reagan elevated the RDJTF, naming it the Central Command (because it encompasses the "central region" between Europe and Asia) and putting it on an equal footing with the other regional commands.[3]

Centcom's critical role in protecting the nation's and its allies' oil supply finds blunt expression in the testimony its commanders in chief regularly deliver to Congress. "America's vital interests in the Central Region are long-standing," General J. H. Binford Peay III told a House subcommittee in 1997. "With over 65 percent of the world's oil reserves located in the Gulf states of the region—from which the United States imports nearly 20 percent of its needs; Western Europe, 43 percent; and Japan, 68 percent—the international community must have free and unfettered access to the region's resources." Any disruption in this flow, he warned, "would intensify the volatility of the world oil market [and] precipitate economic calamity for developed and developing nations alike."[4] All of Peay's successors have echoed this judgment.

Centcom's forces got their first taste of combat in 1987, when President Reagan ordered U.S. warships to escort Kuwaiti tankers—hastily reflagged with the American ensign—while traversing the Persian Gulf and to protect them from attack by Iran and Iraq, then in the final throes of their bloody eight-year war. Such action was essential, Reagan declared, to demonstrate the "U.S. commitment to the flow of oil through the

Gulf."[5] Three years later, in August 1990, President George H. W. Bush used similar language to justify the deployment of Centcom forces in Saudi Arabia, to deter a possible attack by the Iraqi forces then encamped in Kuwait. "Our nation now imports nearly half the oil it consumes and could face a major threat to its economic independence," he said in a nationally televised address on August 8. Hence, "the sovereign independence of Saudi Arabia is of vital interest to the United States."[6]

The ensuing Persian Gulf War introduced the American public and the international press to Centcom's most memorable leader: General H. Norman Schwarzkopf, the brash and forceful architect of Operation Desert Storm. General Schwarzkopf is widely credited with the dramatic "Hail Mary" maneuver that led to the rapid encirclement and defeat of the Iraqi forces in Kuwait.[7] At that point, Schwarzkopf—acting under orders from the president—ceased military operations and commenced what was to become the "containment" of Iraq. Enforcing the containment strategy—including the no-fly zone in southern Iraq and the UN-imposed blockade in the Gulf proper—occupied Centcom forces for the next twelve years, until the onset of Operation Iraqi Freedom in March 2003.

The degree to which the 2003 war with Iraq was driven by American concern over the safety of Persian Gulf oil supplies is a complex and controversial issue that I will examine carefully later in this book. Suffice it to say here that, from the vantage of officers and enlisted personnel in the U.S. Central Command, the invasion of Iraq is only the latest in a series of military engagements in the Gulf proceeding from the Carter Doctrine. This history helps to explain why the very first military objective of Operation Iraqi Freedom was to secure control over the oil fields and refineries of southern Iraq, and why, following the initial U.S. incursion into Baghdad, American forces seized and occupied the Oil Ministry while allowing looters to overrun all the other government buildings in the neighborhood.[8]

Although Saddam Hussein no longer controls Iraq, and his military has been largely destroyed, Centcom's work is far from finished. American troops continue to guard the pipelines that carry Iraqi crude to the Turkish Mediterranean port of Ceyhan and to protect oil facilities elsewhere

in the country. Some of this work is being turned over to private guards
and Iraqi police units, but American forces will continue to play a crucial
role in defending Iraq's highly vulnerable petroleum infrastructure
against attack for some time.[9] Elsewhere in the Gulf, Centcom ships and
planes continue to monitor the incessant oil-tanker traffic and guard the
Strait of Hormuz. Farther north, still other Centcom units serve at American military bases in Afghanistan, Kyrgyzstan, and Uzbekistan. No other
regional command shoulders so many responsibilities or faces so much
danger on a day-to-day basis.

From every indication, Centcom's responsibilities—and the perils
they entail—will grow, not diminish, in the years ahead. The United
States is becoming ever more dependent on petroleum from the Persian
Gulf area and Central Asia, and ensuring access to that energy source will
inevitably entangle American forces in the multitude of ethnic, religious,
and political conflicts that trouble the region. Notwithstanding the many
American troops now deployed in Centcom's AOR and the many battles
they have fought and won, the area is no more stable today than it was in
January 1980, when President Carter issued his proclamation. Although
we cannot foresee the precise nature and timing of the next crisis the
Central Command will address, it's safe to predict that its forces will see
combat in the Persian Gulf once more—and that such intervention will
be repeated again and again until the last barrel of oil is extracted from
the Gulf's prolific but highly vulnerable reservoirs.

Moreover, soldiers from the other regional commands are increasingly
being committed to oil-related operations of this sort. Already troops
from the Southern Command (Southcom) are helping to defend Colombia's Cano Limón pipeline, a vital link between oil fields in the interior
and refineries on the coast, which has been under recurring attack from
leftist guerrillas. Likewise, soldiers from the European Command (Eurcom) are training local forces to protect the newly constructed Baku-
Tbilisi-Ceyhan pipeline in Georgia. Eurcom also oversees all U.S. forces
deployed in Africa (except in the Horn, which falls under Centcom's ju-
risdiction) and has begun seeking bases from which to support future
operations to defend the region's oil facilities. Finally, the ships and

planes of the U.S. Pacific Command (Pacom) are patrolling vital tanker routes in the Indian Ocean, the South China Sea, and the western Pacific.[10]

Taken together, these developments lead to an inescapable conclusion: that the American military is being used more and more for the protection of overseas oil fields and the supply routes that connect them to the United States and its allies. Such endeavors, once largely confined to the Gulf area, are now being extended to unstable oil regions in other parts of the world. Slowly but surely, the U.S. military is being converted into a global oil-protection service.

How did this situation arise? Why have America's armed services been assigned this demanding and hazardous role? What are the long-term consequences of this decision? To answer these critical questions, it is first necessary to look at petroleum itself and consider its pivotal role in shaping the American economy. Likewise, it is essential to assess oil's place in the evolution of American security policy and the implications of the nation's growing dependence on imported supplies.

"Petroleum," the energy expert Edward L. Morse says, "has proven to be the most versatile fuel source ever discovered, situated at the core of the modern industrial economy."[11] This has certainly been the case in the United States, where oil is a major source of energy and a key driver of economic growth. Petroleum provides approximately 40 percent of the nation's total energy supply—far more than any other source. (Natural gas supplies 24 percent, coal 23 percent, nuclear power 8 percent, and all others 5 percent.) Oil serves many functions—powering industry, heating homes and schools, providing the raw material for plastics and a wide range of other products—but it is in transportation that its role is most essential. At present, petroleum products account for 97 percent of all fuel used by America's mammoth fleets of cars, trucks, buses, planes, trains, and ships.[12]

Most analysts believe that oil will remain the nation's principal source of energy for many years to come. This is so because other sources of energy are either too scarce (natural gas, hydropower), too costly (wind, solar), or too harmful in generating by-products (carbon dioxide in the case of coal, radioactive waste in the case of nuclear power). Petroleum, by contrast, is relatively abundant, reasonably affordable, and generates less CO_2 than coal does. So it will likely remain the primary source of fuel for America's industries, communities, and transportation systems for the foreseeable future. In fact, the Department of Energy predicts that petroleum will account for approximately the same proportion of America's total energy supply in 2025, 41 percent, that it does today.[13]

The United States was the first country in the world to develop a large-scale petroleum industry—an endeavor that began in 1859, when pioneering developers struck oil in Titusville, Pennsylvania—and this industry has played a central role in sustaining the nation's economic growth for the past 145 years. Copious domestic oil output gave rise to America's first large multinational corporations, among them John D. Rockefeller's legendary Standard Oil Company, the progenitor of such industry giants as Exxon Mobil, Chevron (now combined with Texaco), Amoco (now part of British Petroleum [BP]), and Atlantic Richfield (now also part of BP). Abundant and relatively cheap oil was also essential to the rise of such other mammoth enterprises as the Big Three automobile manufacturers, DuPont and other chemical companies, and the large airline and freight companies. These firms and others like them have generated much of the nation's wealth and employed many of its workers over the past century.[14]

It is nearly impossible to chronicle all the ways petroleum contributes to the vibrancy of the American economy. Because rapid and reliable transportation is so vital to the functioning of virtually every industry and enterprise, an abundant supply of affordable oil has been a major spur of economic growth and expansion. Private automobiles and cheap gasoline made possible the suburbanization of America, with all its housing developments, malls, office parks, and associated infrastructure. Petroleum provides the "feedstock," or basic raw material, for paints, plastics, pharmaceuticals, textile fibers, and a host of other products. The nation's highly productive agricultural industries also rely on petroleum to power farm machinery and provide the feedstock for pesticides, herbicides, and other key materials. And the booming tourism and recreation industry utterly relies on affordable car, bus, and airplane travel.[15]

A painful reminder of the critical role that oil plays in the U.S. economy is the fact that nearly every economic recession since World War II has come on the heels of a global petroleum shortage and an accompanying surge in prices. Many readers will remember the Arab oil embargo and the OPEC price increases of 1973–74, which resulted in endless lines at gas stations and a severe economic contraction. Long gas lines and another contraction followed the Iranian Revolution of 1979, and a similar if shorter episode followed the August 1990 Iraqi invasion of Kuwait. More recently, a global shortage of petroleum triggered the lingering economic downturn of 2001–2002 and threatened to slow or abort the recovery of 2004. To be sure, other factors have played a role in these events, but in each case a shortage of petroleum set the downturn in motion.

Just as petroleum fuels the economy, it also plays an essential role in U.S. national security. The American military relies more than that of any other nation on oil-powered ships, planes, helicopters, and armored vehicles to transport troops into battle and rain down weapons on its foes. Although the Pentagon may boast of its ever-advancing use of computers and other high-tech devices, the fighting machines that form the backbone of the U.S. military are entirely dependent on petroleum. Without an abundant and reliable supply of oil, the Department of Defense could neither rush its forces to distant battlefields nor keep them supplied once deployed there.[16]

This combination of factors is what makes petroleum central to America's economic and military strength. "Oil fuels more than automobiles and airplanes," Robert E. Ebel, of the Center for Strategic and International Studies, told a State Department audience in April 2002. "Oil fuels military power, national treasuries, and international politics." Far more than a simple commodity to be bought and sold on the international market, petroleum "is a determinant of well being, of national security, and international power for those who possess this vital resource, and the converse for those who do not."[17]

For most of the petroleum age, the United States was among those very fortunate nations that possessed this vital resource. From 1860 until World War II, this country was the world's leading oil producer, easily supplying its own needs and often generating a surplus for export.

Petroleum self-sufficiency played a significant role in America's economic growth and emerging military predominance. During World War II, for example, the United States was able to extract enough oil from domestic fields to satisfy the massive requirements of its own forces and those of its major allies. American wells supplied six out of every seven barrels of the oil the Allied powers consumed over the course of the war. After World War II, rising U.S. oil output helped generate this country's great prosperity and kick-start economic recovery in Europe and Japan.[18] Secretary of Energy Spencer Abraham boldly affirmed this close relationship between oil supply and global power in a June 2002 speech to U.S. energy company officials: "You and your predecessors in the oil and gas industry played a large part in making the twentieth century the 'American Century.'"[19]

But however accurate in some respects, this characteristically exuberant message conceals a critical flaw: America's oil inheritance, while abundant, is not limitless. In the late 1940s, the United States began to rely on foreign oil to satisfy rising energy demand, and the proportion of imports has been rising more or less steadily ever since. During the 1950s, foreign oil accounted for 10 percent of total U.S. consumption; in the 1960s, it accounted for about 18 percent, and in the 1970s approximately twice that much.[20] For a while, domestic production continued to rise as well, thus mitigating to some degree the economic impact of rising energy imports. But U.S. production began an irreversible decline in 1972, and since then it has taken an ever-expanding flow of imported oil to satisfy rising demand *and* compensate for the decline in domestic output. Slowly but surely, the United States has become dependent on foreign petroleum for its economic vibrancy. In Ebel's words, it has gone from being a country for which oil abundance has been a source of security and strength to one for which the converse is true.

The onset of petroleum dependency created a troubling situation for American leaders and the public at large. Briefly stated, abundant petroleum has helped the U.S. economy and the U.S. military dominate the world, and to propel further growth we will have to consume more and more of it, yet the United States is producing less oil, and thus will have to import ever increasing quantities from abroad. At present, the

United States—with something less than 5 percent of the world's total population—consumes about 25 percent of the world's total supply of oil. In 2025, if current trends persist, we will be consuming half as much petroleum again as we do today; however, domestic production will be no greater than it is today, and so the entire increase in consumption—approximately 10 million barrels of oil per day—will have to be supplied by foreign producers.[21] And because we can't really control what goes on in those countries, we become hostage to their capacity to ensure an uninterrupted flow of petroleum.

And herein lies the dilemma. Oil makes this country strong; dependency makes us weak. It weakens us in a number of ways. First, it leaves us vulnerable to supply disruptions abroad, whether accidental or intentional. Such disruptions, like the oil shocks of 1973–74 and 1979–80, typically result in widespread shortages of oil, sharply higher prices, and a worldwide recession. Dependence also entails a massive shift in economic resources from the United States to our foreign suppliers. Assuming that oil is priced at $30 per barrel, the total bill for imported oil over the next twenty-five years should reach a colossal $3.5 trillion; if oil prices rise above this amount, the bill obviously will be much greater.[22] On the political side of the ledger, dependence often requires us to grant all sorts of favors to the leaders of our major foreign suppliers, whether we like them or not. Though they may sell us their petroleum, they frequently expect more than money in compensation: support at the United Nations, transfers of advanced weaponry, military protection, and so forth. As reluctant as our leaders may be to grant such perquisites, they often feel bound to do so to facilitate the flow of oil. Worst of all, dependence can jeopardize our very security, by entangling us in overseas oil wars or by arousing the violent hostility of political and religious factions that resent a U.S. military presence in their midst.[23]

America's leaders have never succeeded in resolving the energy/security dilemma. They have sometimes taken this step or that to slow the growth in oil consumption, such as improving the fuel efficiency of American cars. Or they have proposed the exploitation of untapped domestic reserves in protected wilderness areas, such as the Arctic National Wildlife Refuge (ANWR). But they have never embraced a sustained and comprehensive energy strategy for reducing the demand for foreign petroleum. Instead, in order to minimize the nation's vulnerability to overseas supply disruptions, they have chosen to *securitize* oil—that is, to cast its continued availability as a matter of "national security," and thus something that can be safeguarded through the use of military force. As Secretary of Energy Abraham suggested, "energy security is a fundamental component of national security."[24] This premise underlies a great deal of American foreign and military policy since World War II.

The procurement of foreign petroleum first became a national security matter under the Franklin D. Roosevelt administration during the final years of World War II. Although the United States was then the world's leading producer of oil, President Roosevelt and his aides feared that the accelerated wartime production was rapidly exhausting domestic reserves and hastening the onset of our reliance on imports—a development they thought had grave implications for the nation's long-term security and well-being. But believing, as they did, that such a reliance was inevitable, they attempted to protect future U.S. energy imports by establishing an American protectorate over Saudi Arabia and a permanent military presence in the Persian Gulf.[25] I will discuss the specific steps they took to achieve these ends in chapter 2; the important point here is that Roosevelt set in motion the process of ever-increasing American military involvement in the greater Gulf area.

After World War II, American leaders continued to see foreign petroleum through the lens of national security. Both Presidents Harry S. Truman and Dwight D. Eisenhower regarded the protection of Persian Gulf oil as a vital component of cold-war military strategy, and both introduced major policy initiatives—the Truman and Eisenhower doctrines, respectively—dealing with the strategic equation in the Persian Gulf region. As a result, the United States sharply increased its military aid to friendly producers in the Gulf, especially Saudi Arabia, and sent additional combat forces to the area.[26] President John F. Kennedy built on these precedents, ordering U.S. planes to the region in 1963 when Yemeni forces linked to President Gamal Abdel Nasser of Egypt attacked Saudi Arabia.[27] That America's reliance on imported oil was still relatively modest at this point—no more than 20 percent of total consumption—

only underscores the degree to which the administration viewed dependency as a significant threat to national security.

Not surprisingly, American leaders grew far more deeply concerned over the implications of dependency as the level of such reliance rose. The share of America's petroleum supply that is accounted for by imports crossed the 30 percent mark in 1973 and the 40 percent mark in 1976, reaching 45 percent in 1977.[28] It was this trend, along with the Iranian revolution of 1978–79 and the Soviet invasion of Afghanistan, that led President Carter to regard the safe flow of oil from the Gulf as a matter of national security and to order the formation of what later became the U.S. Central Command. As I noted earlier, the Carter Doctrine provided the justification for the protection of Kuwaiti oil tankers during the later stages of the Iran-Iraq War and the deployment of American forces in Saudi Arabia following the Iraqi invasion of Kuwait.

The expulsion of Saddam Hussein's forces from Kuwait in February 1991 and the subsequent containment of Iraq produced a degree of stability in the Gulf that supported an increase in petroleum output and a drop in prices. These developments, in turn, helped foster the growing American reliance on foreign oil: the share of imports in the nation's total annual supply rose from 42 percent in 1990 to 49 percent in 1997. And then the once unthinkable occurred: in April 1998, American dependence on imported petroleum crossed the 50 percent mark. It increased still more in the months that followed, and so the United States entered the twenty-first century among those great powers with a net reliance on foreign oil. (See figure 1.)

As we crossed the psychologically important 50 percent threshold, a fresh debate over the strategic implications of dependency broke out among American policy makers.[29] Some analysts argued that petroleum, having become a globally traded commodity with many willing suppliers, no longer required government involvement in its procurement.[30] Others argued that it would take concerted action at the national level to mitigate the handicaps of dependency. This latter group proposed all sorts of initiatives both to reduce American reliance on imported oil and to cushion the impact of future disruptions in the global flow of energy. Their ideas ranged from a major expansion of the Strategic Petroleum

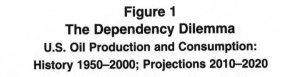

Figure 1
The Dependency Dilemma
U.S. Oil Production and Consumption:
History 1950–2000; Projections 2010–2020

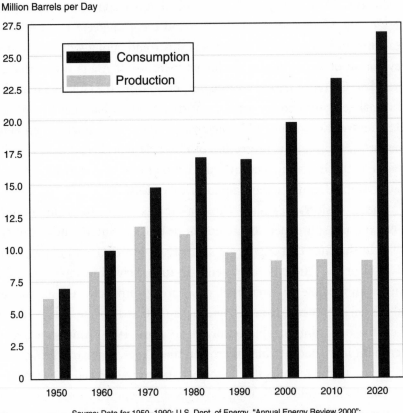

Source: Data for 1950–1990: U.S. Dept. of Energy, "Annual Energy Review 2000";
Data for 2000–2020: U.S. Dept. of Energy, *International Energy Outlook 2003.*

Reserve (a vast reservoir of stockpiled oil available for use in an emergency) to the rapid introduction of alternative forms of energy, such as wind and solar.[31] Still, most policy makers anticipated a deepening dependence on imports, and with it an ever-increasing role for American soldiers in guarding the global flow of oil. "As the world's only superpower, [the United States] must accept its special responsibilities for preserving access to worldwide energy supply," a high-level task force established by the Center for Strategic and International Studies concluded in 2000.[32]

This debate gained wide attention during the 2000 presidential election, when for the first time oil dependency and energy security became important campaign issues. With worldwide shortages sending up oil prices and California reeling from blackouts, both major candidates spoke of a looming energy crisis and promised forceful action to overcome it. After taking office, President George W. Bush pledged to make energy security a top White House priority. "This administration is concerned about [the energy crisis]," he told a group of energy officials on March 19, 2001, "and we will make a recommendation to the country as to how to proceed."[33]

In the weeks that followed, Bush identified our growing petroleum dependency as a significant threat to the nation's security. "If we fail to act," he declared in May 2001, "our country will become more reliant on foreign crude oil, putting our national energy security into the hands of foreign nations, some of whom do not share our interests."[34] To counter this danger, the White House proposed a variety of measures: drilling in ANWR and other protected sites, speeding the development of hybrid (gas/electric) and hydrogen-powered vehicles, and pursuing other technological innovations. But nothing in these proposals really sought to reverse the nation's growing reliance on imported oil; nor did they eliminate America's dependence on the Persian Gulf. Instead, Bush—like every one of his predecessors—turned to the U.S. military to provide insurance against the hazards associated with dependency.

In the early years of the twenty-first century, then, the United States is no closer to solving the dilemma of dependency than it was in Roosevelt's era. We remain highly reliant on foreign petroleum, much of it from the Gulf and other conflict-prone areas. This reliance exposes us to a host of perils, including supply disruptions, unsavory alliances, and entanglement in deadly oil wars. For many policy makers, this is a tolerable level of threat: if dependence on imports is what it takes to satisfy America's gargantuan thirst for petroleum, that is just the way it is. But dependency is not a static condition. The farther we head into the future, the deeper our reliance on imported energy will be and the greater the perils we will face. To fully appreciate the severity of our dilemma, we need to project current trends into the future and see where they are taking us.

The first of these trends is the steady, unrelieved growth of our dependence on imports. The reasons for this growing dependency is simple: America's oil consumption is rising while domestic production is falling. The situation will continue as far into the future as we can see, according to the long-range projections of the Department of Energy. Its *Annual Energy Outlook 2004* foresees that total U.S. oil consumption will rise from an average of 19.7 million barrels per day in 2001 to 28.3 million barrels in 2025, an increase of 44 percent. At the same time, domestic crude-oil production is expected to drop from 5.7 to 4.6 million barrels per day. The drop will be offset to some degree by a slight gain in the production of liquid petroleum from natural gas, but the yawning gap between consumption and production—a gap that only imports can fill—will continue to widen throughout this period.[35] (See figure 2.)

The reasons for the decline in domestic petroleum output are steeped in geology and history. At its founding, the United States was blessed with a substantial but fixed amount of conventional (i.e., liquid) petroleum. Debate rages over the magnitude of that original inheritance—some geologists set it at 345 billion barrels of oil, others at considerably less—but most experts agree that the country's largest and most productive fields have already been discovered and exploited.[36] Because naturally occurring petroleum is stored in porous rock under considerable pressure, any given reservoir or producing area will initially yield great quantities of oil—the well-known gusher effect—but output will drop as time goes on and underground field pressure diminishes. The United States achieved maximum domestic production in 1972; petroleum output has been in decline ever since. The development of new fields in Alaska can slow the rate of decline to some extent but cannot reverse this long-term process of depletion.[37]

The factors behind the increase in consumption are more diffuse but no less identifiable. Petroleum is an unusually efficient and versatile energy source, performing many vital functions for individuals and for the economy as a whole. These include, as I already noted, its many industrial and agricultural applications and its use as a home heating fuel. But to explain the steady increase in consumption we must look primarily to transportation, which accounts for about two-thirds of our current petroleum usage. The numbers are staggering: as Americans buy more and bigger vehicles and drive them longer distances every year, the 13.5 million barrels per day devoted to transportation use in 2001 will jump to an estimated 20.7 million in 2025[38]—at which point such usage will commandeer approximately three-quarters of America's total petroleum supply and over one-sixth of the entire world's.[39]

Consumption on this scale cannot help but boost the demand for

Figure 2
DOMESTIC U.S. OIL PRODUCTION, CONSUMPTION, AND IMPORTS, 2001–2025
(In million barrels per day, unless otherwise noted)

	History	Projections				
Category	2001	2005	2010	2015	2020	2025
U.S. crude oil production	5.74	5.58	5.93	5.53	4.95	4.61
Other domestic petroleum inputs*	3.12	3.40	3.59	3.72	3.94	3.99
Total U.S. domestic supply	8.86	8.98	9.52	9.25	8.89	8.60
Total U.S. oil consumption	19.71	20.48	22.71	24.80	26.41	28.30
Estimated petroleum imports†	10.85	11.50	13.19	15.55	17.52	19.70
Imports as a percent of total consumption	55.0	56.2	58.1	62.7	66.3	69.6

Source: U.S. Department of Energy, *Annual Energy Outlook 2004* (Washington, D.C.: DOE/EIA, 2004), table A11, p. 150. Projections for 2005 from 2003 edition of this annual reference.

*Includes natural gas plant liquids, refinery processing gain, and other inputs (alcohol, ethers, coal-derived liquids, and other synthetic products).

†Includes crude petroleum and refined products.

imports. "The single biggest factor in our ever-increasing dependency on foreign oil is our seemingly endless capacity to consume," former deputy secretary of the Treasury Stuart E. Eizenstat told Congress in 2002. "And, on this subject, the facts are overwhelmingly clear: increased capacity to supply energy from domestic sources cannot match the increased demand that American consumers will have for oil."[40] Accordingly, our dependence on foreign petroleum will continue to grow, rising from 55 percent of U.S. consumption in 2001 to an estimated 58 percent in 2010, 66 percent in 2020, and 70 percent in 2025—the furthest into the future that the Department of Energy is currently prepared to project.[41]

The second trend we need to consider is that more and more of our imported oil will be coming to us from countries that are unstable, unfriendly, or located in the middle of dangerous areas (or some combination of all three). And it is *this* trend, more than any other, that makes our reliance on foreign energy so worrisome. After all, we wouldn't be so anxious about our growing dependency if all our energy was coming to us from Canada, Norway, Australia, and other friendly producers located in peaceful parts of the world. But those countries have limited reserves and are slowly running out of oil, and so it is to the Middle East, Central Asia, Africa, and other less stable but more prolific areas of the world that we will increasingly have to turn for our future petroleum supplies.

Here, too, it is geology that underlies our predicament. Conventional petroleum is not distributed evenly across the planet; it is highly concentrated in a few giant reservoirs. The United States has the good fortune of owning a number of these, as do a few other industrialized nations— Canada, Russia, and North Sea countries. But most of the earth's remaining large deposits are in the developing world, notably the Persian Gulf area, the Caspian Sea basin, northern and western Africa, and South America. And because the industrialized nations generally started exploiting their own deposits at the beginning of the petroleum era, most of the world's as yet untapped oil is now lodged in the developing areas.[42]

As figure 3 shows, six Persian Gulf countries—Saudi Arabia, Iraq, the United Arab Emirates (UAE), Kuwait, Iran, and Qatar—jointly possess 674 billion barrels of proven reserves, or about 64 percent of the world's known supplies. Venezuela, Nigeria, and Mexico jointly claim another 114 billion

Figure 3
PROVEN RESERVES OF THE MAJOR OIL-PRODUCING COUNTRIES, AS OF END 2002

Major producer (in rank order)	Proven reserves (billion barrels)	Percentage of world total
1. Saudi Arabia	261.8	25.0
2. Iraq	112.5	10.7
3. United Arab Emirates	97.8	9.3
4. Kuwait	96.5	9.2
5. Iran	89.7	8.6
6. Venezuela	77.8	7.4
7. Russian Federation and Caspian Sea states	77.1	7.4
8. United States	30.4	2.9
9. Libya	29.5	2.8
10. Nigeria	24.0	2.3
11. China	18.3	1.7
12. North Sea (Norway, U.K., Denmark)	16.3	1.6
13. Qatar	15.2	1.5
14. Mexico	12.6	1.2
All others	90.2	8.6
World total	1047.7	100.0

Source: BP, *BP Statistical Review of World Energy* (London: BP, June 2003), p. 4.

barrels (11 percent of known reserves), and Russia and the Caspian Sea states have some 77 billion barrels (7 percent of reserves). This leaves only 18 percent of the world's remaining petroleum supply in the hands of all other countries, including the United States and its European allies.

It doesn't take a vivid imagination to grasp the essence of America's energy predicament: only the Middle East and other regions that have long suffered from instability and civil unrest have sufficient untapped reserves to satisfy our (and the world's) rising petroleum demand in the years ahead. Like it or not, for as long as we continue to rely on petroleum as a major source of energy, our security and our economic well-being will be tied to social and political developments in these unpredictable and often unfriendly producers. Just how tight this bond has become was made painfully evident in the spring of 2004, when violence in three countries—an assault on an offshore oil terminal in Iraq, a series of bombings and shootings in Saudi Arabia, and the killing of oil workers in Nigeria—depressed global petroleum output and produced record-high gasoline prices in the United States.

Our biggest problem, of course, is our growing reliance on the oil kingdoms of the Persian Gulf. No matter how hard the United States tries to diversify its energy imports by turning to producers in other regions, it will *still* need to acquire more and more oil from the Gulf, the only region whose reserves are large enough to satisfy the rising U.S. and international demand. And sustained dependence on Persian Gulf oil means continued vulnerability to the political unrest, conflict, and terrorism that has long plagued the region. "In the end," former deputy secretary Eizenstat told Congress, "our dependence on Persian Gulf oil in general and Saudi oil in particular leaves us vulnerable to attack, both abroad and at home."[43]

In an effort to reduce America's exposure to this danger, successive administrations have attempted to increase the nation's reliance on producers in other areas of the world, particularly Africa, Latin America, and the Caspian Sea basin. But there is no reason to assume that these non-Gulf suppliers ultimately will prove any more safe and reliable than those in the Middle East. "Even a cursory glance at the list of [major oil suppliers] reveals that most have either experienced noteworthy internal stress in the past or contain incipient sources of stress that could flare up in the future," the energy task force established by the Center for Strategic and International Studies (CSIS) noted in its November 2000 report. While we can assume that the North Sea countries and North America will remain stable, "it is not difficult to conceive of future situations in most of the other [suppliers] that could lead to internal strife at a level sufficient to cause a reduction of oil exports."[44]

The third critical trend follows from the second. The growing American reliance on unstable suppliers in dangerous parts of the developing world is creating social, economic, and political pressures that are exacerbating local schisms and so *increasing* the risk of turmoil and conflict. This is the case for a number of reasons. First, the conspicuous presence of U.S. oil firms is bound to arouse hostility from people who reject American values or resent the great concentration of wealth and power in America's hands. Second, the very production of oil in otherwise underdeveloped societies often skews the local economy—funneling vast wealth to a few and thus intensifying the preexisting antagonism between the haves and the have-nots.

That the presence of U.S. oil companies in the Middle East foments resentment is nothing new; Al Qaeda was by no means the first anti-American or anti-Western organization to target foreign oil facilities and pipelines. But the projected expansion of the American presence in the area, most notably in Iraq, is certain to trigger fresh hostility from such groups. Indeed, the U.S.-protected oil infrastructure in Iraq has already come under repeated attack by opponents of the occupation, severely disrupting American efforts to restore Iraqi production and thereby help finance the costs of reconstruction. In May 2004, moreover, several gunmen attacked the headquarters of an American oil company in Saudi Arabia, killing five employees and wounding several others before they were themselves slain. A more conspicuous U.S. presence in other Gulf countries is likely to provoke similar expressions of anti-American venom.[45]

The growing American reliance on alternative producers in Africa, Asia, and Latin America could also provoke hostility of this sort. In some cases, it will stem from the same sort of religious extremism as in the Middle East. There are already offshoots of Al Qaeda in Central Asia and the Caucasus region and even in parts of Africa. But there are also other forms

of violent opposition in these areas. In Colombia, for example, several revolutionary guerrilla groups have already targeted U.S.-linked oil installations. Venezuela, Mexico, and parts of Africa also harbor guerrillas and
militant groups with radical agendas. New U.S. oil facilities in these areas
will in many cases invite a new round of anti-American violence.

The risk of disorder and conflict in these countries has a good deal to
do with the destabilizing impact of oil production itself. When countries
with few other sources of national wealth exploit their petroleum reserves, the ruling elites typically monopolize the distribution of oil revenues, enriching themselves and their cronies while leaving the rest of the
population mired in poverty—and the well-equipped and often privileged security forces of these "petro-states" can be counted on to support
them. When the divide between privileged and disadvantaged coincides
with tribal or religious differences, as it often does, violence is a likely
outcome. The Western press may describe such strife as "ethnic" in char-
acter, but it comes largely from the perversive effects of oil production.[46]

The dangers arising from this phenomenon received particular emphasis from the energy task force established by CSIS in 2000. Many of
the non-Gulf suppliers upon which the United States is coming to rely,
the group noted, "share the characteristics of 'petro-states,' whereby their
extreme dependence on income from energy exports distorts their political and economic institutions, centralizes wealth in the hands of the state,
and makes each country's leaders less resilient in dealing with change but
provides them with sufficient resources to hope to stave off necessary reforms indefinitely." There is, then, "a significant risk that a crisis in one or
more of these key energy-producing countries could occur during the
span of the 20 years at the beginning of the century."[47]

All of which leads to the fourth and final worrisome trend: to an ever-
increasing extent, all other oil-consuming nations will have to draw on
the same unstable sources of petroleum as will the United States. Europe
and Japan have, of course, long relied on the Middle East and Africa for a
large share of their energy requirements, but now China and other rapidly industrializing countries will join them in competing for this petroleum. According to the Department of Energy, oil consumption by
developing Asian nations (all but Australia, Japan, and New Zealand) will

double over the next twenty-five years, jumping from 15 to 32 million barrels per day. China's consumption alone will climb from 5.0 to 12.8 million barrels, while India's will rise from 2.1 to 5.3 million barrels.[48] Because these countries, and other rising powers like them, have only limited domestic supplies of their own, they will be forced to jostle with the United States, Europe, and Japan in seeking access to the few producing zones with surplus petroleum, greatly exacerbating the already competitive pressures in these highly volatile areas.

At the very least, these pressures will lead to periodic shortages and price spikes, causing worldwide economic instability. This peril can only increase as many older reserves become depleted and global supplies begin to dwindle. Experts disagree as to when the world's oil fields will attain maximum (or "peak") production and begin an irreversible decline—some say this will occur by 2010, others in the second or third decade of this century—but *all* acknowledge that the planet's original petroleum inheritance has been substantially exploited and that a reduction in output is inevitable.[49] (We'll come back to this point in chapter 7.) The eventual contraction of global oil supplies will produce economic hardships aplenty, but we face an even greater danger: that China, the United States, and other countries will respond to scarcity by emphasizing the security dimensions of energy and strengthening their military ties with friendly producers in the Gulf and other producing areas. Russia, China, and the United States are all supplying arms and military services to states in these areas already, and the tempo of these activities is rising. As I will argue in chapter 6, this behavior could lead to a classic great-power geopolitical struggle in the oil zones—significantly increasing the risk that a localized conflict might escalate into something far greater.

In summary, then, four key trends will dominate the future of American energy behavior: an increasing need for imported oil, a pronounced shift toward unstable and unfriendly suppliers in dangerous parts of the world; a greater risk of anti-American or civil violence, and rising competition for what will likely prove a diminishing supply pool. Clearly, the perils of dependency are growing more severe. Yet American leaders are trapped in their same old policy paralysis, proposing feeble steps to reduce our reliance on imported oil even as they acquiesce in our ever-increasing dependency.

If history is any guide, U.S. policy makers will be tempted to respond to the dependency dilemma by relying on military means to ensure the uninterrupted flow of energy. And, as before, the burden will fall on the officers and the enlisted personnel of the U.S. Central Command. At the same time, soldiers from other regional commands, including Southcom, Eurcom, and Pacom, will be assigned similar tasks.

The implications for American society are grim. Senior officials appear to believe that the use of military force is not just a legitimate but also an *effective* response to foreign threats to the flow of petroleum. When Presidents Kennedy, Reagan, Bush senior, and Bush junior ordered American troops into combat in the Gulf, they certainly thought so. But the Gulf is no more stable today than it was before Washington launched these costly operations. And it should be obvious by now that the use of force can have unintended and perilous consequences. For example, when the United States sent warships to protect Kuwaiti oil tankers in 1987–88, the Iranians regarded the move as part of a covert U.S. strategy to aid their opponents, the Iraqis, and so Tehran grew even more hostile toward the United States. Meanwhile, America's indirect support of Iraq in that conflict undoubtedly contributed to Saddam Hussein's sense of invincibility—and so influenced his decision to invade Kuwait in August 1990.[50] As our growing reliance on military force parallels our growing dependence on imported energy, the risks of miscalculation are bound to increase. Indeed, the magnitude of this danger became terribly obvious in late 2003 and early 2004, when the American troops who had assumed responsibility for protecting Iraq's vulnerable oil infrastructure found themselves under almost daily attack from opponents of the occupation.

The economic consequences of these developments are equally grim. To begin with, we will have to devote vast sums of money—hundreds of billions of dollars per year—to maintain our military presence in the Persian Gulf and other volatile oil regions. This expenditure comes, of course, on top of the hundreds of billions of dollars we will have to pay for all this imported petroleum. Such mammoth outlays will sap the vigor of the U.S. economy and deplete the Treasury of the funds we need to address our domestic concerns, such as our fraying educational and health-care systems. Most terrible of all, perhaps, is the huge moral cost of Washington's growing subservience to the autocratic and often anti-American regimes that govern many of the world's leading oil-producing countries.

None of these far-reaching implications, it appears, has played any part in the policies the current American leadership have chosen to pursue. Our existing policies seem to rest on the delusion that an uninterrupted supply of abundant and cheap energy will be ours forever, despite all the evidence to the contrary. Yes, lip service is being paid to the need for energy independence—most notably in the drive to initiate oil drilling in ANWR—but nothing proposed by President Bush or any other senior White House official will actually reverse the trends I have outlined. Yet without a decisive change in policy the United States will sink deeper and deeper into its dependence on foreign oil, with all the costs—including those measured in human blood—that this condition entails. Only by subjecting these policies to close and careful scrutiny, as I have attempted to do in the following chapters, and by devising alternative energy strategies will it be possible for us to avoid either the perils of dependency or the unconscionable costs they incur.

2

Lethal Embrace:
The American Alliance with Saudi Arabia

It is impossible to overstate the importance of the U.S.-Saudi relationship. Not only is Saudi Arabia the leading foreign supplier of crude petroleum to the United States—accounting for approximately 18 percent of imports in mid-2003—it is also the *only* major supplier we can be sure will significantly increase its deliveries of oil to us in times of crisis. Because it has so much of the world's untapped oil—some 262 billion barrels, or one-fourth of proven world reserves[1]—and because it has so much capacity for extra (or "spare") production, Saudi Arabia can single-handedly boost its deliveries enough to compensate for any cutoffs from other major suppliers. This capacity was critically important in 1990 when, following the Iraqi invasion of Kuwait, Saudi Arabia's increased production offset the loss of oil from Iraq and Kuwait, thereby averting a severe economic downturn in the United States. With no other supplier capable of replacing Saudi Arabia in this critical role, the United States will remain dependent on the kingdom both for day-to-day imports of oil and for increased supplies in times of crisis and conflict.

Just as significant is the impact of this relationship on American security. In return for providing the United States with so much of its oil, the Saudi government—which is to say the Saudi royal family—relies on the United States for defense against its adversaries, both foreign and domestic. Over the decades, we have provided the kingdom with vast quantities of sophisticated weaponry, along with large numbers of military advisers, instructors, and technicians. In 1990, the United States demonstrated the extremes to which it would go to defend Saudi Arabia when it deployed hundreds of thousands of its troops to ward off a possible attack by the Iraqi forces then occupying Kuwait. But this intervention, successful as it was in its immediate aims, introduced a new set of complications. After expelling the Iraqi forces from Kuwait, the United States retained a large military presence in Saudi Arabia in order to maintain the no-fly zone over southern Iraq and to deter Saddam Hussein from any further assaults on the Persian Gulf oil kingdoms. This lingering foreign presence stirred up powerful anti-American sentiment among some sectors of Saudi society and fueled the terrorist campaign that Osama bin Laden launched in the early 1990s. The drastic consequences of this new antagonism are still unfolding.

With America destined to grow even more dependent on Saudi Arabian oil in the years ahead, the U.S.-Saudi military relationship can only expand. What shape it will take is not yet entirely clear—I will say more about this in chapter 4—but there is no doubt that American security policy will continue to reflect our need for reliable access to Saudi oil supplies. And because this area of the world is so unstable and the likelihood of crisis there so great, it is almost certain that more American blood will be spilled defending Saudi reserves. How we got to this precarious position will be examined in the following sections.

Oil, War, and U.S. National Security

The United States first forged its alliance with Saudi Arabia during World War II, at a time of mounting government concern over the national security implications of declining U.S. oil reserves. Early in the war, it became apparent that we would have to accelerate the production of domestic petroleum in order to sustain our hard-pressed allies (especially Great Britain) and to provide American combat forces with adequate fuel supplies. Although American leaders worried about the rapid depletion of our domestic reserves, they did not stint on the petroleum they allocated to U.S. allies and our own forces: between the attack on Pearl Harbor in 1941 and the defeat of Japan in 1945, the United States contributed 6 billion out of the 7 billion barrels of oil that the Allied forces consumed.[2] In approving these deliveries, however, senior officials knew they might be exposing the nation to the risk of future petroleum scarcity; accordingly, they believed that it would take extraordinary measures to shore up America's long-term energy security.

It is hard, from our present vantage, to appreciate the extent to which the prospect of seriously depleting America's domestic oil reserves alarmed U.S. officials during World War II. Today the United States can draw on many countries to satisfy its oil requirements—for the short term, at least—but this was not always so. In 1942, when the United States entered World War II in earnest, it was the world's leading oil producer and was thought to possess nearly half of total world reserves— meaning that we had few other suppliers to turn to should our own reserves be exhausted. This situation, in turn, implied that we would face serious difficulties if the war lasted longer than expected, or if another serious conflict erupted in the coming years.

It is also important to appreciate the critical role petroleum played in the Allied victory. Far more than they had in any previous conflict, oil-powered weapons—tanks, airplanes, submarines, aircraft carriers, and armored troop carriers—dominated the theaters of war. In addition, huge numbers of oil-powered ships and planes transported millions of American troops and their equipment to combat zones in Europe, Asia, and Africa. The demands for fuel were prodigious: a typical armored battalion required seventeen thousand gallons of oil to travel only one hundred miles; the U.S. Fifth Fleet alone consumed 630 million gallons of fuel oil during a single two-month period.[3] To satisfy these needs, the United States pushed domestic oil production to record levels and delivered the required fuels to fleets and armies all over the world. "If the internal combustion engine was the heart of the modern military machine," a team of historians noted after the war, "its life blood was oil."[4]

The need to supply so much oil to American and Allied combat forces naturally prompted U.S. officials to pay close attention to global supply-and-demand patterns. At the start of the war, it was estimated that the United States possessed approximately 20 billion barrels of oil—at that time the greatest concentration of known reserves on earth. But as early as 1942, the nation was drawing on these reserves at a rate of about 4 million barrels per day, or 1.45 billion barrels per year. At that rate (assuming no new discoveries of domestic oil) the United States would consume its entire national supply in just thirteen years—a dangerously short period. True, future exploration in such places as Alaska and the Gulf of Mexico was expected to yield additional capacity, but every contemporary projection indicated that rising consumption—driven both by wartime military needs and by the anticipated postwar reconstruction effort—would far outstrip the acquisition of new supplies, leading to the rapid exhaustion of U.S. reserves.[5]

Needless to say, these projections produced widespread anxiety in Washington.[6] "It has become more and more apparent," Commodore Andrew F. Carter of the Army-Navy Petroleum Board informed Secretary of the Navy Frank Knox in 1944, "that known petroleum reserves within the continental limits of the United States are inadequate to meet over a period of years either the wartime needs of the United States or the needs of the civilian economy once normal conditions are established."[7] Petroleum experts at the State Department reached similar conclusions, adding to the atmosphere of alarm. Unless additional sources of oil were secured, Herbert Feis of the department's economic staff declared, "American security, power, and freedom would be in peril."[8]

These concerns led the Roosevelt administration to undertake the nation's first systematic study of the security implications of declining U.S. oil reserves. This effort was entrusted to William C. Ferris, a career foreign-service officer working under Max Thornburg, the State Department's senior petroleum adviser. In an early working paper, dated November 24, 1941, Ferris laid out the basic principles that were to become formal government policy during the course of the war. If the United States continued to exploit its domestic supplies at current rates, he argued, there would be insufficient remaining oil reserves left to deal with future crises. To provide for future contingencies, therefore, the nation should conserve its domestic reserves and use more oil from foreign sources. Because other nations were also seeking additional supplies from these same sources, the U.S. government should pursue a "more and more aggressive foreign oil policy aimed at assuring access to petroleum overseas."[9]

As the war proceeded, other government officials embraced and refined this basic approach. By 1943, a consensus had emerged in the higher levels of the Roosevelt administration, as codified in the *Foreign Petroleum Policy of the United States,* a policy statement released by the State Department in April 1944. "In order to assure the adequacy for military and civilian requirements of strategically available reserves," the paper read, "a broad policy of conservation of Western Hemisphere petroleum reserves should be adopted." Instead of exporting oil from Western Hemisphere sources to markets elsewhere, the United States should promote the "substantial and orderly expansion of production in Eastern Hemisphere sources of supply, principally the Middle East."[10]

From the perspective of American officials, the development of new sources of supply in the Middle East would enhance our security by reducing the pressure on U.S. and Latin American reserves. But it would also introduce a new security concern: by becoming more reliant on Persian Gulf oil, the United States would become more vulnerable to the adverse effects of any interruption in deliveries from that area. It thus became U.S. policy to seek new supplies of petroleum in those parts of the Gulf where American oil companies were already active and the local government was considered friendly to further U.S. exploitation. For all practical purposes, this meant increased American reliance on the one country that satisfied all these requirements: the kingdom of Saudi Arabia.

"A Stupendous Source of Strategic Power"

American firms first began looking for petroleum in Saudi Arabia in 1933, when the Standard Oil Company of California (SOCAL) obtained a sixty-year concession over a large area in al-Hasa (the Eastern Province) along the kingdom's Persian Gulf coast. Two basic considerations had drawn SOCAL to this area, one geologic and the other political. Geologically, al-Hasa looked especially promising, because it shared many of the characteristics of nearby areas in Kuwait, Iraq, and Persia, where oil had already been discovered. More important, Saudi Arabia's potential drilling areas had not yet been parceled out among the major European companies, as those of the other countries had. With its acquisition of the al-Hasa concession, SOCAL became the first American-owned firm to win control over a major Middle Eastern oil zone.[11]

In return, SOCAL gave the kingdom's ruler, Abdul Aziz ibn Saud (known in the West as Ibn Saud), thirty-five thousand pounds sterling in gold, and a promise of future royalties and loans—a remarkably small payment for what turned out to be the world's largest reservoir of untapped oil. SOCAL also agreed to build the infrastructure to develop the field, a project the Saudis lacked the skills and resources to undertake. To that end, SOCAL created a subsidiary, the California-Arabian Standard Oil Company (CASOC), and established a small American outpost at Dhahran, on the Persian Gulf coast opposite Bahrain. After overcoming daunting logistic and technical challenges—at that time there were no large ports or airfields in the area, and roads were nearly nonexistent—CASOC struck oil in 1938 and began commercial production a year later.[12] And while CASOC's initial output was not particularly impressive—between 1941 and 1945, the al-Hasa wells produced about 42.5 million barrels of petroleum, or less than 1 percent of the simultaneous output of wells in the United States[13]—many American geologists became convinced that the kingdom possessed immense reserves.

When SOCAL and its partners (Texaco had acquired a half interest in CASOC in 1936) first began producing oil in Saudi Arabia, in 1939, official Washington barely noticed. Although the United States had recognized Ibn Saud's government in 1931, we did not see fit to establish formal diplomatic relations with the kingdom until 1939 and did not post a resident ambassador there until 1943.[14] As news of the discoveries

Saudi Arabia and the Surrounding Region

in Saudi Arabia filtered into Washington, however, top U.S. officials—anxious by then about the rapid depletion of our domestic reserves—began taking a serious interest in the kingdom's long-term petroleum potential. By the end of World War II, the exploitation of Saudi Arabia's vast petroleum reserves had become a major foreign policy objective. "In Saudi Arabia," the head of the State Department's Division of Near Eastern Affairs informed President Truman in 1945, "the oil resources constitute a stupendous source of strategic power, and one of the greatest material prizes in human history."[15]

As soon as our top officials recognized Saudi Arabia's immense strategic value, they moved to bolster America's ties to the kingdom. The Roosevelt administration opened a legation in the country and, in 1943, elevated its chargé d'affaires to full ministerial rank. That was merely a start, and a tardy one; other countries, including Great Britain, had established far more elaborate ties with the Ibn Saud regime. Believing that a significant American presence was necessary to ensure access to Saudi oil, Washington sought to ingratiate itself with King Ibn Saud and to assert some degree of control over the vital CASOC concession. These efforts, which continued throughout World War II, were invariably described in official statements as a matter of national security. "This was more than a business enterprise," Harold Ickes, the secretary of the interior, said of one such endeavor; "this involved the defense and safety of the nation."[16]

Roosevelt's first move was to approve the delivery of Lend-Lease aid to Saudi Arabia—no simple matter. The Lend-Lease Act of 1941 gave the president the authority to sell, exchange, lend, lease, or otherwise transfer military equipment to "any country whose defense the president deems vital to the defense of the United States." In passing the act, Congress had clearly meant to establish a means of providing assistance to friendly nations that had come under attack by the Axis powers. But Saudi Arabia was not under attack and had no prior ties with the United States, and so it was up to President Roosevelt to make the case that aiding the kingdom was in America's national security interest. Although he was initially reluctant to take this position, his aides eventually convinced him that preservation of the Saudi oil concession was, in fact, crucial to the nation's security. On February 16, 1943, he declared that "the defense of Saudi Arabia is vital to the defense of the United States" and approved the extension of Lend-Lease aid to the kingdom. For the rest of the war, American assistance was a major source of Saudi government revenue.[17]

Many government officials thought that the Lend-Lease aid and the increased diplomatic presence were a sufficient show of U.S. support for the Ibn Saud regime. Others, including the president, feared they were not enough. Apprehensive lest an inadequate American effort lead to the loss of this major oil concession to other powers—especially Great Britain, which already held concessions in neighboring countries—they set out to establish unassailable control over CASOC's holdings with a strategy that had no precedent in American history: the establishment of a state-owned oil company to buy out CASOC's Saudi Arabian concession and place it under direct U.S. government control.

The Committee on International Petroleum Policy, an interdepartmental body that the State Department had just organized, first floated the idea of government ownership of CASOC's Saudi Arabian holdings in March 1943. In a memo to Secretary of State Cordell Hull, the committee proposed that the government establish a state-owned firm, the Petroleum Reserves Corporation (PRC), to buy up options on CASOC's future oil production and sequester these supplies for future military use. Secretary of the Interior Harold Ickes advanced an even more ambitious plan: rather than rely on option contracts—which, he argued, would give Washington little leverage over Saudi Arabia—the PRC could buy CASOC's concession outright on behalf of the U.S. government.[18]

The Ickes proposal won strong support from the Joint Chiefs of Staff and the Navy Department, both of which were very concerned about the depletion of American oil reserves. Writing for the Navy, Under Secretary William C. Bullitt informed President Roosevelt in June 1943 that "we cannot squeeze out of our own soil enough petroleum for our war needs." By imposing direct government control over the Saudi Arabian concession, however, "the estimated oil reserves of the United States would be approximately *doubled*."[19] This argument evidently carried great weight with the president, who on June 26, 1943, approved the plan for the Petroleum Reserves Corporation. He also instructed Secretary Ickes to begin negotiations with CASOC for the purchase of all its stock.[20]

At first it appeared that these efforts might succeed. But opposition from CASOC's owners, along with resistance in Congress to any government involvement in the oil business, hampered the negotiations. The British government, which then had great influence in Washington, also opposed such a dramatic American intrusion into what it viewed as its own traditional sphere of influence. Although talks between Ickes and

CASOC's owners dragged on for months, the plan eventually collapsed, and the PRC was dissolved. CASOC went on to develop the Saudi reserves and, later, renamed the Arabian-American Oil Company (Aramco), became one of the world's leading producers.[21] (In 1948, the Standard Oil Company of New Jersey—later Exxon—and the Standard Oil Company of New York—later Mobil—became part owners of Aramco.)

Despite the failure of the PRC proposal, the federal government continued to play a critical role in efforts to expand American involvement in the development of Persian Gulf oil reserves. From that point on, however, Washington chose to collaborate with rather than supplant the giant American oil companies, spurring their efforts to gain concessions in the region and providing them with diplomatic and military support when deemed useful. The result was what David S. Painter of Georgetown University has termed a *public-private partnership* in foreign oil development: "Even though private interests rather than government agencies were given primary responsibility for implementing U.S. foreign oil policy, the U.S. government was nevertheless deeply involved in maintaining an international environment in which private companies could operate with security and profit."[22]

As Painter suggests, the government's primary role in the partnership was to be the maintenance of security and stability in the major oil-producing regions.[23] And it was this imperative that prompted one of the most remarkable encounters of World War II: the February 14, 1945, meeting between President Roosevelt and King Ibn Saud. After concluding his celebrated summit conference with Winston Churchill and Joseph Stalin in Yalta, Roosevelt flew to Egypt, meeting with Ibn Saud aboard the USS *Quincy,* an American cruiser anchored in the Great Bitter Lake, the southern portal of the Suez Canal. Those who witnessed this event remembered it as nothing short of extraordinary: on one side, the acknowledged leader of the Allied powers and a passionate defender of democratic ideals; on the other, an absolute monarch who had never traveled farther from home than neighboring Kuwait and adhered to an extremely strict form of Islam. Among Ibn Saud's entourage of forty-eight retainers were Bedouin bodyguards, household slaves, and the royal astrologer.[24]

Roosevelt and Ibn Saud sat together and talked, through an interpreter, for five and a half hours. No records were kept and no American save Roosevelt participated in the discussions, so it is impossible to reconstruct their conversations exactly. Roosevelt later said that he had solicited the king's views on proposals for a Jewish homeland in Palestine, then a British-controlled territory, but he gave no other indication of what they talked about.[25] From other evidence, however, it is apparent that he asked for and received Ibn Saud's blessing for the construction of an American air base at Dhahran and discussed other aspects of the burgeoning U.S.-Saudi security relationship.[26]

Just how far Roosevelt and Ibn Saud's discussion of security affairs went we will never know. Most historians and government officials think the two leaders forged a tacit alliance—one which obliged the United States to protect Saudi sovereignty and independence in return for a Saudi pledge to uphold the American firms' dominance of the oil fields.[27] Whether or not this was really the case, leaders of both countries have acted as if it were.[28] Thus, when Iraq invaded Kuwait in August 1990 and positioned its forces on the Saudi Arabian border, the Bush administration cited the Roosevelt–Ibn Saud meeting as part of the justification for its decision to send American troops to the kingdom. "We do, of course, have historic ties to governments in the region," Dick Cheney, then secretary of defense, told the Senate Armed Services Committee on September 11, 1990. Those ties "hark back with respect to Saudi Arabia to 1945, when President Franklin Delano Roosevelt met with King Abdul Aziz on the USS *Quincy,* at the end of World War II, and affirmed at that time that the United States had a lasting and a continuing interest in the security of the kingdom."[29]

The security relationship that Roosevelt and Ibn Saud initiated has evolved considerably since 1945. But its basis was fully established during World War II, when American officials first identified the oil fields of Saudi Arabia as a vital national interest. "The oil resources of Saudi Arabia [are] among the greatest in the world," the State Department observed in a 1945 memo, and they "must remain under American control for the dual purpose of supplementing and replacing our dwindling reserves, and of preventing this power potential from falling into un-friendly hands."[30]

Defending Saudi Arabia:
The Truman, Eisenhower, and Nixon Doctrines

The circumstances that led to the Roosevelt–Ibn Saud meeting of Febru-ary 1945—anxiety over the depletion of U.S. petroleum reserves and a new appreciation of the link between oil and war—were just as com-pelling to Washington in the postwar era. If anything, petroleum took on even more strategic significance as the United States and the other major powers came to rely on cheap and abundant oil to fuel their booming economies. In the quarter century following World War II, America's an-nual consumption of petroleum products tripled, from 1.8 billion barrels in 1946 to 5.4 billion barrels in 1971. Much of this petroleum came from domestic sources, but after 1955 an ever-increasing share was imported from the Middle East. And with every jump in the percentage of energy consumption that foreign sources satisfied, Saudi Arabia acquired greater importance in the eyes of American policy makers.

In 1946, the first year of the postwar era, Saudi Arabia produced a mere 60 million barrels of oil—just 3 percent of the amount extracted from wells in the United States. But Saudi production grew so prodi-giously that in 1976 the kingdom's wells delivered 3.1 billion barrels—fifty-two times the 1946 amount. By that point, Saudi Arabia had become the world's number three producer of petroleum (after the United States and the Soviet Union) and its number one exporter. Without the oil that Saudi Arabia and the other Gulf producers supplied, the United States and its European allies could never have achieved the spectacular eco-nomic growth they posted in the postwar era. Nor could Washington have sustained the great armies, navies, and air forces it deployed in every theater of possible confrontation with the Soviet Union and its allies.[31]

At the same time, however, this Saudi oil imposed a significant strate-gic burden on American leaders. Saudi Arabia's military forces were no match for those of its more heavily armed neighbors, and so it fell to the United States to ensure the kingdom's defense, as well as the safety of its oil fields and pipelines and the sea-lanes that connect the Gulf to markets abroad. Moreover, President Roosevelt had made a promise, implicit or otherwise, to defend the Saudi government itself—which meant, in practice, the Saudi royal family. And because the royal family periodically came under attack from its own subjects, the United States became mired in Saudi Arabia's internal affairs, primarily through its aid to the monarchy's police and internal-security forces.

Whatever their views of Saudi Arabia and its royal family, American policy makers have consistently agreed that access to Saudi oil is a vital national security interest that must be defended.[32] Thus, in a 1947 telegram, Acting Secretary of State Robert Lovell assured the U.S. ambassador in Riyadh that if another power attacked Saudi Arabia, the United States "would take energetic measures to ward off such aggression."[33] But however unanimously they embraced this fundamental proposition, senior officials often disagreed over the tools and strategies with which to back it up. Some argued that American combat forces were the most reliable defense of the Saudi oil fields; but stationing them there was not only prohibitively expensive, it was also sure to arouse native hostility—smacking as it did of colonialism. For these reasons, American strategists preferred more indirect methods of protection: we could deputize friendly local powers to shield the area from external attack and we could beef up the kingdom's own military capabilities.[34]

This policy quandary—how to devise an effective and affordable strategy for protecting Persian Gulf oil fields in the face of the many and complex challenges—is a major theme of cold-war history. Harried not only by Soviet efforts to gain a foothold in the region but also by the powerful currents of Arab nationalism, U.S. officials were constantly being forced to reconsider their approach and launch new initiatives to bolster America's position in the area. It was this recurring cycle of crisis, reassessment, and response that produced the three great presidential edicts of the early cold-war era: the Truman, Eisenhower, and Nixon doctrines.

The Truman Doctrine addressed what many regarded as Soviet adventurism in the eastern Mediterranean and northern Gulf states, the region immediately adjoining the Saudi Arabian oil fields. In the first of a series of crises that gripped the region, Washington and Moscow clashed over the status of Iran—then the Gulf's leading oil producer. At the onset of World War II, Great Britain and the USSR had occupied Iran in order to protect their interests and ensure that the country did not fall into German hands. They had also agreed to withdraw their troops within six months of the end of the war; all Soviet troops should therefore have been out of Iran by March 2, 1946. But as the date approached, Moscow gave no sign that it was planning to remove its forces. Instead, the Soviets assisted in the creation of an independent regime in the north—the Autonomous Republic of Azerbaijan—and repulsed the Iranian forces trying to reoccupy the area. At that point the Truman administration (which up to then had sought to avoid a direct confrontation with Moscow) assumed a more truculent posture. George Kennan, the U.S. ambassador in Moscow, was instructed to communicate Washington's displeasure over Soviet meddling in Iran, and the Navy received orders to beef up its presence in the eastern Mediterranean. Faced with this level of resistance and unwilling to risk a head-to-head confrontation with the United States, Stalin chose to defuse the crisis; Moscow withdrew all of its forces from Iran in May 1946.[35]

The Iranian crisis is usually cited as the opening salvo of the cold war, an early Soviet-American struggle for influence in key areas of Eurasia. But the documentary record makes it clear that American leaders saw the dispute more as a geopolitical contest, with the oil fields of Saudi Arabia and the other Persian Gulf producers as the ultimate prize.[36] In early 1946, President Truman described Soviet actions in Iran as part of a "giant pincers movement against the oil-rich areas of the Near East and the warm-water ports of the Mediterranean."[37] Even though Moscow withdrew its forces from Iran, American policy makers continued to fret about the safety of Western oil supplies in the Persian Gulf area. Noting that access to these resources would be critical in any future U.S.-Soviet conflict, the Joint Chiefs of Staff declared in October 1946 that it was "to the strategic interest of the United States to keep Soviet influence and Soviet armed forces as far as possible from oil resources in Iran, Iraq, and the Near and Middle East."[38]

At the same time, the Soviets were also trying to make political inroads into Greece and Turkey—efforts that Truman and other high officials viewed as closely tied to Moscow's ambitions in the Persian Gulf. Fearing that the installation of pro-Soviet regimes in these countries would threaten American access to Middle Eastern oil supplies, the White House sought to devise a new form of Lend-Lease aid as a means of providing friendly governments with American arms and other forms of military assistance. But in the aftermath of World War II, many members of Congress were reluctant to open the way to fresh U.S. involvement in overseas conflict zones. To overcome this resistance, Truman portrayed the aid proposal in apocalyptic terms—as a global contest between good and evil, freedom and tyranny. Hence his famous Truman Doctrine speech of March 12, 1947, in which he pledged unstinting American assistance to any nation threatened with Communist subjugation.[39]

Greece, Turkey, and Iran—the three countries we then considered most at risk from Soviet expansionism—were the first to benefit from U.S. assistance under the Truman Doctrine. By strengthening these "northern-tier" nations, American strategists hoped to construct a solid phalanx of anti-Soviet powers that would protect the more vulnerable—and valuable—oil kingdoms to the south.[40] But American leaders also sought to boost Saudi Arabia's own defensive capabilities, and so U.S. military aid was soon flowing directly to the kingdom. In 1949, in the renegotiation of the three-year U.S. lease on the military airfield at Dhahran that Ibn Saud had granted in 1946, the Department of Defense agreed to help the Saudis create a modern army. The plan was formalized in the Mutual Defense Assistance Agreement of June 18, 1951, authorizing the delivery of American arms and combat gear and the deployment of the U.S. Military Training Mission (USMTM) to Saudi Arabia.[41] The USMTM helped assemble and train the first Saudi army units and equipped them with basic infantry gear; it also assisted in the formation of the Royal Saudi Air Force and arranged for the delivery of its first modern combat planes.[42]

The United States stepped up its military aid program in 1957, in accordance with the second of the presidential edicts bearing on Saudi Arabian security affairs, the Eisenhower Doctrine. Like the Truman Doctrine, the policy was triggered by growing U.S. unease over Soviet involvement in the Middle East—in this instance, the strengthening military ties between the Soviet bloc and Gamal Abdel Nasser's Egypt. Nasser, a passionate advocate of Arab nationalism, had sought to enhance Egyptian autonomy, first by signing an arms agreement with Czechoslovakia, in 1955, and then, in July 1956, by nationalizing the Suez Canal—a move that immediately prompted Great Britain, France, and Israel to send in troops.* After the invading forces were finally withdrawn, Nasser adopted an even more antagonistic stance toward the Western powers and began buying arms directly from the USSR. In response, Washington initiated a fresh effort to bolster friendly regimes in the region under a policy that came to be known as the Eisenhower Doctrine. First enunciated in a presidential address of January 5, 1957, and later incorporated into a joint congressional resolution, the doctrine authorized the president to use American combat forces to defend friendly Middle Eastern countries against Soviet-backed aggressors and to provide additional arms and military assistance to pro-American regimes.[44]

This time around, Saudi Arabia was one of the earliest beneficiaries of the American aid, receiving assurances in April 1957 (in conjunction with another extension of the lease on the Dhahran air base) of a significant boost in military assistance. The bulk of the aid went to the modernization of the kingdom's army and air force—both of which received additional consignments of modern weapons—while additional support was provided for the establishment of a small Saudi navy.[45] Moreover, in a move that would have significant implications for U.S. security later, the Department of Defense began supplying arms and assistance to the Saudi Arabian National Guard (SANG), a paramilitary force under the control of the royal family, whose principal task was and is to defend the regime against internal revolt.[46]

---

*To the surprise of many, President Eisenhower did not support the British-French-Israeli invasion of Egypt, but rather condemned the assault. Despite his intense dislike of Nasser, Eisenhower concluded that the invasion would fan the flames of Arab nationalism and thus pose a significant threat to the survival of the Saudi regime.[43]

Eisenhower and his successors also made good on the pledge to deploy American combat forces to defend key allies. In the first such instance, in July 1958, Eisenhower ordered U.S. troops into Lebanon to help protect the pro-Western government of President Camille Chamoun during a period of mounting unrest there and in the wider region; he withdrew them four months later, when a measure of calm had returned to the country.[47] Then, when Saudi border posts came under attack from rebel forces in Yemen during the Yemeni civil war of 1962–70, the Kennedy administration sent a contingent of American combat planes to the kingdom; while this endeavor was of no great military significance, it is worth mentioning here because it was the first concrete expression of Washington's readiness to shed American blood on behalf of Saudi Arabia.[48]

By the late 1960s, however, the U.S. public was taking a distinctly different view of American bloodshed on behalf of friendly regimes in the developing world. The high cost of such commitments brought about yet another presidential foreign policy edict: the Nixon Doctrine. Unlike the Truman and Eisenhower doctrines, this new policy responded not to the Soviet threat but to the heavy burdens of British and American intervention. In 1968, London had announced that it was withdrawing its military forces from "east of Suez" by the end of 1971, thus ending a century of British dominion in the Gulf. Up to that point, Washington had been able to rely on Great Britain as the ultimate guarantor of Western interests in the region. But with Britain out of the picture, the United States faced a critical decision: whether to take over as the regional hegemon itself or to find some other country (or countries) to do so. President Richard Nixon might have preferred the former course, but with the nation already entangled in Vietnam he had good reason to fear that the American public would reject another major military commitment; accordingly, he reluctantly chose the route of deputizing friendly local powers to protect American interests.

When it was first announced, in July 1969, the Nixon Doctrine was aimed primarily at Southeast Asia. Anxious to extricate U.S. forces from Vietnam and to avoid entangling Americans in any more such conflicts, the White House sought to shift the burden of the fighting to the countries in the region. "We shall furnish military and economic assistance when requested," the president explained in a report to Congress, but "we shall look to the nation directly threatened to assume the primary responsibility of providing the manpower for its defense."[49] The administration was soon applying this principle in the Persian Gulf area, as Nixon reached a decision to enhance the military strength of Iran and Saudi Arabia so that they could take greater responsibility for the region's and their own security.[50] Rather than have the United States assume "the former British role of protector in the Gulf area," Deputy Assistant Secretary of Defense James H. Noyes later told Congress, we would delegate this function to local powers. "In the spirit of the Nixon Doctrine," he testified, "we are willing to assist the Gulf states but we look to them to bear the main responsibility for their own defense and to cooperate among themselves to insure regional peace and stability." In particular, "[we] look to the leading states of the area, Iran and Saudi Arabia, to cooperate for this purpose."[51]

Where previous administrations had ramped up military aid to friendly states in the Persian Gulf area incrementally, the Nixon Doctrine opened the floodgates. Billions of dollars' worth of advanced weaponry were now transferred to the two chosen agents of American strategy.[52] Iran received 190 F-4 Phantom combat planes, 80 F-14 air-superiority fighters, and 460 M-60A1 tanks; Saudi Arabia got 60 F-15 Eagle fighter planes, 200 AH-1S attack helicopters, and 250 M-60A1 tanks.[53] Most of this equipment went to the countries' regular armed forces, but many of the arms were designated for their police and internal security forces, particularly in Saudi Arabia, where the United States backed a major expansion of the National Guard. In addition, the Army Corps of Engineers assumed responsibility for the construction of a new SANG headquarters complex in Riyadh—a site that would later become one of the early targets of Osama bin Laden's terror campaign.[54]

Because Iranian and Saudi military personnel were generally inexperienced in operating and maintaining such high-tech weapons, most of these arms transfers also entailed the deployment of thousands of American military advisers and technicians. By 1977, the number of Americans serving in this capacity was substantial: as many as 6,250 in Iran and 4,140 in Saudi Arabia, not including dependents.[55] Though these advisers were essential to the success of the U.S. arms-transfer programs and thus of the Nixon Doctrine itself, they eventually became a source of friction and unrest. In Saudi Arabia, Muslim critics objected to the presence of so many infidels in the kingdom; in Iran, dissident clerics complained that the Americans were bringing alcohol and pornography into the country. The close American relationship with SANG also became a problem, since reform-minded Saudis and those seeking the abolition of the monarchy came to view the United States as an enemy.

Nevertheless, the Nixon Doctrine did have some success early on. The shah of Iran, who had regained the Peacock Throne in 1953 with American assistance,[56] was particularly enthusiastic. Not only did he jump at the chance to acquire large numbers of modern weapons, spending some $14 billion on American arms during the 1970s alone, but he also provided the sultan of Oman with troops for a campaign against Marxist-inspired rebels in Oman's Dhofar province.[57] Saudi Arabia cooperated with the plan too, by financing an American-supplied air-defense system in Jordan and by assisting North Yemen against the revolutionary regime in South Yemen.[58] But the Nixon Doctrine was not enough to protect all of America's interests in the region. Saudi Arabia's close military ties with Washington did not prevent its participation in the Arab oil embargo against the United States, imposed in October 1973 in retaliation for Washington's support of Israel in the 1973 Arab-Israeli war; although the embargo was lifted after several months, with a pledge by Washington to be more evenhanded in its Middle East policy, it and the simultaneous OPEC oil-price hike caused economic havoc in the United States.* The royal family also commenced the nationalization of Aramco's Saudi concession at this time, finally

---

*According to recently declassified British documents, in December 1973 Secretary of Defense James R. Schlesinger told the British ambassador to Washington that the administration might consider using military force to seize Saudi oil fields if the embargo lasted much longer; but such a move was apparently judged too risky and provocative to be given serious consideration.[59]

terminating the outright ownership of Saudi petroleum reserves by American companies—which were, however, permitted to retain a significant role in the overseas marketing of Saudi oil.[60]

America's interests in Iran also began to suffer at this time. The seemingly invincible shah became the target of a well-organized, broadly based opposition movement organized by militant Shiite clerics, and the closeness of his ties with the United States weakened his position; rumors of bribery around the U.S. arms sales and drunken behavior by American soldiers and arms-company workers fueled the antigovernment campaign. Even the shah's U.S.-equipped military forces turned against him, and, on January 16, 1979, he abdicated and fled. Within a few months, the country was in the hands of the Ayatollah Ruholla Khomeini's revolutionary Islamic regime.[61]

Sending in the Troops:
From the Carter Doctrine to the Gulf War

The fall of the shah spelled the failure of the Nixon Doctrine in the Persian Gulf and forced the American government—then headed by President Carter—to conduct a fresh review of security policy in the region. This time around, there were no obvious candidates for regional policeman: Saudi Arabia was too weak to assume the role, and the only other local power, Iraq, was firmly entrenched in the Soviet camp. Clearly, any U.S. effort to maintain stability in the Gulf and protect our interests there would require a more vigorous and conspicuous role for the American military.

While the White House was struggling to devise a new strategy for the Gulf, two other events occurred that were to have a dramatic and long-term impact on U.S. policy—the takeover of the American embassy in Tehran by Islamic militants on November 5, 1979, and the Soviet invasion of Afghanistan seven weeks later—and in each event Washington saw a significant threat to the safety of the Persian Gulf oil fields. The embassy occupation and the accompanying seizure of fifty-three American hostages brought the United States into an antagonistic relationship with Iran and complicated the defense of Persian Gulf oil routes. Moreover, with the shah out of the picture, Iran was no longer a reliable shield against Soviet incursion into the Gulf—a blow underscored by the Soviet presence in Afghanistan, which at its nearest point lay only three hundred miles away. Suddenly, the Persian Gulf rose to the very top of the U.S. security agenda, a place it has occupied ever since.

Devising a satisfactory response to these developments proved to be the most difficult challenge the Carter administration would face. Critics charged the president with weakness, and, indeed, his failure to free the hostages in Iran may have doomed him in the 1980 presidential election against Ronald Reagan. But Carter did adopt a muscular response in the end. Abandoning reliance on local surrogates, Carter decreed that the United States would henceforth assume the primary responsibility for the defense of the Gulf. This was the Carter Doctrine, enunciated in his State of the Union address on January 23, 1980. Access to Persian Gulf oil was a vital national interest, Carter declared, and to protect that interest the United States was prepared to use "any means necessary, including military force."

In the months that followed, Carter announced a series of steps to facilitate the projection of American military power into the Gulf area. The most significant was the establishment of the Rapid Deployment Joint Task Force, the Tampa-based military command that would take responsibility for managing U.S. combat operations in the region. Although it had no forces of its own, the RDJTF had the authority to assemble an expeditionary army composed of a number of U.S.-based units for service in the Gulf. Carter also ordered the procurement of long-range cargo planes and supply vessels that could transport American forces to likely combat zones; and, to sustain those forces once they were deployed in the Gulf, negotiated access to new basing facilities in Oman, Kenya, and Somalia and on Diego Garcia Island in the British Indian Ocean Territory.[62]

Although Ronald Reagan and his supporters had been highly critical of Carter during the 1980 campaign, the new administration fully endorsed the basic premise of the Carter Doctrine.[63] If anything, Reagan was even more determined to implement the policy. To enhance the RDJTF's authority, he elevated its Tampa office from an ad hoc staff organization to a full-scale regional headquarters, the Central Command, thus placing it on a par with the European Command in Stuttgart and the Pacific Command in Honolulu.[64] Reagan also stepped up the procurement of cargo planes, supply vessels, and other equipment needed to speed the deployment of U.S. forces to the Gulf.

At the same time, Reagan carried on Nixon's policy of arming our Gulf allies to the hilt. Eager to ingratiate himself with the Saudi rulers, the president approved the largest U.S. arms sale to that country ever: an $8.5 billion package comprising 5 Airborne Warning and Control System (AWACS) surveillance aircraft, 7 KC-135 tanker aircraft, 660 Sidewinder air-to-air missiles, 22 ground radar installations, and a large array of air-defense and communications systems. The announcement of this sale provoked a firestorm in Congress: many lawmakers opposed *any* military sale to Saudi Arabia that could be construed as posing a threat to Israel, and certainly one of this magnitude. Despite heavy lobbying by the administration, the House of Representatives voted, on October 14, 1981, to block the AWACS sale; only an emotional eleventh-hour appeal by President Reagan prevented a similar loss in the Senate and the cancellation of the sale.[65] (Under the Arms Export Control Act of 1976, both houses of Congress must vote against a proposed arms transaction to overturn it.)

Beyond testing Reagan's leadership, the 1981 AWACS sale to the Saudis was important in several respects. Above all, it exposed the flip side of American dependence on Saudi oil: American acquiescence to Saudi demands. In seeking to modernize their military forces, the Saudis demanded the most advanced weapons in the American arsenal and thus caused enormous embarrassment to President Reagan, who felt obligated to submit to their extravagant requests. He even had to strong-arm senators in his own party to avoid insulting our major foreign supplier of petroleum. And since the Saudis could not operate or maintain this new high-tech weaponry on their own, Washington had to reinforce the military technicians it had sent to the kingdom in the 1970s, under the Nixon Doctrine, with still more. Having made all these concessions, however, Reagan did seek something in return: Saudi financial support for the Central Intelligence Agency's clandestine campaigns to overthrow the Soviet-backed regimes in Afghanistan, Nicaragua, and elsewhere.[66] Among the beneficiaries of this secret largesse was Osama bin Laden, a wealthy Saudi entrepreneur who helped recruit Islamic zealots to serve with the Afghan rebels. While ultimately successful in repelling the Soviets, these efforts established a pattern of Saudi aid—or "charitable contributions"—to militant Islamic groups in Afghanistan, and so laid the foundation for the rise of Al Qaeda and the Taliban.[67]

Reagan also chose this moment to reaffirm the American pledge to protect Saudi Arabia and the House of Saud. When supporters of Khomeini's revolutionary regime in Iran began to agitate for a similar revolution in Saudi Arabia, the president vowed that the United States would never allow the Saudi royal family to be overthrown the way the shah had been. "There is no way," he told reporters on October 1, 1981, "that we would stand by and see [Saudi Arabia] taken over by anyone who would shut off the oil."[68] In addition, the administration made it clear that the United States would protect Saudi Arabia from such spillover effects of the Iran-Iraq War of 1980–88 as attacks on Saudi oil tankers in the Persian Gulf. When one such tanker was attacked, in May 1984, the president assured King Fahd that Washington was prepared to use military force to protect Saudi shipping in the future.[69]

Although the United States did not take part directly in the Iran-Iraq War, it played an important behind-the-scenes role in determining the outcome. When Iraq invaded Iran, in September 1980, Washington declared itself neutral, imposing an arms embargo on both belligerents. But when Iran gained the upper hand, in 1982, the Reagan administration—perceiving a potential Iranian threat to U.S. oil interests in Kuwait and Saudi Arabia—began to aid the Iraqis with loans, intelligence support, and covert arms transfers. This policy, known in Washington as the "tilt" toward Iraq, rewarded Baghdad with billions of dollars in agricultural credits (much of it spent on arms) and the sale of militarily significant hardware, such as heavy trucks and helicopters.[70]

America's most significant action in the Iran-Iraq War came in 1987–88, when we outfitted Kuwaiti oil tankers with American flags and defended them against Iranian attack. The administration rationalized this step as a natural corollary to the Carter Doctrine. "We would regard as especially serious any threat by either party to interfere with free navigation or act in any way that would restrict oil exports from the Gulf," Deputy Assistant Secretary of State Robert H. Pelletreau told Congress in 1983.[71] When Iran ignored this warning and stepped up its attacks on Kuwaiti tankers—presumably to punish the Kuwaitis for having helped finance Iraqi arms purchases—Washington decided to act. In July 1987, American warships began to escort "reflagged" Kuwaiti tankers through the Gulf, ultimately provoking a number of clashes with Iranian naval vessels.[72] Our decision to aid Kuwait in this way, combined with a series of setbacks on the battlefield, eventually led the Iranians to abandon the war and sue for peace.[73]

The Iran-Iraq War drew to a close in August 1988, with the exhausted and impoverished belligerents agreeing to a cease-fire and peace talks. But peace in the Gulf reigned briefly. Disappointed with the outcome of the war and facing a mountain of accumulated wartime debt, the Iraqi dictator, Saddam Hussein, began to view Kuwait—which was refusing to forgive the debt Baghdad had built up during the war to pay for arms— as the source of his problems. Seizing his small neighbor's rich oil fields looked like a handy way out of Iraq's financial predicament. After issuing a series of increasingly threatening (and unheeded) ultimatums to Kuwait, Hussein ordered Iraqi troops into the country on August 2, 1990.

In the months leading up to the invasion, American leaders had been struggling to develop a coherent policy on Iraq, with some favoring efforts to placate Saddam (in the hope of averting a breakdown in relations), and others calling for a sterner approach. But when Iraqi tanks rolled into Kuwait City, the White House instantly concluded that Iraq posed an indisputable threat to America's interests in the Gulf. At the first National Security Council (NSC) meeting convened to discuss the invasion, on the morning of August 2, President George H. W. Bush expressed considerable alarm over the safety of Saudi Arabia and the global oil supply. Saudi Arabia's major oil fields, which are largely concentrated in al-Hasa, the Eastern Province adjoining Iraq, were immediately vulnerable; if the Iraqis used their beachhead in Kuwait to invade the kingdom,

they stood to gain control over 25 percent of the world's petroleum reserves. Bush ordered the Department of Defense to make plans for military action to defend the Saudi oil fields; by August 4, he had decided that
military action was essential; and, on August 6—just four days after the
Iraqi invasion—he authorized Secretary of Defense Dick Cheney to begin deploying American troops in Saudi Arabia.[74]

Oil, and the fate of Saudi Arabia, stood at the center of White House
deliberations in the early days of the crisis. In a nationally televised address on August 8 announcing his decision to use military force in the
Gulf, Bush cited America's energy needs as his primary impetus. "Our
country now imports nearly half the oil it consumes and could face a major threat to its economic independence," he declared. Hence, "the sovereign independence of Saudi Arabia is of vital interest to the United
States."[75] Secretary of Defense Dick Cheney sounded the same note, high-
lighting the threat to oil in his first major statement on the crisis, at a September 11 appearance before the Senate Armed Services Committee.
"Once [Saddam] acquired Kuwait and deployed an army as large as the
one he possesses," Cheney observed, he would be "in a position to be able
to dictate the future of worldwide energy policy, and that [would give]
him a stranglehold on our economy."[76] Only later, when American troops
were girding for combat with the Iraqis, did administration officials
come up with other justifications for war: the need to liberate Kuwait, to
destroy Iraqi weapons of mass destruction, to bolster international sanctions against aggression, and so forth. The record makes it clear, though,
that the president and his senior associates initially viewed the invasion
of Kuwait through the lens of the Carter Doctrine: as a threat to Saudi
Arabia and the free flow of oil from the Gulf.[77]

The Road to 9/11

Putting troops on the ground in Saudi Arabia, the Bush administration
concluded, was the only way to effectively defend the kingdom; any less
drastic action—such as a punishing round of air strikes, for example—
would be too feeble to deter Saddam Hussein.[78] But having resolved on

direct intervention, the White House came up against an unexpected problem: Saudi reluctance to let sizable numbers of American soldiers into the country. Since the days of Ibn Saud, the royal family had opposed any conspicuous foreign military presence in the kingdom—partly out of fear of colonial occupation (the fate of several neighboring countries) and partly out of fear of domestic protest. In 1945, Riyadh had rejected an American proposal to station a small military training group in the kingdom, because, as William A. Eddy, the U.S. ambassador, explained to his superiors in Washington, King Ibn Saud thought it would provoke "violent criticism from reactionaries and fanatics."[79] Forty-five years later, the monarchy still dreaded such criticism, and so King Fahd resisted Washington's request for permission to deploy its forces there. In a desperate bid to change his mind, Bush sent Cheney to Riyadh to try to convince him of the urgent need for military action.[80]

The August 6 meeting between Secretary Cheney and King Fahd was, in many ways, emblematic of the tortured relationship between the two nations. Senior American officials typically had to assume a servile posture when entreating Saudi leaders to do what (in Washington's view) was in their own best interests—on this occasion, Cheney had to await a royal summons before he could present his case. Only when Fahd was shown satellite photographs of Iraqi tanks allegedly moving toward the Kuwaiti-Saudi border did Fahd conclude that Saddam Hussein posed a greater immediate danger than did the anger of his subjects. The king then granted his permission for the deployment of American ground troops, but not before he added a strict injunction: the troops *must* be withdrawn from Saudi Arabia the minute the danger from Iraq had passed.[81]

Having given Fahd assurances on this point, Secretary Cheney called President Bush and requested authorization to commence Operation Desert Shield, the armed defense of Saudi Arabia.[82] Within hours, the first U.S. combat planes and a brigade of Army paratroopers from the 82nd Airborne Division were on their way to the Gulf. By August 12, only ten days after the invasion of Kuwait, more than one hundred U.S. combat planes had been deployed in the Gulf area, along with most of the

82nd Division and two aircraft-carrier battle groups; at the same time, elements of the Army's 24th Division, 101st Division, and the Marine Corp's 1st Expeditionary Force were being loaded onto ships and planes for transport to the conflict zone.[83] To an extent no one had foreseen, the lives of large numbers of American soldiers—some 250,000 at this point—were being put at risk to ensure the continued flow of oil from Saudi Arabia.

From Washington's perspective, American ground forces were the only sure way to protect Saudi Arabia. But, unbeknownst to the United States, Saudi leaders had been offered another option: reliance on the "Arab-Afghans," a multinational force of Islamic zealots who had battled the Soviets in Afghanistan in the 1980s and had since fought in Bosnia, Kashmir, and elsewhere. Led, or at least financed, by Osama bin Laden, the Arab-Afghans were scattered throughout the Middle East and available for immediate service in any campaign deemed vital to the interests of Islam.[84] Bin Laden enjoyed ready access to the Saudi royal family, having worked closely with Prince Turki bin Faisal, the head of the Saudi intelligence service, while serving in Afghanistan.[85] He now sought to persuade King Fahd to employ the Afghan veterans instead of the Americans. Fahd's decision to reject his offer and to rely instead on an army of "infidels" infuriated bin Laden and turned him into an implacable foe of the royal family.[86]

In 1990, bin Laden was a tiny blip on American radar, while the Iraqi forces in Kuwait looked like an all but overpowering menace. Once sufficient troops had been deployed in Saudi Arabia to repel an Iraqi invasion, the Bush administration shifted gears and began to plan for Operation Desert Storm, the offensive that would drive the Iraqis out of Kuwait. Another 250,000 American troops joined the 250,000 already in the region, and preparations for a full-scale assault on Iraqi positions began in earnest. On January 17, 1991, American and allied aircraft commenced the air campaign; five weeks later, on February 24, Washington launched the ground offensive; and four days after that, on February 28, Iraqi forces abandoned Kuwait and President Bush ordered an end to allied combat operations.[87]

America's leaders decided to refrain from an invasion of Iraq itself, calculating that fierce Iraqi resistance would produce heavy U.S.

casualties.[88] But they had no intention of letting Saddam rebuild his forces and renew his threat to Kuwait and Saudi Arabia. Accordingly, the Bush senior and Clinton administrations adopted a strategy of "containment," designed to isolate Iraq from the rest of the world community. They imposed an air and sea blockade, intended to prevent Saddam from obtaining new arms or the technology to manufacture weapons of mass destruction. They also established a permanent American military presence in Kuwait and declared a no-fly zone (an area prohibited to Iraqi aircraft) over southern Iraq. And they "pre-positioned" vast quantities of arms and ammunition at supply depots in Kuwait and Qatar, so that any American troops airlifted into the region could collect their gear and jump into combat with a minimum of delay.

From the end of the Persian Gulf War in 1991 to the terrorist attacks of 2001, this containment strategy was the driving factor in U.S.-Saudi military relations. Approximately five thousand American pilots and support personnel were stationed at Saudi bases in execution of Operation Southern Watch, the enforcement of the no-fly zone in southern Iraq; between 1991 and 2000, they conducted more than 240,000 sorties (individual flights) for this purpose.[89] The Department of Defense used the sophisticated command center at Prince Sultan Air Base outside Riyadh to oversee U.S. air combat operations in the Gulf and to manage other aspects of the containment policy.[90] As in the 1970s and 1980s, moreover, the United States provided the Saudi military and the National Guard with vast quantities of modern weapons. Between 1991 and 1999, the Department of Defense sold the Saudis some $40 billion worth of arms, ammunition, and military services through the Foreign Military Sales program—four times as much as our combined sales to Egypt and Taiwan, the number two and number three recipients of U.S. weaponry.[91]

Though the containment strategy allowed Saddam Hussein to remain in power, for American officials it possessed one overarching virtue: it eliminated the threat to Kuwait and Saudi Arabia—the ultimate objective of our Gulf policy—without requiring the permanent deployment of hundreds of thousands of American troops. But it created a new and unexpected problem. Conducting Operation Southern Watch required the United States to continue occupying the air bases it had established in

Saudi Arabia during Operation Desert Shield—thus violating Cheney's promise to King Fahd that U.S. forces would leave the kingdom once the fighting was over. For Osama bin Laden, this was the final act of betrayal. Accusing the royal family of subservience to American interests, he called on his followers to use any means, including armed violence, to topple the monarchy and push the Americans out of the country.[92] "For over seven years," bin Laden averred in 1998, "the United States has been occupying the lands of Islam in the holiest of places, the Arabian Peninsula, plundering its riches, dictating to its rulers, humiliating its people, terrorizing its neighbors, and turning its bases in the Peninsula into a spearhead through which to fight the neighboring Muslim peoples." To erase this blight on the Muslim world, he thundered, it was "an individual duty for every Muslim" to "kill the Americans" and drive their armies "out of all the lands of Islam."[93]

Bin Laden would soon prove that he was serious. He and his associates embarked on a dual strategy. On the one hand, they took aim at the physical manifestations of American power in the region, especially military bases and embassies. On the other, they attacked symbolic targets in the United States, hoping thereby to erode Washington's attachment to its bases in Saudi Arabia. As part of the first strategy, bin Laden operatives bombed the SANG headquarters in Riyadh in 1995, killing five Americans, and attacked the Khobar Towers (a residential complex occupied by U.S. Air Force personnel assigned to Operation Southern Watch) in Dhahran in 1996, killing another nineteen. These attacks were followed, in August 1998, by the bombings of the American embassies in Nairobi, Kenya, and Dar es Salaam, Tanzania, and, in October 2000, by the attack on the USS *Cole* while it was berthed in Aden, Yemen. The second strategy produced the 9/11 assaults on the World Trade Center in New York City and the Pentagon in Washington.

In the wake of the 9/11 attacks, analysts in the United States and abroad attributed a wide variety of motives to the perpetrators. Especially popular was the view that 9/11 represented the opening salvo in a new war between the Islamic world and the (mostly) Christian West, as Harvard professor Samuel P. Huntington had predicted in his influential 1993 *Foreign Affairs* essay, "The Clash of Civilizations?"[94] Other thinkers

suggested that the attacks reflected growing rage against economic globalization, or anger at continued American support for Israel in its struggle with the Palestinians. But while these theories may help explain why
so many Muslims have been drawn to Al Qaeda, they do not sufficiently
explain 9/11. Osama bin Laden's hostility toward the United States was
provoked primarily by the deployment of American troops in Saudi Arabia and the continuing alliance between Washington and the Saudi royal
family—the alliance forged in 1945 by President Roosevelt and King Ibn
Saud. And although this alliance may have evolved over the years in response to changing regional and international conditions, it remains, as
before, a product of America's thirst for imported oil and the monarchy's
hunger for protection.

The 9/11 attacks occurred several months into the Bush administration,
but in a sense their grim shadow was already felt when George W. Bush
first entered the White House in February 2001. Bush was deeply aware
that growing U.S. dependence on Middle Eastern oil was a source of danger for the United States, and he campaigned on a promise to address this
peril if elected. How he chose to do so once installed in the White House
is the subject of the next chapter.

3

Choosing Dependency:
The Energy Strategy of the
Bush Administration

George W. Bush assumed the presidency at a critical juncture in the evolution of U.S. energy policy. Just twenty months before, in April 1998, the United States had passed a disquieting milestone of energy dependency: for the first time, the country had imported more than half of the oil it consumed—and the proportion was destined to grow. Two years later, in the summer and fall of 2000, the eastern United States and much of the Midwest suffered a shortage of oil and natural gas, and California endured a series of rolling electricity blackouts. With gasoline prices in many areas topping two dollars a gallon, farmers and truckers descended on Washington to demand federal action. In March 2001, President Bush acknowledged that the nation was undergoing an "energy crisis" and hinted that troubling structural trends were behind it. "The reality is, the nation has got a problem when it comes to energy," he said. "We need more sources of energy."[1]

Recognizing that it was going to take more than a superficial correction to address this crisis, Bush announced plans for a major review of energy policy. The goal, he explained, was to examine the country's consumption patterns, forecast our future needs, and find effective ways to meet them. "One thing is for certain," he warned in March 2001. "There are no short-term fixes.... The solution for our energy shortage requires long-term thinking and a plan ... that will take time to bring to fruition."[2] Responsibility for the plan went to the National Energy Policy Development Group (NEPDG), a new body created by the White House and staffed with high officials from the Departments of State, Commerce, and Energy. Stressing the need for decisive action, Bush ordered the group to complete its work by May 2001, only four months into his administration.

The NEPDG was instructed to examine every aspect of the nation's energy situation, from the need for better electricity-distribution networks to a deficiency of oil-refinery capacity and a shortage of natural-gas pipelines. But the central concern, and the toughest issue the group had to address, was what to do about the nation's growing thirst for imported petroleum. "On our present course," the NEPDG warned in its report, "America 20 years from now will import nearly two of every three barrels of oil—a condition of increased dependency on foreign powers that do not always have America's interests at heart."[3] Viewing this development as a threat to national security and economic well-being, the NEPDG called for action to stem our nation's reliance on imported oil. But even as it was claiming to blaze a new trail, the group was really embracing a more vigorous commitment to the same old path. Energy policy under the new Bush administration was to become more and more tied to fossil fuels—with deeply disturbing implications for U.S. foreign policy.

The Fork in the Road

As the NEPDG set about its work in February 2001, it was obvious that the United States stood at a crossroads. The nation could continue consuming more and more petroleum and sinking deeper and deeper into its dependence on imports. Or it could choose an alternative route, enforcing strict energy conservation, encouraging the use of fuel-efficient vehicles, and promoting the development of renewable energy sources, such as wind and solar power. The incompatibility of these two policy paths had long been apparent to energy experts and, to one degree or another, the general public. But it was only with the creation of the NEPDG that the critical choice was finally addressed at the very highest levels of government.[4]

Clearly, the decision was going to have profound social, economic, and political consequences. Continuing with the status quo would bind the United States ever more tightly to the Persian Gulf oil states. But altering it would require huge investments in new energy-generation and transportation technologies, engendering the rise or fall of entire industries. Either way, Americans would feel the impact in their day-to-day lives and in the world around them. No one, in the United States or elsewhere, would be left untouched by the decision on which energy path we would follow.

In reality, no one much doubted which path the administration would choose. After all, the president had tapped Vice President Dick Cheney to direct the work of the NEPDG and assess the competing options. Cheney was the former CEO of the Halliburton Company, a major oil-field services firm, and he had close ties with senior officials at other large energy firms. Predictably, he sought strategy recommendations from his former colleagues in the oil, gas, and coal industries—in particular senior officials of the Enron Corporation, a giant energy company with close ties to Bush and other members of the administration.[5] (Secretary of the Army Thomas E. White had been vice chairman of Enron Energy Services before joining the administration, and both U.S. trade representative Robert Zoellick and White House economic adviser Larry Lindsey had been on the Enron payroll as consultants.) Secretary of Energy Spencer Abraham, another key figure in the NEPDG review, met with no less than 109 representatives of prominent energy firms between January and May 2001; many of these firms, including ChevronTexaco, Exxon Mobil, and Enron, had been lavish contributors to the Republicans' 2000 election campaign.[6]

Given the extent of the administration's links to the energy industry, not many observers expected that the NEPDG report would buck the status quo. And Vice President Cheney did nothing to change their minds when, on April 30, 2001, he belittled conservation and suggested that upping oil, coal, and natural gas production was our only viable option.

Speaking to reporters at an Associated Press meeting in Toronto, he scoffed at the notion that "we could simply conserve or ration our way out" of an impending energy crisis. "Conservation may be a sign of personal virtue," he sniffed, "but it is not a sufficient basis for a sound, comprehensive energy policy." The reality, he said, was that oil and other fossil fuels would remain America's primary source of energy for "years down the road," and therefore the administration would seek to *increase* their availability, not restrict it.[7]

Cheney made his remarks just two weeks before the NEPDG was scheduled to release its report, and they triggered a barrage of reproof from congressional Democrats and leaders of the environmental community. "They pay lip service to [energy] efficiency, but their whole emphasis is on [increasing] supply," Senator Jeff Bingaman, a Democrat from New Mexico, complained.[8] Stung by such remarks, the White House hastily retooled its message, inserting a new emphasis on conservation, efficiency, and alternative energy into its energy proposal.[9]

The administration released the Cheney team's report and recommendations, formally titled the *National Energy Policy* (*NEP*), on May 17, 2001. The new policy, Bush declared, "reduces demand by promoting innovation and technology to make us the world leader in efficiency and conservation." The plan would "underwrite research and development into energy-saving technology" and would "require manufacturers to build more energy-efficient appliances." This new, green approach, the president maintained, would ensure an adequate energy supply while simultaneously reducing American dependence on imported oil and averting damage to the environment.[10] To add symbolic weight to this claim, he released the *NEP* at an experimental power plant near St. Paul that burns wood chips and other "biomass" fuels as well as oil. In his remarks that day he said that he had just "toured a plant that harnessed the best of the new technology to produce energy that is cleaner and more efficient and more affordable."[11] A day later, he reiterated his commitment to alternative resources: "I hope someday that these renewables will be the dominant source of energy in America," he said at a hydroelectric plant near Conestoga, Pennsylvania.[12]

But although the president's rhetoric stressed a commitment to conservation and self-sufficiency, a close reading of the *National Energy Policy*—also known, after its principal author, as the Cheney report—reveals something radically different. For all the discussion of new energy initiatives, the *NEP* never envisions any reduction in our use of petroleum. Instead, it proposes steps that would *increase* consumption while making token efforts to slow, but not halt, our dependence on foreign providers. In fact, the essence of the *NEP* is a commitment to the *expansion* of America's oil economy. The single concession it makes to the problem of dependence on foreign producers is a call for the intensified exploitation of our own petroleum reserves, including untapped fields in Alaska and other protected wilderness areas.

The proposal to increase domestic oil production by drilling in the vast, untouched wilderness preserve in Alaska known as the Arctic National Wildlife Refuge, or ANWR, won immediate praise from congressional Republicans and from entrepreneurs who favor the use of federal lands for oil, gas, and coal production. Not surprisingly, it also provoked denunciations from Democrats and environmentalists who were outraged over the prospective spoliation of a pristine wilderness area. The debate over ANWR was so vitriolic that it wholly monopolized the public discussion of the president's energy plan—thus obscuring many of its more alarming features.

As the ANWR fracas intensified, the White House and conservative commentators attempted to spin the president's proposal as a choice between energy "independence" and excessive environmental protection. In a July 2001 address before the National Press Club, for example, Secretary of Energy Spencer Abraham avowed, "Our plan confronts our increasing dependency on foreign sources of energy by calling for—yes, it's true, I admit it—increased domestic production of energy."[13] But while comments of this sort were intended to suggest that the administration was pursuing a policy of self-sufficiency, the facts told another story. Even if ANWR really contains the 10 billion barrels of oil the drilling lobby claims it does, extracting it would reduce U.S. imports by only about 3 percent per year during the next two decades—an almost negligible change.[14]

Aside for the ANWR proposal, nothing in the Cheney plan offered any prospect for lowering our dependence on imported petroleum. In-

deed, one searches the *NEP* in vain for any evidence of the Bush administration's commitment to a fundamental shift in American energy behavior. Yes, it earmarks limited funds for research on new propulsion
systems, including hydrogen-powered fuel cells for automobiles. But
these timid moves will no more change America's oil-consuming behavior than will drilling in ANWR. Instead, the Bush-Cheney plan aims to
sustain our petroleum habit—and the complicated geopolitical arrangements that support it.

No doubt Bush was influenced by Kenneth Lay, the CEO of Enron,
and other friends in the oil and gas industry. Any significant alteration in
U.S. energy policy would inevitably affect the future prospects and prof-
its of these companies, so naturally they lobbied long and hard against
one. And like his predecessors in the White House, Bush recognized the
critical role petroleum plays in driving the American economy and thus
was reluctant to do anything that would diminish it. He understood that
shifting to other sources of energy would entail a change in lifestyle that
the American public might not easily accept, and was unwilling to take
the political risk. And so he chose the path of least resistance.

Perpetuating Dependency

The greater rather than smaller dependence on imported petroleum that
the Bush energy plan envisions does not jump out at a reader of the May
2001 *National Energy Policy*, at least not right away. The first seven chapters focus on boosting domestic energy output, particularly by removing
the regulatory bars to greater exploitation of domestic oil, gas, and coal
deposits and by relying more widely on nuclear power. It is only in the
eighth and final chapter, "Strengthening Global Alliances," that the pivotal feature of the administration's strategy emerges: increasing petroleum imports. At this point, the tone changes markedly, from deference
to conservation and energy efficiency to emphasis on our need for foreign oil. "U.S. national energy security depends on sufficient energy supplies to support U.S. and global economic growth," the chapter begins,
going on to explain that, because the United States cannot generate
enough oil from domestic reserves, it has to secure more petroleum from

abroad. To this end, the *NEP* enjoins the president and his associates to "make energy security a priority of our trade and foreign policy."[15]

While acknowledging the need for increasing imports, the Cheney report is very circumspect about just how vast this need is going to be. The only hint appears in a chart showing the nation's projected oil production vs. consumption over the next twenty years. (See figure 4.) According to the chart, domestic production will decline by about 18 percent between 2000 and 2020, falling from 8.5 to 7.0 million barrels per day, while total consumption will grow by 31 percent, from 19.5 to 25.5 million barrels. This means that imports—the difference between the two—will have to rise by approximately 68 percent, from 11 to 18.5 million barrels per day, the equivalent of current consumption by China and India combined.[16] Most of the recommendations in chapter 8 of the *NEP* are geared toward finding ways to guarantee this huge increase.

Our future demand for foreign oil, in other words, will be staggeringly large—and getting it won't be easy. This is a subject upon which the *NEP* has much to say. In fact, the report makes thirty-five foreign-policy recommendations—one-third of its total proposals—on how to facilitate America's acquisition of imported oil. Most of these recommendations are region- or country-specific ideas for enhancing our access to particular sources; but the overall thrust of the report is on removing the economic and political obstacles to overseas procurement. Indeed, the Cheney report can be read as a sort of grand blueprint for American foreign policy, calling as it does for a vigorous effort, led by the president himself, to bolster our ties with oil-rich countries and expand our presence in key producing areas.

Not surprisingly, it also envisions a close working relationship between the federal government and the American oil giants. This sort of collaboration, as I pointed out in chapter 2, was a hallmark of U.S. strategy in the Persian Gulf during the early cold-war era.[17] In the Cheney-Bush version, the partnership entails a novel division of labor: the government will work with foreign governments to overcome obstacles to American investment and maintain stability in key producing areas; the energy companies will put up the investment capital, assemble the technical and logistic capabilities to extract the oil, and arrange for its delivery to refineries in the United States. "American energy firms remain world leaders, and their investments in energy producing countries enhance efficiencies and market linkages," the *NEP* explains. "Promoting such investment will be a core element of our engagement with major foreign oil producers."[18]

Under the Bush-Cheney plan, this partnership would operate in all the regions that harbor potential sources of additional petroleum, beginning with the Persian Gulf. Although cognizant of the risks of relying too heavily on Gulf producers, the plan nevertheless calls for increasing imports from them. "This region will remain vital to U.S. interests," the report avows; Saudi Arabia, in particular, will continue to play a critical role as "the world's largest oil exporter."[19] The Cheney report is relatively

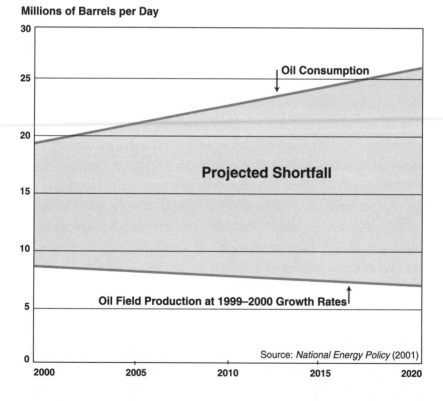

Figure 4
U.S. Dependence on Imported Petroleum, 2000–2020

Millions of Barrels per Day

Oil Consumption

Projected Shortfall

Oil Field Production at 1999–2000 Growth Rates

Source: *National Energy Policy* (2001)

mum as to how much oil the Gulf states will have to pump to meet the growing demand. But other government documents and reports are more forthcoming; for example, projections of global energy patterns released in 2003 by the Department of Energy show that the major Persian Gulf oil producers—Iran, Iraq, Kuwait, Qatar, Saudi Arabia, and the United Arab Emirates—will have to *double* their total daily output between 2001 and 2025, from 22.4 to 45.2 million barrels, to satisfy projected American and international demand.[20]

It is not at all certain that the Gulf countries can meet these expectations. To even come close, they will have to attract much more capital than they can raise internally for necessary infrastructure improvements—new drilling rigs, pipelines, pumping stations, storage tanks, and the like.[21] With this factor in mind, the Cheney report calls on the president and other U.S. officials to "support initiatives by Saudi Arabia, Kuwait, Algeria, Qatar, the UAE, and other suppliers to open up areas of their energy sectors to foreign investment"[22]—an uphill struggle at best, given these states' ingrained resistance to foreign ownership of their assets.

The Lure of Diversification

Even if such resistance could be overcome, large-scale foreign investment alone would not ensure that the Gulf countries would be able to deliver their resources as the United States expects them to. No matter how much oil these countries manage to produce, the world economy will still be vulnerable to shock if war or terrorist attacks disrupt the supply flow. The *NEP* does not discuss this danger, but it must have occurred to the authors, since they do devote considerable attention to expanding the worldwide system of emergency oil reservoirs modeled on the U.S. Strategic Petroleum Reserve.[23] Of course, another kind of insurance for the continued flow of oil is military might, but the *NEP* tactfully omits any discussion of that option. Instead, it recommends that the United States assiduously court suppliers around the world, so that increased petroleum in one area might compensate for a supply disruption in another.

The "concentration of world oil production in any one region of the world is a potential contributor to market instability," the *NEP* contends; therefore, "greater diversity of oil production . . . has obvious benefits to all market participants." To promote such diversity, it enjoins American officials from the president on down to pressure and cajole leaders of non-Gulf producers to increase their exports to the United States. The advice extends to virtually every potential source of petroleum, but the report places special emphasis on several key areas, among them the Western Hemisphere, the Caspian Sea basin, and West Africa. "Growing levels of production and exports [from these regions] are important factors that can lessen the impact of a supply disruption on the U.S. and world economies."[24]

The first goal of the diversification plan is to increase imports from Latin America, notably Mexico, Venezuela, and Colombia. The *NEP* portrays these three countries as especially attractive because they have large reserves, are relatively close, and fall within the American sphere of influence.[25] But, like the Persian Gulf states, they will need substantial investment in new infrastructure to boost production in older fields and start the development of new ones; and, again, they will have significant problems assembling the necessary capital. Mexico's constitution bans foreign investment in its oil industry. Venezuela's fiercely nationalistic president, Hugo Chávez, opposes any deeper American involvement. And Colombia's government, while it would love to expand its oil exports to the United States, cannot do so because of the continuing civil war. Overcoming these barriers to American investment will not be easy, but doing so is vital to the Bush energy plan.

The report also views Russia and the major Caspian Sea producers— Azerbaijan, Kazakhstan, Uzbekistan, and Turkmenistan—as promising new sources. These countries were significant components of the once prolific Soviet oil industry but suffered a decline in oil production following the collapse of the USSR, in 1992. Their collective output began to rise again in the past few years, and now they seek to boost their exports to the West. Still, like the Latin American countries, Russia and the Caspian states are up against serious capital shortfalls. They rely on the

Soviet-era pipeline system and other rapidly deteriorating infrastructure, and since the Caspian Sea has no outlet to the world's oceans, the need for additional pipeline capacity is critical. After a long struggle, partners in the Baku-Tbilisi-Ceyhan (BTC) pipeline—a giant conduit stretching from Azerbaijan to Turkey via Georgia—were able to secure sufficient funding to complete the project; but other such endeavors are being held up due to a lack of adequate financing. Here again, the *NEP* advises American officials to work with political leaders in the region to remove the impediments to foreign investment.[26]

"Along with Latin America," the *NEP* asserts, "West Africa is expected to be one of the fastest-growing sources of oil and gas for the American market."[27] The area's reserves, many of them offshore, are especially inviting because they have yet to be fully developed and because they can be so easily shipped across the Atlantic. Together, Nigeria and Angola, the two leading producers in the area, supplied the United States with 1.2 million barrels of oil per day in 2000, and the *NEP* envisions doubling or tripling this amount over the next ten years.[28] But there are good reasons to question whether the West African countries will be able to increase their production enough to satisfy Washington's long-term expectations. These states have even less capital for large-scale investments in new infrastructure than do the Caspian and Latin American producers. Much of Africa is also bedeviled by ethnic unrest, political corruption, and organized crime, and—as I will explain in a later chapter—these factors have repeatedly frustrated expectations for higher output levels.

Indeed, recent events suggest that *all* these alternative producers, whether in Latin America, the Caspian, or Africa, face a high risk of supply disruptions and shutdowns as a result of political discord and conflict. Ethnic violence has hampered output in Nigeria. Political turmoil has plagued Venezuela. Insurgent warfare has crippled Colombia. Georgia, a major transit state for the BTC pipeline, faces an array of separatist conflicts. Diversify its imports as it may, the United States will not be able to escape the violence and disorder that seems to follow the oil industry wherever it goes. And the more we shift our reliance to suppliers outside the Gulf, the more likely it is that we will eventually have to send troops to these countries as well.

The Military Dimension of Energy Security:
Enhancing America's Power-Projection Capacity

The authors of the *NEP* were perfectly aware how vulnerable the global oil trade is to serious disruption, especially in the Persian Gulf. And they certainly knew that a deepening dependence on energy from vulnerable suppliers would, in turn, make the United States itself more susceptible to oil shocks. It was self-evident to them that the only force capable of quelling such disorder would be, in many cases, the U.S. military. This line of reasoning has long informed American security policy in the Middle East, and the possible necessity of military intervention has always been viewed as a concomitant to dependence on imported oil. But as it became clear that such dependence would place even harsher burdens on U.S. combat troops in the future, the question arose as to whether America was prepared to assume the endless and inescapably bloody task of policing overseas oil zones.

Unless we increased the defense budget and otherwise enhanced U.S. military capabilities, a growing burden of this sort would place an enormous and possibly intolerable strain on the morale and readiness of American forces. But President Bush had entered the White House with every intention of expanding the nation's combat capacity. This determination reflected both his own views and those of his close associates, many of whom had served in senior Pentagon positions in prior Republican administrations and came to power strongly convinced of the need for enhanced fighting power. These figures—notably Vice President Dick Cheney, Secretary of Defense Donald Rumsfeld, and Deputy Secretary of Defense Paul Wolfowitz—had used their years of exile from power during the Clinton era to devise plans for an expanded U.S. military establishment; now, back in power again, they quickly moved to put their plans into effect.

Many of the ideas in the administration's new strategic template had first been articulated in the *Defense Planning Guidance (DPG)* for fiscal years 1994–99, a top-secret policy statement crafted by the Department of Defense in February 1992 and leaked to the press a month later. Prepared by Wolfowitz, then under secretary of defense, for his boss, Secretary of

Defense Cheney, the *DPG* was designed as a basic policy guide for Pentagon budgetary and organizational planning over the next five years. The Wolfowitz text basically spelled out a plan for permanent U.S. military superiority and world dominance. "Our first objective is to prevent the re-emergence of a new rival, either on the territory of the former Soviet Union or elsewhere, that poses a threat on the order of that posed formerly by the Soviet Union," the document began. This task would require "that we endeavor to prevent any hostile power from dominating a region whose resources would, under consolidated control, be sufficient to generate global power." The rest of the document mostly detailed the particulars of implementing the strategy, among them holding on to America's lead in military technology, bolstering the Pentagon's efficacy to prevail in regional conflicts, and blocking any "European-only security arrangements" that marginalized the United States. Petroleum figured prominently: "In the Middle East and Southwest Asia, our overall objective is to remain the predominant outside power in the region and preserve U.S. and Western access to the region's oil."[29]

The arrogant and unilateralist tone of these and other extracts from the *DPG* set off a howl of criticism in the U.S. Congress and around the world when they were published in March 1992. "What these Pentagon planners are laying out," said Senator Joseph R. Biden of Delaware, a senior Democratic member of the Senate Foreign Relations Committee, "is nothing but a Pax Americana."[30] In response, the Department of Defense toned down the language of the final document, erasing the explicit call for global dominance. One year later, the authors were out of power, replaced by Clinton administration officials who favored a more multilateralist approach to world affairs.[31] But the tone of the original draft of the *DPG* reflected the real views of its creators, and conservative security analysts continued to circulate these ideas throughout the 1990s in literature generated by prominent Washington think tanks.

No tract these conservative analysts issued during the Clinton era had greater influence than *Rebuilding America's Defenses: Strategy, Forces and Resources for a New Century*, released by the Project for the New American Century (PNAC) in September 2000 and written by Paul Wolfowitz and other Republican hawks who soon would have high positions in the new Bush administration. *Rebuilding America's Defenses* reiterated many of the ideas from the *DPG* draft of February 1992. "At present, the United States faces no global rival," the report observed. "America's grand strategy should aim to preserve and extend this advantageous position as far into the future as possible." To accomplish this aim, it called on the government to increase spending on advanced weapons substantially and to build up our combat capacity in regional conflicts, especially in the Middle East and Asia.[32]

Even before he entered the White House, George W. Bush had made these concepts the foundation of his own military policy. In his most important preelection speech on security affairs, a talk delivered at the Citadel, the military academy in Charleston, South Carolina, on September 23, 1999, he declared that his principal goal was "to take advantage of a tremendous opportunity—given to few nations in history—to extend the current peace into the far realm of the future. A chance to project America's peaceful influence not just across the world, but across the years." To do so it would be necessary to "transform" the U.S. war machine, better equipping it to face the emerging threats of the post-cold-war era: "As President . . . I will give the Secretary [of Defense] a broad mandate—to challenge the status quo and envision a new architecture of American defense for decades to come." This new "architecture" would include both missile defense and other high-tech systems designed to protect the United States against hostile attack, plus a vastly enhanced capacity to "project our power" into distant combat zones.[33]

Most commentators reporting on this seminal speech focused on the call for missile defenses and other aspects of what has been called the "revolution in military affairs"—the use of computers and other high-tech devices to defeat less technologically advanced adversaries. But the text of the speech makes it clear that Bush's primary concern was with enhancing America's capacity to project power into distant combat zones and prevail in regional conflicts of the sort his father had encountered in the 1991 Persian Gulf War. "Our forces in the next century must be agile, lethal, readily deployable, and require a minimum of logistical support," he said. "We must be able to project our forces over long distances, in days or weeks rather than months." Thus every branch of the armed services would be reconfigured. "On land, our heavy forces must be lighter. Our light forces must be more lethal. . . . On the seas, we need to pursue promising ideas like the arsenal ship—a stealthy ship packed with long-range missiles to destroy targets from great distances. In the air, we must be able to strike from across the world with pinpoint accuracy."[34]

Upon taking office, Bush quickly gave the new secretary of defense, Donald Rumsfeld, full authority to implement the proposals he had made in his Citadel address. In his first major presidential address on security policy, Bush again described the "new architecture" of defense: national missile defenses, advanced weapons technologies, and—once again taking precedence—enhanced power-projection capabilities. "We do not know yet the exact shape of our future military," he observed, "but we do know the direction we must begin to travel." And then he repeated the essence of his Citadel address, with its call for agile, easily deployable combat forces.[35]

This emphasis on power-projection capabilities is extremely significant, because these are precisely the kind of forces it takes to fight regional oil wars and protect distant pipelines, refineries, and delivery routes. Bush never specifically linked these military priorities to his energy plan, but White House officials clearly understood that the protection of an ever-expanding array of overseas energy assets was going to require the enhancement of our long-range projection capabilities. In a top-secret document, dated February 3, 2001, a high-ranking official of the National Security Council directed the NSC staff to cooperate with the NEPDG in assessing the military implications of the administration's energy plan. According to Jane Mayer of the New Yorker, who has seen a copy of the document, it envisioned the "melding" of two White House priorities: stepped-up pressure on "rogue states," such as Iraq, and "actions regarding the capture of new and existing oil and gas fields."[36]

What further action resulted from the February 3 NSC directive cannot be determined at this time, but there is no doubt that a "melding" of this sort was very much on the mind of Vice President Dick Cheney, who had long affirmed both the strategic importance of Persian Gulf energy and the need for robust power-projection forces in securing it. As secretary of defense during the first Bush administration, he had advocated the use of force to protect Saudi Arabian oil fields following the Iraqi invasion of Kuwait, and then, after the 1991 war, argued for the further enhancement of America's power-projection capabilities. "The Gulf war presaged very much the type of conflict we are most likely to confront again in this new era—major conventional contingencies against foes well armed with advanced conventional and unconventional munitions," he told the House Foreign Affairs Committee in March 1991. In response, "we must configure our forces to effectively deter, or quickly defeat, such regional threats."[37]

The Cheney imprint is especially evident in the most fully developed expression of the Bush administration's military policy: the September 2001 report of the Quadrennial Defense Review (QDR), a congressionally mandated assessment of America's strategic posture. Although it was released after September 11, the QDR report was largely prepared before the terrorist attacks and so reflects a combination of pre- and post-9/11 concerns. As might be expected, the report places great emphasis on homeland security and the war on terrorism and calls for the establishment of a national missile defense (NMD) system, another administration priority. But, once again, the QDR devotes particular attention to the enhancement of America's power-projection capacity: "The United States must retain the capability to send well-armed and logistically supported forces to critical points around the globe, even in the face of enemy opposition." It also explicitly identifies overseas oil-producing regions as "critical points" that American military forces may conceivably have to invade, going on to assert that because the Middle East, in particular, includes several states with formidable conventional capabilities as well as the capacity to manufacture weapons of mass destruction (WMD), American forces must be strong enough to overpower them and eliminate their WMD stockpiles.[38]

The release of the QDR report was accomplished by a major expansion in the responsibilities of and the number of troops assigned to the Central Command. "The Central region is of vital interest to our country and allies," Centcom commander General Tommy Franks testified in 2002. "Sixty-eight percent of the world's proven oil reserves are found in the Gulf region, and 43 percent of the world's petroleum exports pass through the Strait of Hormuz." Suggesting that threats to these resources, both from terrorists and from hostile powers like Iran and Iraq, were growing, Franks requested congressional support for the administration's plan to bolster the command's power-projection capacity in the region: "Our ability to deploy forces and equipment quickly remains the linchpin for responding to contingencies in Centcom's area of responsibility."[39] The upgrade was also crucial, Franks argued, because Centcom's AOR had been enlarged to include the eastern Caspian Sea basin—the former Soviet republics of Kazakhstan, Kyrgyzstan, Tajikistan, Turkmenistan, and Uzbekistan, whose oil and natural gas deposits are of major interest to Washington. The United States has also established new bases in Kyrgyzstan and Uzbekistan and has lavished military assistance throughout the area. As chapter 5 will show, this buildup aims not only at supporting antiterrorist operations in the region but also at ensuring access to its oil and natural gas reserves.

In fact, it is getting harder to distinguish U.S. military operations designed to fight terrorism from those designed to protect energy assets. And the administration's tendency to conflate the two is obvious in more than just the Gulf and Caspian areas. In Latin America, the U.S. Southern Command has been ordered to strengthen the Colombian army's ability to defend oil pipelines against guerrilla attack—again on the basis of expanding the war against terrorism. In the Caucasus, the European Command is doing its part in the war on terror by training Georgian forces to protect the soon-to-be-completed Baku-Tbilisi-Ceyhan pipeline; terrorism and the vulnerability of oil supplies are also providing the justification for Eurcom's efforts to enhance America's power-projection capacity in Africa. And, in Asia, the Pacific Command has announced plans for a small-boat squadron to protect oil shipping and deter terrorism in the Strait of Malacca, a major sea route adjoining Sumatra and Malaysia.[40]

All of which points to the president's preference for responding to the risks of oil dependency by relying more and more on military force. Indeed, it appears that the administration has merged its three main foreign-policy and security priorities (increased access to overseas oil, enhanced power-projection capabilities, and intensified antiterror operations) into a single, unified strategic plan—and even if the components are sometimes ends in themselves, they usually work in tandem. Thus the protection of foreign oil supplies—routinely described as part of the war on terror—is normally conducted by the Pentagon's myriad power-projection forces. This conflation of strategic objectives is most evident in the Persian Gulf area—the subject of the next chapter—but can also be seen in the Caspian Sea basin, Latin America, and Africa.[41]

By the end of 2003, therefore, the Bush administration's energy policy had become thoroughly integrated into the nation's security strategy. As Energy Secretary Abraham phrased it in 2002, "Energy security is . . . national security."[42] The consequences are not hard to imagine. American forces will speed overseas to protect oil fields, pipelines, refineries, and tanker routes more and more frequently, and they will often encounter enraged local populations. The American military can help deter attacks on vital oil facilities and ensure the continuing flow of petroleum, but it can never guarantee that our rising demand for imported oil will be satisfied. All that is certain is that we will pay for it with an increasing sacrifice of blood.

4

Trapped in the Gulf:
The Irresistible Lure of
Bountiful Petroleum

In May 2001, when the National Energy Policy Development Group endorsed America's long-standing and prodigious oil habit, it took another, equally fateful stand: it committed the United States to perpetual dependence on Persian Gulf oil. While some members of the group may, perhaps, have worried about the implications of this obviously risky proposition, there was really no other plausible option—given their ingrained reluctance to consider reductions in our utilization of fossil fuels. And of all the oil-producing regions of the world, it was clear, the Gulf alone had enough untapped reserves to satisfy the burgeoning American and international demand in the coming decades of the twenty-first century. We might try to increase imports from non-Gulf suppliers, such as Russia and Nigeria, so as to enlarge our net supply of petroleum and acquire a modest degree of protection against disruptions in the flow of Middle Eastern oil; but none of these suppliers would ever produce enough oil to reverse, or even slow, the nation's growing reliance on the major Gulf producers.

Data amassed by the Department of Energy and the major oil companies, such as BP, make it clear how utterly dependent the United States and other oil-importing nations are going to be on the major Gulf providers. First, there is the matter of *proven reserves*—an area in which the Persian Gulf has no rivals. Proven reserves are the supplies of untapped petroleum that are known to exist and can be extracted from their underground reservoirs with existing technology. There may be additional, unknown reservoirs of petroleum out there somewhere—beneath the frozen Arctic or the hidden depths of the deep Atlantic, for example—but known reserves are the ones that will produce the oil we will rely on for the foreseeable future. And the overwhelming majority of the world's proven reserves are in just five nations: Iran, Iraq, Kuwait, Saudi Arabia, and the United Arab Emirates (UAE)—which together possess some 658 billion barrels of untapped petroleum, or 63 percent of known reserves. Add the supplies of neighboring Oman and Qatar, and the Gulf's total share rises to 65 percent, just shy of two-thirds of the world's total remaining petroleum supply.[1]

Equally important is the matter of *production capacity*, or day-to-day output. Several non-Gulf producers, including the United States, Mexico, and Russia, currently extract more petroleum on a daily basis than most of the Gulf suppliers; they began developing their resources a long time ago, and so possess elaborate and sophisticated oil infrastructures. Most of the Gulf producers, on the other hand, started drilling only in recent decades and have yet to develop all their known fields; as a result, they will be able to boost production substantially in the years ahead, while the older suppliers will have a hard time sustaining their current output. Saudi Arabia is especially critical in this regard—already the planet's number one producer, its share of total world output is expected to grow steadily in the decades to come. And so, with each passing year, the Gulf producers will supply an ever-increasing share of the world's oil intake.[2] According to the Department of Energy (DoE), this share will rise from approximately 27 percent in 2000 to 36 percent in 2025[3]; it will reach an estimated 43 percent by 2030.[4] (See figure 5.)

The Persian Gulf's share of global production capacity is even more significant because the countries it comprises consume such a small portion of their total oil yield, while most of the other major producers consume a substantial share of their output at home. Mexico, for example, should see its oil production rise from 3.6 to 4.8 million barrels per day between 2001

Figure 5
PETROLEUM RESERVES AND PRODUCTION
IN THE PERSIAN GULF AND OTHER REGIONS,
2002 AND 2025

Country and region	Reserves		Production			
	At end of 2002 (bbl)	As percent of world total	Actual production, 2002 (mbd)	As percent of world total	Estimated production capacity, 2025 (mbd)	As percent of world total
Iran	89.7	8.6	3.37	4.6	4.9	3.9
Iraq	112.5	10.7	2.03	2.7	5.2	4.2
Kuwait	96.5	9.2	1.87	2.5	5.1	4.1
Oman	5.5	0.5	0.90	1.2	n.a.	n.a.
Qatar	15.2	1.5	0.76	1.0	0.8	0.6
Saudi Arabia	261.8	25.0	8.68	11.7	23.8	19.1
United Arab Emirates	97.8	9.3	2.27	3.1	5.4	4.3
Persian Gulf, total	679.0	64.8	19.88	26.9	45.2*	36.3*
United States	30.4	2.9	7.70	10.4	9.4	7.6
Canada and Mexico	19.5	1.9	6.44	8.7	8.9	7.1
North Sea countries	16.3	1.6	6.16	8.3	4.5	3.6
Former Soviet Union	77.1	7.4	9.35	12.6	15.9	12.8
Africa	77.4	7.4	7.94	10.7	16.2	13.0
Asia	38.7	3.7	7.99	10.8	7.5	6.0
South, Central America	98.6	9.4	6.65	9.0	12.3	9.9

Country and region	Reserves		Production			
	At end of 2002 (bbl)	As percent of world total	Actual production, 2002 (mbd)	As percent of world total	Estimated production capacity, 2025 (mbd)	As percent of world total
Rest of world	10.7	1.0	1.83	2.5	4.6	3.7
World, total	1047.7	100.0	73.94	100.0	113.5	100.0

Sources: For 2002 data, BP, *Statistical Review of World Energy 2003* (London: BP, June 2003), pp. 4, 6, 9; for 2025 data, U.S. Department of Energy, Energy Information Administration (DoE/EIA), *International Energy Outlook 2003* (Washington, D.C.: DoE/EIA, 2003), table D1, p. 235.

*Excludes Oman.

Abbreviations: bbl = billion barrels; mbd = million barrels per day

Note: Totals may not add up precisely due to rounding.

and 2025—which would be good news for the United States were it not for the fact that Mexico's daily consumption is projected to climb by even more, from 1.9 to 4.1 million barrels. In other words, *less* Mexican oil will be available for export to the United States in 2025 than in 2001. The same pattern holds for other producers in Latin America and Asia.[5] The Gulf producers, on the other hand, will continue to funnel the overwhelming bulk of their output to international markets, because their domestic demand is so small.[6] According to the DoE, total petroleum consumption by all Middle Eastern countries (including nonproducers like Turkey) will reach 8.9 million barrels per day by 2025, while output will soar to 47.9 million barrels.[7] That leaves 39 million barrels for export—without which the United States and the other importing nations would starve for oil.

The DoE's projections cannot show precisely how much oil the United States will acquire from any particular supplier at any given point; that figure always depends on the prevailing price and supply conditions at the moment. But they do show that the 54 percent of its oil that America imported in 2001 will rise to 68 percent in 2025.[8] Some of this oil will come from Canada and Mexico, but most of it will have to come from the interregional flow of petroleum (that is, oil exported beyond its immediate region)—a commerce in which the Gulf countries will play an increasingly dominant role. At present, the Gulf countries plus Syria account for approximately 41 percent of the interregional trade in oil; by 2030, their share is expected to climb to 70 percent.[9]

And this isn't the end of our reliance on the Gulf. Our continued prosperity will depend not only on having sufficient supplies of oil but also on keeping it affordable; otherwise, the costs of energy will rise, and the entire economy will fall into recession. This means that the United States has an interest in ensuring that *all* major consuming countries have an adequate supply of petroleum, lest shortages elsewhere lead to panic buying that boosts prices everywhere, including this country. Here again, large increases in Persian Gulf production will be critical, even if we manage to obtain the bulk of our imports from other suppliers, since the Gulf *alone* has the reserves and the production capacity to satisfy future global demand and keep prices affordable for all.[10]

This circumstance no doubt weighed heavily on the deliberations of the NEPDG. And while the Cheney report never put the situation so bluntly, it could not entirely conceal our deepening dependence on the Gulf. "By any estimation," the *NEP* declares, "Middle East oil production will remain central to world oil security"; as a result, "the Gulf will be a primary focus of U.S. international energy policy."[11] Even this bland restatement of conventional wisdom acknowledges the critical importance of the Gulf; but emphasize just two words in the report, and America's real dilemma comes into focus: Middle East oil "will remain *central* to world oil security," and so "the Gulf will be a *primary* focus" of American energy policy. From this, everything else in the administration's Gulf policy follows.

The Gulf in 2001: Confronting the Obstacles to Increased Production

Having determined that the United States had no choice but to rely more and more on Persian Gulf oil, the Bush-Cheney team confronted a new challenge: although the major Gulf producers might have sufficient untapped reserves to satisfy future global requirements, there was no guarantee they would do what was necessary to boost their output enough to meet those needs. To achieve the level required, they would have to invest hundreds of billions of dollars in new infrastructure and acquire new production technologies from the major international oil firms—steps they might be neither able nor willing to take. And whether they welcomed foreign investment or not, they were often torn by disputes and conflicts that could easily hamper their capacity to sustain their output and deliver it to international markets. Increased reliance on the Gulf, therefore, would saddle the United States with the responsibility for ensuring both higher output levels and regional stability.

To fully grasp the magnitude of this burden, consider the data available to the national energy group when it began its work in early 2001. According to that year's edition of the *International Energy Outlook*, total world oil production would have to grow by 60 percent between 1999 and 2020 to meet anticipated world consumption of 119 million barrels per day. But because of flat or declining production in many other areas of the world, output in the Gulf would have to climb by *85 percent* to satisfy this enormous rise in demand.[12] Put another way, combined Persian Gulf production would have to rise from 24.0 million barrels per day in 1999 to 44.5 million barrels in 2020, a jump of 20.5 million barrels.[13] (See figure 5.) This means that the Gulf suppliers would have to be cajoled, coerced, or somehow compelled into doubling their combined production of oil for the Bush-Cheney plan to succeed. But to make all this happen would require overcoming a number of prodigious obstacles—political, economic, technological, and military.

The most obvious obstacles were economic and technological. First there was the task of raising the copious funds it would take to upgrade the required improvements in oil-production infrastructure. According to the International Energy Agency (IEA), the Persian Gulf producers would have to spend an estimated $523 billion on new equipment and technology between 2001 and 2030 to increase their output enough to meet anticipated world demand.[14] While the Gulf states were both rich and attractive candidates for loans from the major international banks, it was unlikely that they could assemble such a vast sum without allowing foreign firms to invest in their largely state-controlled oil industries; but this expedient ran counter to their long-standing determination to retain full control over their nationalized energy sectors. As the NEPDG recognized, changing the minds of key Persian Gulf governments on this matter would require substantial American effort.

The challenge was particularly daunting in the case of Saudi Arabia. As the Department of Energy's 2001 projections showed, Saudi Arabia would have to *double* its production capacity between 1999 and 2020—pushing it from 11.4 to 23.1 million barrels per day—in order to satisfy anticipated American and world demand.[15] Most analysts believed that Saudi Arabia had the untapped petroleum to support an increase of this magnitude, but they were far less convinced that the kingdom either could or would make the necessary infrastructure improvements. Even the legendary wealth of the Saudis was insufficient to double total petroleum output by 2020; to do so would require substantial foreign financing. And because the Saudi leadership was loath to allow foreign companies to play any role at all in the extraction of domestic petroleum—such "upstream" activities were normally reserved for the national oil company, Saudi Aramco—it was doubtful that Saudi Arabia would reach the DoE's production target for 2020.[16]

The situation was roughly the same in Kuwait, where the constitution prohibits foreign ownership of petroleum reserves and government policy limits the participation of foreign firms in most other aspects of energy production. The ruling al-Sabah family was known to favor the lifting of these restraints, but the country's parliament strongly opposed any such changes; and so, as with Saudi Arabia, the country's ability to boost petroleum output significantly was in doubt.[17] The other Persian Gulf sheikhdoms, Qatar and the United Arab Emirates, were more open to foreign investment, but there, too, legal and technical obstacles stood in the way of increased production.[18]

Iraq and Iran presented the Bush administration with a different set of problems. Both countries harbored large reserves of untapped petroleum—Iraq, it was thought, possessed 112.5 billion barrels, Iran 89.7 billion—and both had been major exporters in the past. But two decades of war and economic sanctions (UN-imposed in Iraq's case, U.S.-imposed in Iran's) had damaged their domestic oil facilities and constrained their ability to raise output. Iraq was producing only 2.5 million barrels a day in 2001, far below its 1979 peak of 3.7 million barrels; Iran's daily output had fallen from 6.0 to 3.7 million. Clearly it would take substantial foreign investment in both these countries to restore their facilities and boost their output—but such investment was hardly likely to turn up so long as economic sanctions remained in place.[19]

And then there were the equally formidable political and military obstacles. They, too, were complex and disparate. Although the United States was on friendly terms with many of the key producers—especially Saudi Arabia, Kuwait, Qatar, Oman, and the UAE—these countries were not so eager to be seen embracing the United States, especially when it appeared to be so entwined with Israel. To make matters worse, some of the regimes that had collaborated with Washington in the past—notably the House of Saud—were themselves being threatened by militant antigovernment forces. How to curry favor with and help out those regimes while avoiding the appearance of intrusion into local affairs was—and remains—a major quandary for the United States.

Overshadowing all these concerns in early 2001 was the threat posed by Saddam Hussein. Although Operation Desert Storm and the intermittent U.S. air strikes conducted during the Clinton era had substantially downgraded Iraq's combat capabilities, Saddam still possessed a large and potent military. "Iraq remains the most significant near-term threat to U.S. interests in the Gulf region," General Anthony C. Zinni of Centcom testified in 2000. "Iraq's conventional military force continues to pose a threat to our regional partners who do not possess the capability to deter or stop an Iraqi invasion without U.S. assistance."[20] And while most of Iraq's known weapons of mass destruction (WMD) had been destroyed as a result of Operation Desert Storm or the efforts of the UN Special Commission on Iraq, many analysts believed that Baghdad retained at least a limited WMD capability and was secretly trying to augment it. So long as Saddam remained in power, we could not entirely discount the danger of a future Iraqi assault on Kuwait and Saudi Arabia.[21]

The second greatest threat to U.S. interests came from the radical Islamic regime in Iran. Although the Iranian government had been careful to avoid a direct clash with the United States in the years following the costly Iran-Iraq War, and the Iranian military was considered relatively weak,

Washington perceived a continuing danger from Iran, particularly in its ability to obstruct tanker traffic through the Strait of Hormuz—the vital passage connecting the Persian Gulf to the world's oceans.[22] The Iranians also possessed a substantial supply of ballistic missiles and chemical agents and were thought to be developing nuclear weapons.

And, finally, there was the threat of terrorism. Many of the world's most violent terrorist organizations are based in the Persian Gulf, and the region's oil facilities—inherently vulnerable, and often linked to American firms—have long been a target for them. Terrorist groups have also surfaced in other parts of the world, of course, and they have carried out some of their deadliest attacks elsewhere. Nevertheless, there was no escaping the fact that Al Qaeda and its many kindred organizations arose in the Persian Gulf area and had absorbed its deep-seated antagonisms. For many of these groups, the United States was the very embodiment of the West's centuries-long assault on the Arab-Muslim world; and because the lure of oil was what had brought the United States into their midst, they viewed anything having to do with oil—including a local government cooperating with U.S. oil companies—as a legitimate target.[23]

In the face of these problems and dangers, the Bush-Cheney team could draw only one conclusion: that, on their own, the Persian Gulf countries had neither the will nor the capacity to increase their petroleum output *and* protect its outward flow. If the administration's energy plan was to succeed, the United States would have to become the dominant power in the region, assuming responsibility for overseeing the politics, the security, and the oil output of the key producing countries. The buildup of American power and influence in the area that had begun with Presidents Roosevelt, Truman, and Eisenhower would have to be taken to an entirely new level.

The Strategy of Maximum Extraction

In the months before and after 9/11, the Bush administration fashioned a comprehensive strategy for American domination of the Persian Gulf and the procurement of ever-increasing quantities of petroleum. It is unlikely that this strategy was ever formalized in a single, all-encompassing

White House document. Rather, the administration adopted a series of policies that together formed a blueprint for political, economic, and military action in the Gulf. This approach—I call it the strategy of maximum extraction—was aimed primarily at boosting the oil output of the major Gulf producers. But since the sought-after increases could be doomed by instability and conflict in the region, the strategy also entailed increased military intervention.

The strategy of maximum extraction called for American officials to exhort friendly regimes to open their energy sectors to the investment by foreign companies that would provide them access to advanced exploration and drilling technology. Washington has long relied on the giant oil corporations to oversee the hands-on aspects of energy production in the Gulf; with motives of their own for obtaining greater quantities of Persian Gulf crude, U.S. firms could always be counted on to pursue fresh opportunities in the region. But while these companies could be delegated certain functions, other tasks—including the critical effort to persuade the major Gulf producers to open their energy sectors to outside investment—would have to fall on the U.S. diplomatic corps and other high officials.

Increased government involvement in the effort to boost Persian Gulf exports was one of the *National Energy Policy*'s principal recommendations, and the administration has carried it out scrupulously. Energy Secretary Spencer Abraham has met repeatedly with Saudi Arabia's minister for petroleum and mineral resources, Ali al-Naimi, to convince him of the benefits of greater energy cooperation with the United States. "One thing that has become clear to me from our conversations over the last year is the need for even more dialogue between producer countries and consumer countries," Abraham told a conference on U.S.-Saudi relations in Washington, D.C., on April 22, 2002. Beyond dialogue, "we also need more opportunities to develop energy supplies"—an effort that requires, of course, that we "strengthen our relations with Saudi Arabia and other long-term energy partners."[24] Abraham and his colleagues have delivered similar messages to Kuwait and neighboring countries.

Increasing output in the Gulf, however, is only one part of the equation. For the strategy of maximum extraction to succeed, Washington would have to ensure that these added supplies could be safely delivered to the United States and other major consumers—which means propping up imperiled allies in the Gulf and quashing any threats to American dominance in the region. As the administration saw it, a greater level of security in the Gulf required progress on three fronts: first, the stabilization of Saudi Arabia under the House of Saud; second, the removal of Saddam Hussein in Iraq and his replacement with a stable government capable of substantially boosting oil output; and, third, an escalation of pressure on the Iranian government leading, eventually, to the emergence of a leadership friendly to the United States. Together, these three goals—joined, after 9/11, by the war on terrorism—constituted the core elements of the Bush administration's Persian Gulf security policy.

Stabilizing Saudi Arabia

The first and possibly most formidable challenge facing the United States in 2001 was to preserve the status quo in Saudi Arabia. Just how difficult this task would prove became apparent on August 6, 2002, when the *Washington Post* revealed that a consultant to the Defense Policy Board— a high-level advisory group of senior officials—had designated Saudi Arabia an enemy of the United States and called for the seizure of Saudi financial assets, including its oil fields, if the government did not terminate its support for Islamic terrorism. According to the *Post,* the consultant, Laurent Murawiec of the Rand Corporation, accused senior Saudi officials of complicity with terrorist attacks on the United States: "The Saudis are active at every level of the terror chain, from planners to financiers, from cadre to foot-soldier, from ideologist to cheerleader," he told the group. As "the most dangerous opponent" of U.S. interests in the Gulf area, he continued, Saudi Arabia must change its ways or face severe American reprisals. Murawiec's presentation reportedly received strong support from prominent Republicans at the meeting, leading to speculation that key officials of the Bush administration had endorsed it—and it was *this* aspect of the story that aroused so much comment in Washington.[25]

That so many prominent conservatives would applaud a critique of this sort and endorsed a call for the seizure of Saudi assets should not have come as a total surprise. Ever since it had been determined that most of the 9/11 hijackers had been recruited in Saudi Arabia and that members of the royal family had subsidized some of the charities linked to Al Qaeda, many conservatives had come to view the kingdom as an adversary of the United States. The editors of the *Wall Street Journal* were particularly strident in their demands for strong punitive measures against Saudi leaders. "We must work against the Saudis' campaign of religious hatred and subversion around the world," one pundit wrote. "We must be prepared to seize the Saudi oil fields and administer them for the greater good."[26] Other contributors to the *Journal* and conservative commentators on radio and television expressed equally harsh views.[27]

But if many in Washington—even among the upper echelons of the Republican leadership—shared these views, the White House anxiously disassociated itself from Murawiec and his recommendations. On August 6, the morning the story broke, Secretary of State Colin Powell telephoned the Saudi foreign minister, Prince Saud al-Faisal, in Riyadh to reassure him. "These views that have been bandied about by certain individuals do not reflect the views of the President nor of the U.S. government, and the Secretary made that quite clear in his telephone conversation," the State Department's spokesperson, Philip Reeker, disclosed later that afternoon. "The United States and Saudi Arabia have excellent relations." Dismissing charges that the Saudis had been slow to cut off funds for charities linked to terrorism, Reeker expressed gratitude for "steps taken by Saudi Arabia to help combat the problem of terrorist financing." The two countries might have "differences" on some issues, he acknowledged, but not enough to damage their warm and cooperative relationship.[28]

The State Department briefing was the first of several efforts at damage control. On August 26, President Bush telephoned Crown Prince Abdullah, the kingdom's de facto ruler, to assure him of Washington's continued friendship. According to an official account of their eighteen-minute conversation, Bush said that Murawiec's views "had nothing to do with the views of any senior-level government administration officials, including himself, including the Secretary of Defense or the Vice President." He then invited Saudi Arabia's ambassador to the United

States, Prince Bandar bin Sultan, to his ranch in Crawford, Texas, where he again promised continued close relations.[29]

These efforts, widely publicized by the White House and the State Department, were a predictable response to a diplomatic embarrassment. With plans for an attack on Iraq already far advanced, the president needed to dispel any hint of a rift between the United States and a key Persian Gulf ally. But the urgency with which the administration responded to the *Washington Post* article and the personal solicitousness of both Powell and Bush toward the Saudis revealed a much deeper concern—about the stability of Saudi Arabia, not the forthcoming invasion of Iraq. Bush would not have made such haste to advertise America's enthusiastic support for the Saudi government if he and his advisers had not been so worried about its durability, a factor bearing directly on the safety of U.S. oil interests.

The administration's nervousness can be traced to secret U.S. intelligence data suggesting that the Saudi royal family's hold on power was far more tenuous than the absence of any overt opposition movement might suggest. Although this secret data has never been made public, it is evident from newspaper and magazine accounts that senior analysts at the Central Intelligence Agency and the National Security Agency were deeply worried about the potential for an Iranian-style insurrection in Saudi Arabia.[30] "Like pre-revolutionary Iran, Saudi Arabia is an authoritarian, oil-rich monarchy," Elaine Sciolino wrote in the *New York Times*, in a synopsis of these concerns. "It is notorious for corruption and profligate spending, resistant to democratization, viewed increasingly as subservient to the will of Washington, dependent on American weaponry, and criticized by radicals in exile and some conservative clerics for not being Islamic enough."[31]

As U.S. analysts had discovered, Saudi Arabia had become a scene of social, economic, political, and religious ferment.[32] To start with, there were the demographics: propelled by one of the highest birthrates in the world, the population had surged from 3.2 million people in 1950 to 21.7 million in 2002 and was expected to reach 40 million in 2025.[33] Not surprisingly, such a high birthrate had produced an extremely youthful population: 75 percent of Saudi citizens in 2002 were under the age of thirty, and 50 percent were under eighteen. Such a high concentration of young people would pose a significant social and economic problem for any developing country, but was particularly troublesome in Saudi Arabia because per capita income had dropped from $28,600 in 1981 (when it was roughly equivalent to that of the United States) to a mere $6,800 in 2001. This plunge was exacerbated by a sharp rise in unemployment among young, college-educated Saudi men, from almost zero a decade earlier to more than 30 percent. The result, inevitably, was a surplus of well-educated, ambitious, and often alienated young men with high expectations and few economic opportunities—perfect fodder for political or religious extremists.[34]

And, indeed, Western analysts saw discontent seething just below the surface of Saudi society. Although public expression of dissent is not permitted in the kingdom—those who speak out against government policies are routinely arrested and jailed or exiled[35]—critics of the regime were finding ways to make their views known, primarily through religious associations, kinship networks, and private discussion groups. "Political, economic, and social problems in the country have provided a fertile field for dissent—dissent that can no longer be managed from above," Professor Gwenn Okruhlik of the University of Arkansas wrote in 2002. Popular grievances with the royal family, she reported, included "authoritarianism and repression, maldistribution and inequity, the absence of representation in the political system, and the seemingly permanent stationing of United States military forces in Saudi Arabia."[36]

Several of these many grievances deserve particular attention. First and foremost was the continuing American military presence in the kingdom. As I noted in chapter 2, the United States established combat bases in Saudi Arabia in 1990 to support operations against Iraqi forces in Kuwait, but these facilities were supposed to be temporary. By failing to leave at the conclusion of Operation Desert Storm, as promised, we enraged those who abhorred the presence of infidels in the spiritual heart of Islam. "Despite official denials, the U.S. troops . . . are highly unpopular," the French journalist Eric Rouleau noted in 2002 in an article for *Foreign Affairs*. Obviously, nothing could be said about the American military presence in public; "in private, however, many Saudis complain that they consider it a form of occupation," he wrote.[37] This resentment was one of the main sources of discontent that Osama bin Laden tapped into when he was seeking recruits for his strikes against the United States and the Saudi leadership.

A second grievance was the monarchy's refusal to respond to Washington's continuing support for Israel's war against the Palestinians by severing or downgrading ties. "The deterioration of the Arab-Israeli situation has started to threaten the very stability of the Saudi state," Rouleau observed. "Outsiders have underestimated the anger roused in the Saudi population by the suffering of the Palestinian people—and the fact that this suffering is blamed less on Israel than on its American protector." Given the close ties between Washington and Riyadh, "this anger has also started to focus on the House of Saud itself."[38]

These two factors combined with a third—a widespread perception of corruption in the royal family—to further undermine support for the monarchy. Although the family's many princes (there are some seven thousand of them) are supposed to be strictly bound by Islamic law and ritual, they often turn up in tabloid reports after drunken nights on the town, frequently with prostitutes in tow. Many were known to extort bribes or "commissions" from foreign companies seeking to do business in the kingdom. American contractors, for example, allegedly paid substantial bribes to well-connected senior princes in order to secure orders for costly and sophisticated arms.[39] The endless stories of "mismanagement, maldistribution, and waste of national assets," Okruhlik observed, convinced many Saudi citizens that the regime had "deviated from the straight path" of Islam and thus lost its mantle of legitimacy.[40]

Equally worrisome was the monarchy's favored response to these grievances: the ill-considered strategy of subsidizing militant Islamic foundations and charities as a way of containing dissent in the kingdom. Ever since the 1979 uprising in Mecca, in which Islamic fundamentalists challenged the religious authority of the royal family, the monarchy had sought to court militant clerics by showering them with funds and offering them positions of authority in prominent religious and educational institutions. But as one terrorist attack after another has shown, the tactic backfired. While most of the co-opted clerics avoided any direct criticism of the royal family—which in all likelihood would have landed them in jail—many used their positions to denounce the United States and its allies and to glorify the fighters waging jihad, or militant resistance to the infidels.[41] And because the House of Saud was so closely aligned with Washington, it inevitably became a target of the extremists' wrath. "Fear of losing power has led the Saudis to pay off just about everyone," Neela Banerjee wrote in the *New York Times*. "But that protection money has not stemmed a growing domestic restiveness, as many Saudis have become fed up with a sprawling ruling family they believe is insatiably corrupt."[42] The upshot was an explosion of anti-Americanism, a deepening anger at the royal family, and a steady stream of recruits to Al Qaeda and other extremist organizations.

Together these factors added up to the hornets' nest that U.S. intelligence officials discerned in late 2001. Although barred from speaking out on their own, some of these analysts confided in Seymour Hersh, the prominent investigative journalist. "In interviews last week," Hersh reported in the *New Yorker* in October 2001, "current and former intelligence and military officials portrayed the growing instability of the Saudi regime—and the vulnerability of its oil reserves to terrorist attack—as the most immediate threat to American economic and political interests in the Middle East."[43] If other experts in the U.S. intelligence community shared this opinion (and there is every reason to assume that they did), we can safely conclude that the administration was fully aware of the regime's deepening plight, and that it resolved to do whatever it took to ward off a future catastrophe.

But what action could the White House take? To replace the royal family with a handpicked successor regime, as we are now attempting in Iraq, was one possible solution. But this option would have been summarily rejected, because of the close ties between Republican leaders and the House of Saud. Many prominent Saudis, such as Prince Bandar, the Saudi ambassador, were friends of senior American officials (including the two Bush presidents) and investors in firms managed by prominent Republicans, including former secretary of state James Baker III and former secretary of defense Frank Carlucci.[44] Moreover, the fall of the House of Saud could release explosive social forces and possibly even foster the rise of a Taliban-like anti-American junta; such a regime might well sever the remaining links between state-owned Saudi Aramco and American energy companies and impose an embargo on petroleum sales to the United States as punishment for American support of Israel.[45] The Bush administration, collectively shuddering at this prospect—which could easily lead to a global economic meltdown—saw no other option but to bolster the royal family as best it could and seek to eliminate, or at least contain, the sources of discontent.

To do so required vigorous action on several fronts. The United States would have to vacate its combat bases in Saudi Arabia, bring the Arab-Israeli imbroglio to some sort of resolution, and persuade the Saudi leadership to rid the ruling class of corruption and crack down on terrorists and terror-linked charities. But each of these imperatives was fraught with problems.

On the matter of the bases, the United States was in a bind as long as Saddam Hussein remained in power. While the containment strategy had eliminated the immediate risk of another Iraqi assault on Kuwait or Saudi Arabia, it had not erased the danger altogether—which meant that American forces had to stay. White House officials saw only one way out of the dilemma: to abandon containment, remove Saddam Hussein, and thereby eliminate the need for the bases.[46] It is difficult to determine just how heavily this calculation weighed in the decision to invade Iraq, but it was clearly a factor. Just a few weeks after the fall of Baghdad to U.S. troops (and long before the city was fully secure), Secretary of Defense Donald Rumsfeld flew to Riyadh and announced that the Pentagon was closing its bases in Saudi Arabia. "It is now a safer region because of the change of regime in Iraq," he told reporters on April 29, 2003; as a result, "the U.S. aircraft and those involved [in enforcing the no-fly zone over Iraq] will now be able to leave."[47] The departure of the combat troops began shortly thereafter, and by the end of September 2003 they were gone.[48]

In withdrawing the troops, the administration was in no way downgrading Washington's commitment to protecting the kingdom, and its oil, against attack. The Department of Defense still has a sizable military training mission in Saudi Arabia—the latest incarnation of the contingent first deployed in 1951, during the Truman administration—and

American defense contractors still provide advisory and technical support to the Saudi Arabian National Guard and other Saudi military units. Many of the combat troops that were withdrawn from Saudi Arabia during the summer of 2003 went no farther than nearby Qatar, where the Central Command has established a new, multibillion-dollar command center and operations facility at Al Udeid Air Base.[49] Other facilities that the United States acquired during the 1990s and when preparing for the invasion of Iraq will also be available in the event of a future clash in or around Saudi Arabia. (See map, page 92.)

Addressing the second major source of discontent in Saudi Arabia, the conflict between Israel and the Palestinians, was, if anything, even trickier. For the Bush administration to make any meaningful concessions to Saudi public opinion on this issue would cost it dearly at home. The Saudis had long been calling on American leaders to force Israel to moderate its harsh treatment of the Palestinians and to cease construction of Israeli settlements in the Occupied Territories. But many in Washington and in the American media endorsed the tough measures the government of Ariel Sharon was employing to suppress Palestinian resistance groups.[50] Bush's public expressions of support for the Israeli prime minister—he once called him a "man of peace," infuriating much of the Arab world—seemed to reflect his true leanings. Out of deference to the Saudis, however, he sought to project a more evenhanded stance, pressing for eventual Israeli recognition of Palestinian sovereignty in return for more vigorous efforts by the Palestinian Authority to combat terrorism.[51] Bush also voiced his personal support for the "road map" to Middle East peace, the internationally backed plan for step-by-step concessions on both sides ultimately leading to Palestinian statehood.[52] While the fate of this initiative obviously has implications far beyond the political situation in Saudi Arabia, the administration has embraced it at least in part to defuse Saudi anger over continuing American support for Israel.

There was not much the White House could do about the profligacy and corruption of the royal family. The most promising tack seemed to be to support Crown Prince Abdullah, the Saudi heir apparent and a major advocate of reform within the monarchy. Although hardly

Major U.S. Bases in the Persian Gulf Area

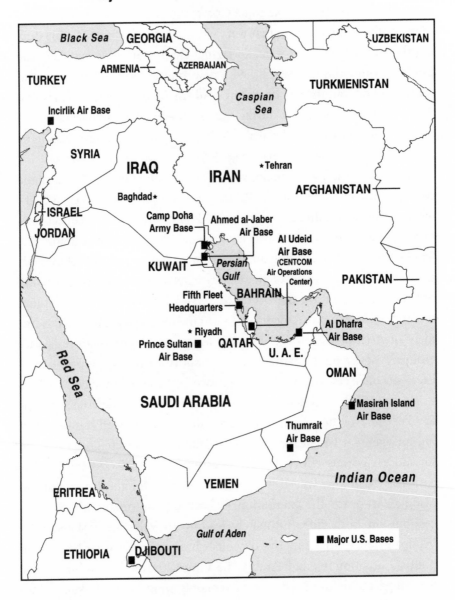

groundbreaking, Abdullah's calls for the princes to show greater financial accountability and for the election of local officials had aroused significant popular support in Saudi Arabia (and fervent opposition from senior princes).[53] By inviting Crown Prince Abdullah to his ranch in

Crawford, listening soberly to his counsel on the Arab-Israeli conflict, and otherwise showing him respect, Bush sought to bolster Abdullah's domestic authority and thereby quicken the pace of reform.

The related issues of terrorism and security within Saudi Arabia were probably the most delicate ones for the White House to address, since many members of the royal family were either sympathetic to the fierce anti-Western views of the extremist organizations or, at least, willing to fund them in return for their tacit agreement to conduct their attacks elsewhere.[54] American efforts to convince the House of Saud that supporting extremism and doling out protection money would not, in the end, spare the regime from attack had little effect. Since 2001, White House emissaries have repeatedly entreated Saudi officials to seize the bank accounts of figures linked to terrorism and to cut off charities suspected of subsidizing Al Qaeda, but the Saudis have rarely followed through on their promises to comply.[55] True, there were some joint efforts to constrict the flow of funds to terror-linked entities.[56] But it was not until May 2003, following a string of powerful bombings in Riyadh—later traced to Al Qaeda—that the regime finally started to impose tough controls on suspect charities and religious foundations.[57]

None of these efforts has brought the hoped-for stability to Saudi Arabia. As the May 2003 bombings in Riyadh and a second round of attacks the following spring made all too clear, strong forces are still at work against the regime. And the royal family is still riven by disputes between a faction that favors some degree of reform and a faction that wants to preserve the status quo—brawling that is likely to intensify when King Fahd dies and the two factions maneuver to seat their preferred senior prince on the throne. Nevertheless, the withdrawal of American combat troops has eased some of the pressure on the monarchy, and the regime has helped its own cause by at least making noises about loosening political restraints. Any further progress will require an easing of the Arab-Israeli conflict and the triumph of the pro-reform faction in the long-expected succession struggle.

But however frustrated American officials may find themselves at the creeping pace of change in Saudi Arabia, they cannot afford to remain aloof—not as long as the United States relies on steady supplies of

Saudi petroleum. According to the Department of Energy, Saudi Arabia *alone* will have to provide nearly a third of all the additional petroleum it will take to satisfy world demand in 2025—13.6 million barrels per day, or more than the added output of the United States, Canada, Mexico, South America, Europe, Asia, and Africa *combined*.[58] Most experts think the Saudis have enough untapped reserves to meet that need, but there is considerable doubt as to whether the kingdom can make the extremely costly and technically demanding infrastructure improvements required.[59] Only in a reasonably stable political environment—which means, in Washington's view, one bolstered by American military power—can this colossal and indispensable effort move forward.

Regime Change in Iraq

As we have seen, in 2001 the Bush administration identified two major policy goals with respect to the oil-producing nations of the Persian Gulf: a substantial increase in oil output, and an improvement in the security climate. The two goals were closely linked, of course, and nowhere was their conjunction more apparent than in Iraq. For more than two decades, Saddam Hussein had jeopardized the region's stability, hampering foreign investment in new exploration and infrastructure expansion. Washington's desire to see oil production levels rise had also been frustrated by the very means the international community had chosen to pressure Iraq: the maintenance of economic sanctions. Although the sanctions permitted Saddam to sell Iraqi petroleum in order to pay for food and medicine—originally, $2 billion worth every six months; later, an unlimited amount—they did not permit the acquisition of any of the machinery or technology Iraq would need to modernize its existing oil infrastructure and develop new fields. Hence, its output remained at far below potential.[60] Clearly, no real improvement in either the security environment or regional production levels would be possible so long as Saddam remained in power.

George W. Bush did not, of course, face a blank policy slate vis-à-vis Iraq when he took office in early 2001. He inherited the strategy of containment his father had put into place ten years earlier, which aimed at crippling Iraq's military capabilities and, eventually, producing an internal upheaval that would oust Saddam and his top lieutenants. In addition to the UN-imposed sanctions on international trade, containment entailed a naval blockade to enforce them, the stationing of American troops in Kuwait and Saudi Arabia, and the maintenance of no-fly zones over southern and northern Iraq. These efforts proved effective in denying arms to Iraq and deterring further military adventurism: aside from a few low-key military exercises, the Iraqis never again moved their troops near the border with Kuwait and Saudi Arabia. Yet Saddam showed no sign of losing his grip on power. For the incoming Bush administration, therefore, the critical issue was not Iraq per se but, rather, the strategy of containment: whether to reinvigorate it in some fashion so as to increase the internal pressure on Saddam, or to replace it.

The administration immediately initiated a high-level review of the containment strategy and other aspects of U.S. policy toward Iraq. It turned up some disturbing findings. To begin with, the ban on sales of "dual-use" commodities—industrial goods, chemicals, and equipment (such as computers and machine tools) that could be used for military as well as for civilian purposes—had produced a dramatic slump in the economy, causing enormous misery for ordinary citizens. The downturn affected all sectors of Iraqi society, including the health system; hundreds of thousands of young children are believed to have died for lack of adequate food and health care.[61] The UN initiated its oil-for-food program in 1995 to address this crisis, but it could not reverse the decline in living standards.

The widespread suffering provided Saddam with a powerful propaganda tool: by portraying the country's misery as the product of a campaign against the entire nation, rather than the regime, he was able to generate substantial popular support.[62] To make matters worse, this misery was becoming more and more widely known—and resented—by Muslims across the Middle East as a result of growing media attention and the emergence of the Al Jazeera television network. As Secretary of State Colin Powell observed after a trip to the Middle East, "We were being accused, and we were taking on the burden of hurting Iraqi people, hurting Iraqi children, and we needed to turn that around."[63]

That large numbers of people in the Muslim world had turned against the sanctions was creating yet another problem for the United States: governments in the area were becoming increasingly disinclined to carry them out. "One Gulf War ally after another," the *New York Times* reported in February 2001, "[has] denounced the sanctions, and often openly flouted them." At least a dozen countries had broken the air embargo by allowing their national carriers to fly into Baghdad, and three—Egypt, Jordan, and Syria—had begun regularly scheduled flights.[64] These countries also abetted the Iraqis' efforts to circumvent UN rules and engage in various forms of unauthorized commerce, thereby generating billions of dollars in illicit revenues that many American officials believed were being used to rebuild Iraq's military machine and restart its WMD programs.[65]

But although some of Iraq's neighbors were willing to overlook the sanctions on consumer goods and certain dual-use items, the controls remained intact on foreign investment in the energy sector and on the acquisition of modern oil-extraction technology. While the oil-for-food program allowed Baghdad to export as much petroleum as it could produce with its existing infrastructure, it did not permit outside investment in production facilities or the development of untapped reserves—a ban that the large international oil companies were not prepared to violate for fear of facing legal punishment. Nor could Baghdad import the machinery and materials it needed to upgrade obsolete infrastructure. Thus, even as other facets of the sanctions regime were being eroded, the ban on critical oil technology remained in effect and, as a result, Iraq's production continued on its downward slide. By 2001, Iraq was barely capable of producing 2.5 million barrels of oil per day—less than half of its potential capacity.[66]

The corrosion of the sanctions system presented American officials with a serious dilemma. On the one hand, Saddam was taking advantage of it to strengthen his military position, thus magnifying the threat to U.S. security interests in the Gulf; on the other, it was preventing him from helping to satisfy the rising world demand for oil. From Washington's perspective, in other words, the situation was a complete disaster. "When we took over," Powell told Congress on March 8, 2001, "I discovered that we had an Iraq policy that was in disarray. And the sanctions part of that policy was not just in disarray, it was falling apart. . . . We discovered that we were in an airplane that was heading to a crash."[67]

What could be done to avert this crash? We now know that senior White House figures devoted enormous time and effort to this question in the early months of 2001, reflecting their belief that relations with Iraq would prove a defining issue for the new administration. For some, the answer was self-evident: invade Iraq, oust Saddam Hussein, and install a new regime friendly to U.S. interests. Indeed, several top officials, including Secretary of Defense Donald Rumsfeld and Deputy Secretary Paul Wolfowitz, had indicated their support for such a plan before Bush's election (having signed a highly publicized letter to this effect in January 1998) and continued to push for military action once in office. But other figures, including Secretary of State Colin Powell, counseled against an invasion, suggesting that public support was lacking and that the international response would be harshly critical. Another possible option—to abandon sanctions altogether and let the chips fall where they may—was rejected out of hand because it would represent a victory for Saddam Hussein and thus frustrate American efforts to gain greater control over developments in the Gulf.[68] In the end, therefore, President Bush decided on a middle course: to scrap the existing sanctions regime and adopt Secretary Powell's proposal for a new system of "smart sanctions," aimed directly at the Iraqi leadership and the military.[69]

As Powell viewed them, smart sanctions would lift curbs on the delivery of most basic commodities—thereby alleviating the lot of ordinary Iraqis—while tightening restrictions on high-tech goods with potential military applications.[70] Acknowledging the widespread Arab resentment of the existing system, he told Congress in March 2001 that the best approach would be "to eliminate those items in the sanctions regime that really were of civilian use and benefitted people, and focus them exclusively on weapons of mass destruction and items that could be directed toward the development of [these] weapons." Such a system, he argued, would meet the objections of local governments and thus be easier to enforce. At the same time, it would isolate and immobilize the regime, thus hastening its collapse.[71]

Powell inserted his proposal into a draft Security Council resolution and brought it before the United Nations, hoping for quick approval. But while many Security Council members were dissatisfied with the existing sanctions, few were willing to embrace a new system devised entirely by Washington and entailing a complicated ledger of dos and don'ts. (It reportedly included a crowded list, twenty-eight pages long, of prohibited items ranging from sophisticated telecommunications gear to night-vision goggles and underwater television cameras.[72]) When Chinese and Russian diplomats were first presented with the proposal, in May 2001, they insisted on a lengthy review, dooming Powell's hopes for its rapid adoption. Instead the Security Council voted to retain the existing unwieldy (and unpopular) scheme while deliberating possible modifications.[73]

This is where things stood on September 11, 2001. In the wake of the attacks, many in Washington began calling for vigorous action against Saddam Hussein, even though U.S. intelligence agencies had found no connection between the Baghdad regime and Al Qaeda.[74] Colin Powell continued to argue for the smart-sanctions plan, but the tide had turned against him. Top administration officials discussed proposals for an American-led invasion of Iraq at a meeting at Camp David on September 14 and at subsequent meetings in the White House. President Bush chose to hold off on any such action while the war in Afghanistan was monopolizing the Pentagon's attention, but in the early weeks of 2002 he finally gave the go-ahead for the development of a detailed invasion plan.[75]

Why did the president choose to abandon the Powell plan and seek the forcible ouster of Saddam Hussein? No single factor can account for this momentous decision.[76] Security considerations were certainly an important part of the equation: White House officials were obviously worried about the continuing buildup of Iraq's military capabilities and the threat they posed to regional stability.[77] But, as I have argued, security was directly tied to the safety of Persian Gulf oil supplies and thus to the prospects for increased output. So long as Saddam Hussein remained in power, the Gulf would never be entirely stable, and the United States would never be able to boost Iraqi petroleum production.[78]

Top administration officials took great pains to keep from mentioning oil as a casus belli—an admission that would undoubtedly have under-mined public support for the war. Nevertheless, a few moments of candor from Vice President Cheney provide hints as to the administration's deep anxiety about oil production in the Gulf. Cheney's August 2002 address to the Veterans of Foreign Wars was widely viewed as an unvarnished ex-pression of administration thinking, both because he was Bush's most in-fluential adviser and a key architect of the war and because it was the only speech on Iraq he gave.[79] "Should all [of Hussein's WMD] ambitions be realized, the implications would be enormous for the Middle East and the United States," Cheney declared. "Armed with an arsenal of these weapons of terror and a seat atop 10 percent of the world's oil reserves, Saddam Hussein could then be expected to seek domination of the entire Middle East, take control of a great portion of the world's energy supplies, directly threaten America's friends throughout the region, and subject the United States or any other nation to nuclear blackmail."[80] Viewed from this angle, the continued survival of his regime was unthinkable.

The administration's thinking is further revealed in the elaborate preparations made before the war to occupy Iraqi oil installations at the very onset of combat and to install a friendly oil-management team once the fighting had stopped. The State Department's Future of Iraq Project, an ambitious planning effort supervised by Thomas Warrick of the de-partment's Office of Northern Gulf Affairs, recruited the team with the help of the Working Group on Oil and Energy, which was filled with ex-patriate Iraqi oil officials sympathetic to Washington's war aims.[81] The group met on several occasions in late 2002 and early 2003 under tight security, finishing its work just a few weeks before the onset of hostilities. Although its membership was never made public, the news media did re-port on its meetings; according to these accounts, it called for the open-ing up of Iraq's previously state-owned oil sector to outside investment after an initial period in which U.S.-approved Iraqi managers would su-pervise the rehabilitation of the war-damaged infrastructure.[82]

A key player in all this was Ahmed Chalabi, a former Iraqi banker and the founder of the anti-Hussein Iraqi National Congress (INC).[83] In the months leading up to the war, Chalabi—who had established close ties with the American Enterprise Institute and other conservative think tanks in Washington—met with high officials of American energy firms, reportedly promising them a significant role in the reinvigoration of Iraq's oil industry. "American companies will have a big shot at Iraqi oil"[84] once Saddam was deposed and representatives of the INC were installed in top positions, he announced.[85] Evidently the arrangements he and the American oil officials quietly worked out were sufficiently sweeping to unnerve executives of British Petroleum (BP), who pleaded for equal access to Iraqi petroleum under a new regime.[86] (As of this writing, Chalabi had been cut off from official American support because of suspicions that he had provided secret U.S. intelligence data to Iran.)

Meanwhile, the Department of Defense was preparing to seize the oil fields and installations at the very outbreak of hostilities in order to keep Iraqi forces from sabotaging them. "Without going into great detail," a senior Pentagon official explained at the time, "it's fair to say that our land component commander and his planning staff have crafted strategies that will allow us to secure and protect these fields as rapidly as possible in order to preserve those prior to destruction, as opposed to having to go in and clean them up after."[87] But protecting the installations was only the beginning. According to the *Wall Street Journal*, the special Army units assigned to occupy the fields were also being given intensive training in oil-field maintenance.[88] At the same time, the Department of Defense awarded a multibillion-dollar, no-bid contract to a subsidiary of Dick Cheney's old firm, the Halliburton Company, to repair any damage Iraqi forces inflicted on the installations during the war and to commence the rehabilitation of the country's massive oil infrastructure once it was over.[89]

Just how much importance the White House placed on these endeavors was further demonstrated by the actions of U.S. forces during the war itself. In one of their very first combat operations, American forces seized Iraqi oil-export facilities north of Kuwait. "Swooping silently out of the Persian Gulf night," an excited reporter for the *New York Times* wrote on March 22, "Navy Seals seized two Iraqi oil terminals in bold raids that ended early this morning, overwhelming lightly armed Iraqi guards and claiming a bloodless victory in the battle for Iraq's vast oil empire."[90] Other forces then secured Iraq's southernmost oil fields in the Basra area, and, when American forces later entered Baghdad, they quickly occupied the Oil Ministry—protecting this one facility against looters while (in a widely reported public relations disaster) ignoring the wholesale destruction of other government buildings in the vicinity.[91]

Nevertheless, key elements of the oil infrastructure were badly damaged by the looting and violence that erupted in the days immediately following the collapse of the regime. "Everything we need for our work is gone," Hameed Abdul Razzaq, the engineering director of the North Oil Company (a major component of Iraq's state-owned oil industry), lamented in late April. "If it is not taken, it is broken; if it's not broken, it's burned."[92] As a result, American contract personnel and their Iraqi collaborators had a much harder time restoring production at the main oil fields than they had anticipated. Once the fields were back in operation, the U.S.-Iraqi oil team encountered another obstacle: sabotage of the country's far-flung pipelines and pumping stations. Near-daily attacks on the pipeline from Kirkuk to the Turkish port of Ceyhan—eighty-five between May and December 2003 alone[93]—put the line out of commission repeatedly, frustrating efforts to resume exports of Iraqi crude via Turkey.[94] These attacks and the looting damage moved the Bush administration to request $2.1 billion for protection and rehabilitation of Iraqi oil facilities as part of the $87 billion occupation and reconstruction package it submitted to Congress in September 2003.[95]

The persistent sabotage also prompted the Department of Defense to take greater responsibility for protecting the infrastructure. Although it assigned some duties to private security firms—in August 2003, for example, the occupation authorities contracted with a South African company, Erinys International, to supply 6,500 guards for oil-field security work[96]— American forces continued to perform the most dangerous jobs. In October 2003, the Department of Defense began using skilled marksmen from the 327th Tiger Force (an elite unit of the 101st Airborne Division first deployed in Vietnam) to shoot saboteurs on the Kirkuk-Ceyhan pipeline. The snipers were reportedly transported into battle by special

Iraq: Major Pipelines

helicopters whose pilots were trained "to fly at night without light and . . . hover within range of targets"—an obviously perilous maneuver.[97]

While the American forces were struggling to protect pipelines and refineries against attack, the American occupation authorities were installing the new leadership of Iraq's oil industry. The civilian official President Bush selected to supervise the occupation, L. Paul Bremer III, played a direct role in shaping the management team. He entrusted day-to-day operations to experienced Iraqi administrators and engineers, but overall direction of the industry went to Philip J. Carroll, an American oil executive who had once run the American office of Royal Dutch/Shell.[98] Carroll hired more American oil executives to devise an "American-style" corporate management structure that would oversee the industry.[99]

Working closely with U.S. defense contractors like Halliburton, these executives established Team RIO (Restore Iraqi Oil) to undertake the rehabilitation of the country's dilapidated infrastructure.[100]

At present, senior Iraqi and American oil managers are concerned primarily with restoring the existing fields and refineries, which, having been severely damaged during the long period of sanctions and again in the 2003 war, need extensive and costly repairs to achieve high levels of output. The Iraqi fields were reported to be producing around 2.0 million barrels per day at the end of 2003 and attained their prewar level of 2.5 million barrels only in the spring of 2004[101]; higher levels will take more time and considerably more investment. According to some analyses, it may cost more than $7 billion to boost Iraqi production to its 1990 level of 3.5 million barrels per day, and at least $20 billion to achieve the 5.5 million barrels that Iraqi petroleum officials envision.[102]

American occupation officials decided to keep the Iraqi oil fields, for the time being at least, under state ownership and control; privatization, they feared, would smack of imperialism and sharpen the already keen opposition to the occupation. Continued state ownership would also allow Iraq's apolitical technocrats to repair infrastructure damage quickly and begin the long-term rehabilitation of the industry. As the *Wall Street Journal* explained in January 2004, "U.S. and Iraqi oil advisers say a politically independent state company would allow Iraqi oil professionals to ramp up production, improve operating standards, and pursue maximum revenue for Iraq without inflaming nationalistic passions about foreign meddling."[103] But although Iraq has many skilled managers and engineers, it does not have the billions of dollars it will take to boost production. And on the question of where those funds will come from, Iraqi and American officials are of one mind: from the major international oil firms. "To develop the oil sector, we need foreign investment," Ibrahim Bahr al-Uloum, Iraq's interim oil minister, said in September 2003.[104] American energy analysts naturally concur.[105]

But which firms will be invited to invest, and under what circumstances? Those are the questions dominating discussion of Iraq in the business press—and, no doubt, the boardrooms of the world's largest oil companies.[106] Under current plans, foreign firms will not be able to purchase existing fields but *will* be allowed to collaborate with the country's state-owned oil company in joint rehabilitation and development projects[107]—an approach that should prove particularly advantageous to American oil-services firms like Halliburton and Bechtel, both of which are expected to win multibillion-dollar contracts for infrastructure repair and modernization.[108]

But while it may solve Iraq's short-term problems, this approach leaves unanswered a much bigger question: what to do with Iraq's prodigious "greenfields," or undeveloped reserves? According to the DoE, these fields may hold as much as 100 billion barrels of oil—probably the largest reservoir of untapped petroleum in the world.[109] Before the war, a number of prominent Russian, French, Italian, and Chinese firms had negotiated for rights to develop some of these fields with Saddam's government, but none of these projects could go forward while UN sanctions were in place.[110] Now that sanctions have been lifted, these firms hope to proceed with their prewar plans. However, the new Iraqi management team has announced that any development contracts signed by the deposed regime will have to be reviewed, and that some may be deemed invalid.[111] The abrogation of these contracts will, of course, open the field to investment by U.S. and British firms, none of which had been allowed by Iraqi authorities or their own governments to bid for development rights while Saddam remained in power.[112] Although the big decisions are still several years away, American oil-company executives are reportedly eager to invest in Iraq. "For any oil company," an executive of one of them has said, "being in Iraq is like being a kid in F. A.O. Schwarz."[113]

Before any of this can come to pass, though, the American occupation authorities will have to resolve the question of how much self-rule Iraq will actually be allowed to enjoy after the formal transfer of sovereignty on June 30, 2004. Supposedly, the Iraqi authorities to be selected in UN-supervised elections in 2005 will have considerable power to govern the country. But news reports from Baghdad and Washington suggest that the U.S. embassy in Iraq (which is to replace the occupation authority) will exercise significant control over major government ministries, including, presumably, the Oil Ministry.[114] This will, no doubt, facilitate the award of oil-development contracts to American energy firms. At the same time, however, it will surely arouse continuing hostility from those Iraqis who resent an overbearing U.S. presence.

And this leads to a final dilemma: before large-scale drilling projects can proceed in Iraq, the United States must quell the violence that continues to rack the country. Major oil companies will not risk large sums in Iraq if their facilities and personnel are going to be at constant risk; in the words of Daniel Yergin, the chairman of Cambridge Energy Research Associates and a noted expert on oil, "No company will write a check for a million dollars without some sense of stability."[115] And so, in the end, America's energy priorities in the Gulf come back to the critical issue of security. Only by retaining sizable forces in Iraq, and risking the blood of its young servicemen and -women, can the United States hope to produce the atmosphere of stability that will encourage investment in Iraq's oil industry and bring about the intensely wished-for increase in its output.

Squeezing Iran

The Bush administration's ultimate goal in Iran is the same as it was in Iraq: a change in regime. If the administration could have its wish, the clerical junta that now controls Iran would be replaced by a Western-oriented government that rejects terrorism and nuclear weapons and throws open the country's state-owned oil industry to outside—especially American—investment. To the degree that it has been able to, the administration has pursued this goal. But, despite some superficial similarities, Iran today is emphatically *not* like prewar Iraq, and so the White House has had to adopt a different, less obviously aggressive approach.[116]

White House officials have been careful not to use the term *regime change* in public. To be sure, the president has made his sentiments known: in his February 2002 State of the Union address, he included Iran in the "axis of evil" along with Iraq and North Korea.[117] He reiterated his feelings in June 2003 when, discussing student protests in Tehran, he said, "This is the beginning of people expressing themselves toward a free Iran which I think is positive."[118] He has even suggested that Iran's fledgling nuclear-weapons program may justify military action; the United

States "will not tolerate the construction of a nuclear weapon" in Iran, he declared on June 18, 2003.[119]

In many respects, the administration's antipathy to the government in Iran stems from the same concerns raised by Saddam Hussein in Iraq: an anti-American agenda that Washington believes includes support for terrorism and the manufacture of weapons of mass destruction.[120] Some American officials also believe that extremist elements within the Iranian government participated or at least somehow assisted in the June 1996 terrorist attack on the Khobar Towers in Saudi Arabia.[121] They further believe the Iranians have apprehended—but have refused to hand over to the United States—senior Al Qaeda operatives sought by Washington for their role in attacks on American citizens and installations.[122]

As for nuclear munitions, although Iranian officials have denied any intent to acquire such weapons and have allowed inspectors from the International Atomic Energy Agency (IAEA) to visit the country's nuclear facilities in accordance with its obligations under the nuclear Non-Proliferation Treaty (NPT), the administration still believes Tehran is pursuing a secret weapons program.[123] These suspicions gained in credibility when, in August 2002, an Iranian opposition group in exile displayed satellite photographs showing the construction of two nuclear facilities in Iran that should have been reported to the IAEA, at Natanz and Arak.[124] In the wake of these disclosures, Tehran came under enormous pressure from the international community to open up these previously unknown facilities for international inspection and to abide fully by its NPT obligations. In response, the Iranians agreed in October 2003 to suspend all objectionable programs and to permit more thorough inspections of its nuclear facilities by the IAEA. However, Tehran subsequently announced that it would start up a uranium-processing plant in Isfahan, raising doubts about its commitment to the October 2003 agreement.[125]

As with Iraq, Washington's concerns about Iran's threat to regional security are closely tied to issues of oil production and safety. There is, to begin with, the question of Iran's own output: as long as American-imposed sanctions remain in effect, the Iranians will not be able to raise it significantly. Iran possesses the world's fifth-largest petroleum reserves (after Saudi Arabia, Iraq, Kuwait, and the UAE); at its peak in 1974, it produced

6 million barrels of oil per day. In recent years, however, net output has rarely surpassed 3.7 million barrels per day, and it is not expected to rise much above this in the foreseeable future.[126] The drop began in 1979, in the tumult accompanying the ouster of the shah, and continued through the long war with Iraq. Since 1988, the nation has been attempting to boost output to prerevolutionary levels but, like Saudi Arabia and Kuwait, has balked at offering the sort of financial incentives that would attract large Western energy firms with advanced production technologies.[127]

The sanctions imposed by the United States have proved an even bigger obstacle to foreign investment. Under Executive Order 12959, signed by President Clinton in 1995 and later renewed by President Bush, American firms are barred from any significant investment in Iran; under the Iran-Libya Sanctions Act of 1996 (extended for five years in 2001), the government is required to penalize any *non*-U.S. company that invests in Iran. Not surprisingly, these measures have deterred many foreign firms from making such investments.[128]

The sanctions on Iran have also hampered international efforts to develop the energy resources of the Caspian Sea basin. Because the Caspian is landlocked, any oil and natural-gas exports must be carried out by pipeline or delivered to ports with access to international waters. At present, energy firms can use the old Soviet-era pipeline system to transport Caspian oil and gas to Russia and thence to eastern Europe, or two newer lines that carry oil to ports on the Black Sea. But many of these companies would prefer a pipeline running across Iran to the Persian Gulf, where oil-export facilities are abundant; that route is much shorter than any of the alternatives, avoids dependence on the narrow and often clogged Turkish Straits (which connect the Black Sea to the Mediterranean), and provides a shorter haul to consumers in Asia. However, no one wants to build such a pipeline with the threat of American economic retaliation looming.[129]

Finally, Washington remains deeply worried about Iran's potential threat to the outflow of oil through the Strait of Hormuz, the vital waterway that connects the Persian Gulf with the Indian Ocean and the world beyond. Every day, giant tankers carrying some 14 million barrels of oil—a fifth of total world output—traverse the strait, making it "the world's most important oil chokepoint."[130] Keeping this chokepoint free and secure was one of the Central Command's original missions when it was established in 1983, and this mission remains among its top priorities today.[131] Hence Washington's anxiety over Iran's continuing deployment of Chinese-made antiship missiles at both entrances to the Strait of Hormuz and on a number of small islands (Abu Musa and the Greater and Lesser Tunbs) that abut the narrow ship channel in the waterway itself. Although Iran's capacity to fight a full-scale war with the United States is obviously limited, it has the power to disrupt or block tanker traffic through the strait, thereby creating a severe shortage in global energy supplies.[132]

All these problems would disappear if the current Iranian regime were replaced by a government more attuned to America's strategic interests. Washington could then lift its restrictions on investment in Iran, clearing the way for the influx of advanced production technologies and facilitating a rise in Iranian oil output, as well as the construction of oil and gas pipelines from the Caspian to the Persian Gulf. But the conditions that made regime change possible in Baghdad—an isolated and widely detested leader with a history of defying UN resolutions and a military establishment with dubious loyalty to him—do not exist in Iran. While the country is effectively controlled by a religious autocracy headed by Supreme Leader Ayatollah Ali Khamenei, it also boasts a popularly elected president, Mohammed Khatami, who is respected abroad. The Iranians have, moreover, offered to comply with the Non-Proliferation Treaty and have persuaded many foreign firms to do business with them, despite the threat of American penalties. A replay of Operation Iraqi Freedom in Iran is not, therefore, a realistic scenario.[133]

What other options does Washington have? No clear blueprint for regime change in Iran has yet surfaced, but it is possible to reconstruct the administration's game plan from its public statements and actions. The senior official who has been most explicit in laying out this plan is Zalmay Khalilzad, the U.S. ambassador in Afghanistan; an American citizen of Afghan origin, he enjoys close ties with senior administration officials, having served as an adviser to Defense Secretary Donald Rumsfeld and as head of the Bush-Cheney transition team for the Department of Defense. The administration's approach toward Iran, he explained in an August 2002 speech, is based on a "dual-track policy," combining economic and diplomatic pressure on the regime with support for antigovernment forces within the country. We will "tell the world what is destructive and unacceptable about Iran's behavior—sponsorship of terror, pursuit of weapons of mass destruction, and repression of the clearly expressed desires of the Iranian people for freedom and democracy—while laying out a positive vision of partnership and support for the Iranian people." Khalilzad distinguished between the antidemocratic elite in control of the Iranian government and the popular masses who have suffered as a result of the elite's recalcitrance and isolation; once the regime has been swept away, he predicted, economic sanctions can be lifted and the Iranian public will enjoy both freedom and prosperity.[134]

Khalilzad dismissed the notion that Iran's elected officials, including President Khatami, have any power at all. "In Iran," he said, "critical decisions on national security issues are made by an un-elected few who have used terrorism as an instrument of policy"—without the authorization of the country's elected officials and "often without their knowledge." The same dictatorial clerics have used their authority to block any of the reform measures sponsored by Khatami and endorsed by the Iranian parliament. Thus, the existence of an elected government in Iran is irrelevant. "Our policy is not about Khatami or Khamenei," Khalilzad declared, "it is about supporting those who want human rights, democracy, and economic and educational opportunity for themselves and their fellow countrymen and women."[135]

For Khalilzad, the most promising engine of transformation was the palpable discontent of the nation's younger citizens, who make up a majority of the population (nearly 65 percent of Iranians are under twenty-five) but suffer from limited opportunities and high levels of unemployment. "This group has been the driving force for change," he said. "But the voices and protests of Iran's young people have been repressed—at times violently." To bolster their defiance, the United States would offer various forms of encouragement and support, including the broadcast of pro-democracy messages in Farsi, the national language, into the country.[136]

At present, the Bush administration appears committed to the multipronged approach Khalilzad described, in the hope that political, economic, and diplomatic pressure will exacerbate existing divisions within

Iranian society and lead to a popular uprising. Just how long the White House is willing to wait is less clear. At this point, with large numbers of American troops tied up in Iraq, the administration is unlikely to do anything drastic. But if, once the situation in Iraq improves, the current approach has failed to produce any results in Tehran, it is entirely possible that the White House will turn to covert operations or even direct military action. Indeed, there are signs that the White House has already considered tactics of this sort.[137] According to a May 2003 report in the *Washington Post*, some Pentagon officials favor a covert alliance with the Mujaheddin-e Khalq (MEK), a large and well-equipped paramilitary force based in northern Iraq. The State Department has designated the MEK a terrorist organization and so has vetoed such an alliance, at least for now. But the very fact that a move of this kind has already been considered at the highest levels suggests that covert military operations are very possibly in the cards.[138]

As this book went to press, in July 2004, the Bush administration was focusing on three key developments in Iran: the election of a conservative majority in parliament after the Guardian Council (a clerical body with sweeping powers) banned most reformist candidates; Tehran's continued defiance of the IAEA; and a major upward revision of Iran's untapped petroleum reserves. The new parliamentary majority is expected to vote fresh restrictions on the press and the pro-reform parties, provoking increased resentment among the young and strengthening the arguments of those who denounce elections as a sham and advocate more forceful action to effect systemic change. Meanwhile, in late March, the Iranians announced the start-up of the nuclear-processing facility at Isfahan, despite their earlier promise to cease all weapons-related activities.[139] And, while all this was going on, Iran's Ministry of Petroleum recalculated the country's proven reserves, raising the total from 89.7 billion barrels at the start of 2003 to 125.8 billion barrels at the start of 2004—the biggest increase of its kind in recent years.[140] This growth in reserves, along with the growing inclination of European and Japanese companies to invest in Iran, is certain to deepen Washington's desire to effect a regime change in Tehran, lift sanctions, and pave the way for substantial investment by American firms in the country's prolific oil sector.

America and the Gulf:
No Exit, No Peace

Between early 2001 and the end of 2003, the Bush administration committed vast resources to subduing the Persian Gulf region and increasing its oil output. These efforts were not fruitless: Saddam Hussein was deposed, the Saudi royal family was shored up, and Al Qaeda was driven from Afghanistan. But this immense effort did not achieve its fundamental objectives. The region was still violent and unstable, and oil production had not increased significantly. After all that expenditure of blood and money, the Gulf still posed the same colossal challenge.

The most troubling situation, of course, was Iraq. Although President Bush had declared an end to major combat operations in May 2003, attacks on American forces escalated in the summer and fall, producing more and more American and allied casualties. "We are going to win this battle, and this war," General Ricardo Sanchez, the U.S. military commander in Iraq, pledged on November 11, 2003.[141] But his very choice of words acknowledged that we were still at war, and that the struggle to pacify Iraq and commence the full-scale exploitation of its petroleum reserves was far from over. This struggle has its ups and downs, with some days less deadly than others, but the overall level of violence had not subsided by May 2004. How long the war will last, and what price it will exact in dollars and in human lives, cannot be foreseen.

Equally uncertain is the future in Saudi Arabia. Although the Bush administration has eliminated one of the most important sources of instability there—the presence of American combat troops—other critical problems, including the corruption of the royal family and its resistance to reform, remain. By striking at residential compounds in Riyadh rather than (heavily defended) government facilities, Al Qaeda may have alienated some of its Saudi supporters. But the continuing attacks nevertheless show there is a deep reservoir of antigovernment sentiment in the country.[142] No matter how fiercely Saudi rulers respond to domestic terrorism, the regime will never be safe from violent attack so long as it is perceived as a tool of American oil interests. And, lacking the strength to defend itself against a major assault or rebellion, it will continue to rely on the protective embrace of American military forces.

As for Iran, the situation is even more unpredictable. At present, the conservative mullahs appear to be in control, but popular discontent could erupt in massive demonstrations or outright rebellion at any time. Whether the status quo will persist, or give way to a peaceful transition of power or to some form of violent upheaval—possibly involving American military intervention—it is impossible to say. What is evident, though, is that Washington's patience is diminishing as its concern over nuclear weapons and its desire to open up Iran's oil sector to outside investment grow.

The pervasive instability of the Persian Gulf undoubtedly portends the continued presence of a large American military force in the region. At the beginning of 2004, approximately 160,000 American soldiers were deployed in Iraq and Kuwait, and several tens of thousands more were stationed in Qatar, Bahrain, and the United Arab Emirates and aboard ships in the Gulf proper. Some of these forces will be recalled when (or if) the fighting in Iraq recedes, but the Department of Defense cannot lower American troop strength too far without impairing Centcom's ability to ensure the outward flow of Persian Gulf oil. With so many issues and disputes still unresolved, the risk of regional conflict—and of armed intervention by American forces—remains high.

But no matter how costly the effort grows, we cannot remove our forces from the Gulf as long as we remain committed to a strategy of maximum petroleum extraction. To meet anticipated U.S. energy demand in the years ahead while also slaking the growing thirst of other oil-importing nations, the Gulf producers must—as we have seen—boost their combined oil output by 85 percent between now and 2020, and these supplies must safely reach their markets. Left to themselves, the Gulf countries are unlikely to succeed; it will take continued American intervention and the sacrifice of more and more American blood to come even close. The Bush administration has chosen to preserve America's existing energy posture by tying its fortunes to Persian Gulf oil. These are the abiding and ineluctable consequences.

5

No Safe Havens:
Oil and Conflict Beyond the Persian Gulf

For the Bush-Cheney energy policy to have even a chance of success, there has to be a mammoth increase in the output of Persian Gulf oil. But even attaining that critical objective—an effort that will tax America's diplomatic and military capabilities to the limit—won't generate enough petroleum to quench the world's thirst. According to the Department of Energy, global oil output must grow by 45.3 million barrels per day between 2001 and 2025 to satisfy anticipated world demand; if all goes according to plan, and all the necessary infrastructure improvements are made, the Gulf countries will provide 22.8 million more barrels per day—only half of the required increase. Another 22.5 million barrels will have to come from suppliers in other regions, few of which have reserves on the scale of the Gulf's. Boosting output in these non-Gulf areas is thus equally vital to the administration's energy goals. And this would accomplish another White House objective as well: making us better able to weather supply disruptions in the Gulf. The administration believes we can achieve both objectives through the avid pursuit of import "diversification."

The Bush administration sees diversification as a vital effort to multiply the number of petroleum suppliers and to prod all those producers into vastly increasing their output. Theoretically, it would both expand the net supply of global energy and diminish the impact of an interruption in any one of them. With this critical goal in mind, the 2001 *National Energy Policy* calls on public servants from the president on down to do everything in their power to encourage production increases in areas outside the Gulf, especially Africa, Latin America, and the former Soviet Union. In the administration's view, diversification is the perfect solution to our energy dilemma—the one great fix that will eliminate the risks and the problems of relying too fully on the Gulf. "Diversity is important not only for energy security, but also for national security," Bush declared in May 2001. "Over-dependence on any one source of energy, especially a foreign source, leaves us vulnerable to price shocks, supply interruptions, and, in the worst case, blackmail."[1]

In my view, price shocks and supply interruptions—and perhaps even blackmail—are precisely what the president's energy strategy holds in store for the United States. His rhetoric, however, aims to convince us that we can dodge this fate—that we can increase our consumption of imported oil without increasing the attendant risks of economic trauma and bloodshed. Imagine that the administration announced an energy policy that relied solely on increased imports from the Persian Gulf. Most Americans would view it as reckless and foolhardy. A strategy of "diversification," on the other hand, suggests that we have alternatives, that enough energy is available elsewhere in the world to minimize the danger of consuming ever more imported oil. Not surprisingly, then, diversification has become a major talking point for the administration—the automatic response to any question raised about the risks of its energy plan.

But is this a viable strategy? By expanding our range of suppliers, can we obtain the petroleum we need to keep the American economy running smoothly? The Bush administration is exceedingly optimistic. "Technological advances will enable the United States to accelerate the diversification of oil supplies, notably through deep-water offshore exploration and production in the Atlantic Basin, stretching from offshore Canada to the Caribbean, Brazil, and West Africa," the *NEP* affirmed with characteristic enthusiasm. "The Caspian Sea can also be a rapidly growing new area of supply."[2] But there are excellent reasons to question the promise of diversification. As a response to America's energy dilemma, it will succeed only if: (a) there is sufficient oil outside the Gulf to significantly reduce our dependence on the Middle East; and (b) we can get that oil while avoiding the sorts of dangers and liabilities we now face there. In reality, *neither* of these conditions holds true. As we shall see, the non-Gulf suppliers do not have enough petroleum to permit a substantial reduction in our reliance on Persian Gulf oil, yet they present a very high risk of American entanglement in regional strife and disorder.

The False Promise of Diversification

Official talk about diversification conveys the impression that all over the globe substantial amounts of crude petroleum are awaiting discovery and development, and that, once tapped, these reserves will substantially reduce America's dependence on Middle Eastern oil. Major producers in the Western Hemisphere, the former Soviet Union (including the Caspian Sea basin), and West Africa are are said to be the key to diversity. The 2001 *National Energy Policy* lists eight countries in particular whose reserves are of potentially great advantage to the United States. For shorthand purposes I'll refer to them as the Alternative Eight. The *NEP* describes them as follows:

- "**Mexico** is a leading and reliable source of imported oil, and its large reserve base . . . makes Mexico a likely source of increased oil production over the next decade."
- Growing international investment in **Venezuela's** energy sector is "enhancing the country's ability to meet its development goals and to keep pace with a growing world energy market."
- "**Colombia** has also become an important supplier of oil to the United States."
- **Russia** has increased its output in older fields, and "new fields are being developed, including those with U.S. and other foreign investors."
- "Proven oil reserves in **Azerbaijan** and **Kazakhstan** are about 20 billion barrels, a little more than the North Sea. . . . Exploration, however, is continuing, and proven reserves are expected to increase significantly."

• **"Nigeria** . . . has set ambitious production goals as high as 5 million barrels per day over the coming decade," more than twice as much as in 2000.
• **"Angola's** growing offshore oil industry, with participation by U.S. and international oil firms, is also a major source of growth [and] is thought to have the potential to double its exports over the next ten years."[3]

These and other official comments proclaim a future of abundance and cooperation. But just how prolific, in reality, are these fields likely to prove? And—more to the point—how much of their future output will be available for export to the United States? To answer these questions, we must look at the Alternative Eight's reserve base and assess their day-to-day production and consumption patterns.

First, let's consider the matter of reserves. In 2003, the energy giant BP estimated the Alternative Eight's combined "proven reserves" at 198 billion barrels, or about 19 percent of the world total.[4] (Proven reserves, you may recall, are those that are *known* to exist and can be exploited with existing technology.) These are conservative calculations, but they are the best indication of how much petroleum is likely to be extracted from these key countries. (See figure 6.)

Most geologists believe that these countries also possess as yet undeveloped and undiscovered supplies of oil, typically described as "possible" or "potential" reserves. For example, the Department of Energy claims that Azerbaijan and Kazakhstan jointly possess proven reserves of 6.6 billion barrels along with possible reserves of 124 billion barrels, for a hypothetical grand total of 130.6 billion barrels.[5] There are similar claims for the other key countries. But many oil-industry analysts are wary of such projections; they insist that the full extent of a country's reserves can be determined only through systematic exploration and testing. And so, until more information becomes available, it makes sense to rely on BP's conservative figures rather than the DoE's speculative (and cheery) projections. From this perspective, the Alternative Eight's 198 billion barrels of oil is a substantial but by no means awe-inspiring amount. If, as expected, daily world oil consumption reaches 108 million barrels per day in 2020, they would meet world requirements for little more than five years. We are not talking about a bottomless well of undeveloped petroleum.

Figure 6
PROVEN RESERVES, PRODUCTION, AND EXPORT CAPACITY
OF SELECTED NON–PERSIAN GULF OIL PRODUCERS,
END OF 2002

Producer	Proven Reserves (bbl)	Reserves as a percent of world total	Production (mbd)	Production as a percent of world total	Domestic consumption (mbd)	Available for export (mbd)
Mexico	12.6	1.2	3.59	5.0	1.79	1.80
Venezuela	77.8	7.4	2.94	4.3	0.50	2.44
Colombia	1.8	0.2	0.60	0.8	0.22	0.38
Russia	60.0	5.7	7.70	10.7	2.47	5.23
Azerbaijan	7.0	0.7	0.31	0.4	0.07	0.24
Kazakhstan	9.0	0.9	0.99	1.3	0.13	0.86
Nigeria	24.0	2.3	2.01	2.8	0.29	1.72
Angola	5.4	0.5	0.91	1.3	0.03	0.88
Total, selected non-Gulf producers	197.6	18.9	19.05	26.6	5.50	13.55
Total, Persian Gulf producers	679.0	64.8	19.9	26.9	2.98	16.92

Sources: Proven reserves: *BP Statistical Review of World Energy 2003* (London: BP, 2003), pp. 4, 6, 9. Data on consumption for Angola and Nigeria: U.S. Department of Energy, Energy Information Administration (DoE/EIA), country analysis brief for Angola (November 2002) and Nigeria (January 2002), electronic documents accessed at www.eia.doe.gov.

Abbreviations: bbl = billion barrels; mbd = million barrels per day

But reserves are just one of several factors to consider when assessing a country's future export potential. Just as important is its *production capacity*. A nation may have enormous reserves of untapped petroleum, but they're of no practical value unless they can be extracted and delivered to global markets. And a country that produces oil at a very high rate may still contribute little to the world market if it consumes most or all of what it takes out of the ground. So we must also take into consideration a producer's *domestic consumption rate*, the share of its output that is consumed locally. The amount of oil a given provider can supply to world markets is the difference between its net production capacity and its domestic consumption rate.

Once we apply this formula to the Alternative Eight, it becomes apparent that they do not hold nearly the promise the Bush administration ascribes to them. At the end of 2002, they were jointly producing 19 million barrels of oil per day, accounting for approximately one-fourth of total world production. But they were also consuming 5.5 million barrels per day, leaving 13.5 million barrels available for export.[6] That is a major contribution to global supply and represents a significant source of America's current imports.[7] But we are concerned here with their long-term potential. If the Alternative Eight are to diminish our reliance on the Gulf, they must substantially increase their production *and* their export potential in the years ahead. Since global petroleum consumption is expected to rise by half over the next two decades, they will have to boost their export potential from 13.5 to 20.8 million barrels just to retain their current market share; if they are to provide us with a *larger* portion of our imported oil, they would have to boost their day-to-day exports by an even greater amount.

This is the goal to which the Bush administration's strategy of diversification is largely devoted. As we have seen, the *NEP* had called on federal officials to persuade oil-rich countries to ramp up their production and to clear the way for American private-sector investment in new drilling projects. And the Bush administration has obliged: figures ranking as high as the president, the secretary of state, and the secretary of energy have met with the leaders of the Alternative Eight to discuss strategies for boosting their energy exports. In his first trip outside the United States as president, for example, George W. Bush met with Mexican President Vicente Fox in Mexico City to discuss ways of increasing Mexican energy exports to this country.[8] The White House has also convened periodic "energy summits" to promote cooperation between the United States and its key suppliers.[9] In countries where bureaucratic and legal obstacles might make private-sector investors fearful, the State Department has sent legal experts to help rewrite the investment laws. "We all have worked together very hard over the past year to develop a legal and commercial framework for the export routes that will stand up to the razor-sharp scrutiny of prospective investors," Assistant Secretary of State John S. Wolf declared in October 2002, speaking of the Caspian Sea region.[10]

The administration has devoted particular attention to Russia, the Caspian Sea states, and West Africa. Secretary of Energy Spencer Abraham has spoken glowingly, for example, of "Russia's vast untapped energy resources."[11] In May 2002, President Bush met with Russian president Vladimir Putin to talk about how these assets might be more readily exploited. Together they inaugurated the U.S.-Russian Energy Dialogue, with the aim of developing "bilateral cooperation in the energy sphere" and promoting "access to world markets for Russian energy."[12] Five months later, the Department of Energy convened the U.S.-Russian Commercial Energy Summit in Houston to solidify ties between the two nation's energy firms. In the optimistic words of Secretary Abraham, these new ventures portended "a bright energy future."[13]

The White House sees similar promise in the Caspian Sea. Among other development efforts, it has endorsed construction of the Baku-Tbilisi-Ceyhan (BTC) pipeline, which will carry oil from Baku, in Azerbaijan, to Ceyhan, in Turkey, via the Georgian capital of Tbilisi—thus breaking Russia's current monopoly on the flow of Caspian Sea energy and facilitating future deliveries to the United States. Signaling the strong American support for the project, Secretary Abraham attended the pipeline's groundbreaking ceremony in Baku in September 2002 and read a letter from President Bush commending the countries and companies that had sponsored it.[14] Voicing his own support, he added that the pipeline "will strengthen international energy security" by adding "a million barrels of oil a day" to global supplies.[15]

Abraham and other senior officials have also made frequent trips to Africa to promote closer cooperation and the elimination of regulatory obstacles to American investment.[16] In June 2002, he attended the third annual meeting of African energy ministers in Casablanca, Morocco.

"We met with government and industry," he testified several weeks later, "to discuss ways to improve energy trade and facilitate energy sector development to better serve U.S. and African economic growth and development." The meeting was a great success, he added, because the African producers had reaffirmed their commitment to "stable regulatory structures" and "discussed additional steps to encourage private investment in the energy sector."[17]

As these comments demonstrate, the U.S. government has assumed a pivotal role in the global energy system, working tirelessly to eliminate the obstacles to increased oil production. In seeking to boost output in Russia, Secretary Abraham observed in 2002, "the governments of the United States and Russia have an important role to play. Our job is to create the framework of laws and rules that allow our companies to form partnerships with confidence in the security of their arrangements."[18] This is exactly the role that President Franklin D. Roosevelt and his successors played when they were opening up Saudi Arabia and its neighbors to American exploitation, except that now the Bush administration is conducting such diplomacy on a far wider scale. American firms will no doubt take advantage of the space it creates for private-sector development; without the work of government officials, there would be few such openings.

Despite these efforts, however, it is highly unlikely that the Alternative Eight will live up to the administration's expectations. Several factors will keep these countries from achieving or sustaining much higher production and export capacities: rising domestic consumption, significant oil-field depletion, and an uninviting investment climate. And—as if all of this were not enough—many of these countries are vulnerable to exactly the same sorts of disorder and conflict that make the Gulf such a perilous area.

Obstacles to Increased Output

The first obstacle the non-Gulf producers face to boosting their oil exports is the anticipated growth in their own and their neighbors' consumption levels. Many of the alternative suppliers the Bush administration is touting, including Mexico, Venezuela, Colombia, Brazil, and Nigeria, are developing nations with rising populations and ever-increasing domestic demand for oil. Russia, though it is a mature industrial power with a sizable demand for energy, is also expected to see an increase in domestic consumption as its economy recovers from the devastating effects of the Soviet Union's collapse.[19] These countries will not be able to supply additional oil to the United States or anyone else unless they boost their total output substantially *beyond* what they need to satisfy themselves.

The Department of Energy does not supply detailed projections of oil production and consumption for all of these key providers. What data it has provided do not exactly bolster one's optimism. Mexico and the South American countries are expected to post a combined increase in production of 61 percent between 2001 and 2025; but their total consumption will rise by an estimated 78 percent, resulting in a net *decline* of exportable energy. Production gains in Russia and the Caspian states (81 percent) will exceed their increase in consumption (59 percent), but not by enough to make a huge difference. Only in Africa will net output grow significantly faster than consumption (91 to 35 percent). But when these three areas are added together, their combined gain in output—76 percent—is not all that much greater than their combined gain in consumption—64 percent.[20]

And these DoE projections are relatively optimistic. Many analysts believe that the Alternative Eight will find it difficult to reach even these increases in output. In some countries, older fields will become depleted. In others, the development of new fields—especially those in difficult terrain or deep offshore areas—will founder for lack of adequate capital and technology. Most of these countries also suffer from corruption, obsolete legal structures, and political instability—factors that tend to discourage foreign investment.

The depletion of older fields is a particularly serious problem for Mexico and Venezuela. The yields of Mexico's most productive source, the Cantarell field in the Bay of Campeche, have declined in recent years as a result of reduced natural pressure, and are not expected to recover.[21] Many of Venezuela's older fields, some of which have been in production for nearly a century, are also yielding less. The government of President

Hugo Chávez is trying to reverse this decline, but many officials of the state-owned oil company were forced out during the political turmoil that roiled the country in 2002 and 2003, and experts fear that their replacements are engaging in drilling practices that will actually accelerate the fields' exhaustion.[22]

Russia's older fields are also facing decline. Russia was once the world's leading producer, extracting 12.5 million barrels per day in the peak year of 1988, but its output plunged to 6 million barrels following the collapse of the Soviet Union. Production has since risen to 8 million barrels per day and is expected to climb further in the years ahead—leading some analysts to speak of an energy renaissance in Russia and even to predict that it will eventually overtake Saudi Arabia.[23] Privatization and advanced Western technology have enabled Russian firms to restore some of the capacity that was lost in the early 1990s; however, many of their older fields are believed to have been substantially depleted in the Soviet era (in order to satisfy high, state-mandated production quotas) and so are incapable of sustaining higher yields. Russia does possess large untapped fields in eastern Siberia and the Far East, and they will undoubtedly augment global supply in the future. But it is highly improbable that Russia's output will ever surpass Saudi Arabia's.[24]

Doubts have also arisen as to Nigeria's capacity to produce substantially more petroleum. In a move that shocked investors, oil giant Royal Dutch/Shell admitted in January 2004 that it had overstated its proven oil and natural gas reserves by 20 percent—or approximately 3.9 billion barrels of oil equivalent. Shell did not disclose which of its previously declared reserves had been eliminated in its reassessment, but the *New York Times* subsequently revealed that the largest concentration of them were in Nigeria. According to the *Times*, Shell concluded that 60 percent of its Nigerian reserves—about 1.5 billion barrels—did not meet international accounting standards for "proven reserves." The Nigerian government has contested these findings, claiming there has been no decline in its own tally of the nation's reserves, but questions remain as to how much oil is actually buried there.[25]

Many of the untapped reservoirs that other key suppliers in this group are thought to possess are in remote locations or offshore areas that pose serious impediments to development. The most promising new reserves in Angola, for example, are located in deep Atlantic waters—in some cases, at depths of a mile—and so require use of the most advanced drilling technologies.[26] Development of the huge Kashagan field in Kazakhstan's section of the Caspian Sea poses a different sort of problem: although relatively shallow, the Caspian freezes over in the winter and so makes year-round drilling operations difficult.[27] And many of Russia's new reserves are in remote areas of Siberia or in the frigid waters of the Bering Sea. All these deposits *can* be developed, but only with a great deal of money and the latest technology.

Older reservoirs are not necessarily doomed to become barren; with "enhanced recovery" techniques, they can now yield far more oil than was once considered possible. But to stay productive, they will need investment, and lots of it. Massive amounts of capital are also the key to exploiting new and undeveloped reserves. According to a recent study by the International Energy Agency, the world community will need to invest $3 *trillion* over the next thirty years to raise global oil production to a level adequate to meet worldwide demand in 2030.[28] This is a colossal sum of money, and assembling it will be a formidable challenge for every government, lending agency, and private company involved. All the oil-producing countries will struggle to raise the necessary funds, and the Alternative Eight will have a particularly hard time. With limited financial reserves and the generally weak condition of their economies, they will have to rely almost entirely on external sources of capital—principally the large American, European, and Japanese energy firms and their respective lenders. But private, profit-driven companies are not likely to invest vast sums unless they can exercise a significant degree of control over local operating conditions and somehow insulate themselves from other problems, and in very few cases will they receive the required assurances.

In a number of these countries, foreign investment in energy exploration and production endeavors—upstream activities, in oil jargon—is banned or saddled with strong disincentives. The constitutions of Mexico and Venezuela strictly prohibit external investment in upstream activities; domestic production is reserved for the state-owned oil companies, Pemex (Petróleos Mexicanos) and PdVSA (Petróleos de Venezuela, S.A.), respectively. Russia does allow foreign investment, but the legal and tax structure strongly favors ownership by domestic firms.[29] The October 2003 arrest of Mikhail Khodorkovsky (chairman and CEO of the Russian oil giant Yukos) for financial irregularities is widely viewed as a blow to outside investment, given his role as a major proponent of foreign involvement in the country's energy industry.[30] Other members of the Alternative Eight claim to welcome foreign investment, but their insistence on tight control tends to scare off prospective suitors.[31]

Most of these countries also suffer from corruption, crime, and political unrest. Mexico's Pemex, for example, loses up to $1 billion a year in bribes and payoffs to company officials and union bureaucrats.[32] Much of the money is believed to find its way into the coffers of the Institutional Revolutionary Party (PRI), which dominated Mexican politics until the election of President Vicente Fox, in July 2000. "Pemex and the oil union were considered the right arm, financially and ideologically, of the PRI," explains George Baker, an independent oil analyst.[33] President Fox has attempted to curb this corruption, but critics complain he lacks either the authority or the necessary will to overcome a problem so deeply entrenched.[34] "The effort to reform the beast has failed," energy expert Edward L. Morse said in January 2003, because Fox did not understand "how thoroughly ingrained in the national political culture the monopoly of Pemex is."[35]

The situation is even worse in Nigeria. According to the U.S. Department of Energy, Nigeria's state-owned oil company reported losses of $4 billion to crime and corruption in 2000 alone.[36] Some of the cash found its way into the bank accounts of the military and business elites that have long controlled the nation.* The organized pilfering of oil supplies by criminal gangs also accounted for a large share of losses, as did the sabotage of pipelines and other oil installations by ethnic groups with grievances against the central government in Abuja.[37] These losses and disruptions

---

*In February 2004, Nigerian president Olusegun Obasanjo ordered an investigation into allegations that a Halliburton subsidiary had paid $180 million in bribes to Nigerian officials in the 1990s—when Dick Cheney was still running the company—to secure a $4 billion contract for the construction of a liquefied natural gas plant. The allegations are also being investigated by the U.S. Justice Department and the Securities and Exchange Commission.

have forestalled the modernization and expansion of Nigeria's energy infrastructure and contributed to a decline in production.[38]

Corruption is also a problem in Angola, one of Africa's most promising new sources of oil. According to the International Monetary Fund (IMF), Angolan officials skimmed as much as $1 billion from the country's oil revenues in 2001—a devastating plunder in a country where most people earn less than a dollar per day and nineteen out of every one hundred babies die before their first birthday. Using unusually blunt language, the IMF asserted, "Governance and transparency issues continue to be of serious concern, with corruption widespread throughout society."[39] Secretary of State Colin Powell cited these allegations in a September 2002 meeting in Luanda with Angolan president Jose Eduardo dos Santos. Unless the government roots out corruption and adopts reforms, Powell told dos Santos, the country will not attract the investment it needs to boost its oil production.[40]

Venezuela owes its disappointing production rates not to corruption but to political unrest. In December 2002, opponents of President Hugo Chávez organized a general strike that nearly shut down state-owned PdVSA.[41] Chávez then took full control of the company and put political loyalists in charge, partially restoring production. But the departure of the company's most experienced managers led foreign analysts to conclude that PdVSA will never return to the high production levels of the 1990s.[42] According to BP, total national output dropped from a high of 3.5 million barrels per day in 1998 to 2.9 million barrels in 2002, a decline of 17 percent; more recent reports, in the *Wall Street Journal,* placed output in 2003 at an even lower level, between 2.5 and 2.7 million barrels per day.[43]

Corruption, crime, and turmoil are all plentiful in the Caspian Sea republics. Kazakhstan, the region's most promising supplier, operates under the iron fist of President Nursultan Nazarbayev, a former Communist Party functionary who enjoys lifelong powers and reportedly expects a big cut of any major oil deal.[44] In April 2003, a federal grand jury in New York City issued an indictment against an American banker, James H. Giffen, for arranging a $78 million bribe to Nazarbayev and his cronies on behalf of several American and European oil companies (including Exxon Mobil and ChevronTexaco) that had sought development contracts in Kazakhstan. Swiss authorities have opened a parallel investigation, claiming that Giffen and his partners used accounts in that country to funnel money to Nazarbayev.[45] In September 2003, a New York court indicted a Swiss banker for providing bribes to Heydar Aliyev, then the president of Azerbaijan; Aliyev's son, Ilham, who succeeded his father as president in October 2003 (in an election marred by numerous irregularities), was also said to be involved in the case.[46]

These circumstances make it highly unlikely that the major oil firms will commit funds on the scale needed to slow the depletion of existing fields and develop new ones in the nations on the administration's "diversified" roster of suppliers. There is no doubt, of course, that investment will occur: every month brings news of a new commitment by the big oil companies in one or more of the Alternative Eight. Reports are nearly as frequent that one or another company has abandoned a once-promising exploration zone or reduced the scale of its proposed operations because of disappointing drilling results, legal problems, or financial troubles.[47] In sum, there is little real hope that foreign investment will ever reach the stratospheric levels it would take to significantly increase these countries' production capacity.

No Escape from Conflict

Let's say that the Alternative Eight were to squeeze out such prodigious oil surpluses in the years ahead that they lived up to the sunny predictions of American policy makers. These supplies would *still* be every bit as vulnerable to instability and conflict as petroleum from the Persian Gulf. The principal attraction of diversification is supposed to be the hedge it affords against violence and disorder in the Gulf; but even a cursory examination of these producers makes it plain that they are riven by the same sorts of ethnic, religious, and political divisions.

Their troubles vary, of course, but we can discern certain similarities and patterns. Five of the Alternative Eight—Angola, Azerbaijan, Colombia, Nigeria, and Russia—have undergone civil wars or ethnic conflicts in recent years; the other three—Kazakhstan, Mexico, and Venezuela—have had riots, strikes, or other forms of political disorder. Violence has also erupted in such other potential supplier nations as Chad, Congo-Brazzaville, Equatorial Guinea, and São Tomé e Principe, as well as in strategically located countries like Georgia that are expected to serve as major conduits for the transport of oil.[48]

The violence is not simply an unfortunate coincidence. As I noted in earlier chapters, the production of petroleum in otherwise undeveloped countries can lead to distortions of the local economy and political system that practically ensures instability. Typically, the ruling clique or clan controls the collection and distribution of oil revenues (or "rents") in such systems, rewarding its own members and the instruments of national authority—especially the military and the police—while ignoring (or repressing) everyone else. When imbalance in the allocation of oil rents coincides with ethnic, religious, or political divisions—as it so often does—you have a natural recipe for internal conflict. The Western press may describe the resulting violence as tribal or sectarian warfare, but all too often it derives from, or is exacerbated by, the distorting effects of oil production.

The ugly relationship between oil and violence has played out along very clear lines in Nigeria, Africa's leading petroleum producer. For years, the country was ruled by military officers who, having bullied their way into power, stole much of the nation's oil wealth while allowing the Delta region—where much of the oil comes from—to remain mired in poverty. This, in turn, has fueled the rise of ethnically based militias among the minority peoples of the Delta, resulting sometimes in attacks on oil facilities and personnel.[49] The nation's current, elected leader, President Olusegun Obasanjo, has promised to increase the share of national oil revenues allocated to the Delta, but reform has been slow and the antigovernment sentiment in the area continues to rise.* Violent attacks on oil installations and oil-company personnel—two Americans working under contract to ChevronTexaco were shot and killed in the Delta

---

*In one of the most remarkable protests against economic deprivation, in July 2003, some 150 women from poor Delta communities peacefully occupied a ChevronTexaco oil terminal. Fearful of inciting more protests by treating the women harshly, ChevronTexaco officials finally agreed to provide the communities with additional development aid.

region in April 2004—have periodically prompted multinational firms operating in the country to suspend production—leading, of course, to a reduction of the country's output.[50]

The destabilizing impact of oil production has also played a part in the decades-long civil war in Colombia. Although many factors have contributed to the persistence and intensity of the fighting, the huge divide between rich and poor has been one major source of friction.[51] In their campaign against the nation's government and business elite, rebel bands associated with the Revolutionary Armed Forces of Colombia (FARC) and the Army of National Liberation (ELN) have taken to attacking oil pipelines and installations in the interior. According to Colombian authorities, the ELN and the FARC bombed the vital Cano Limón pipeline an unprecedented 170 times in 2001, preventing the delivery of some 24 million barrels of crude petroleum. These and other attacks have produced a substantial decline in Colombian oil output—from 830,000 barrels per day in 1999 to 591,000 in 2002.[52]

Venezuela is also suffering from domestic turmoil, although not—as yet—of the acutely violent form experienced in Colombia. Here, too, the discord has been fueled by disputes over the distribution of national wealth, but in this case the government, headed by President Hugo Chávez, is allied with the poor while it is the wealthy and professional classes—fearful of losing their privileged position in the oil industry and related fields—that are spearheading the opposition. So far, the turmoil in Venezuela has been limited to general strikes and massive street demonstrations organized by antigovernment factions, coupled with periodic crackdowns by military forces loyal to President Chávez. Still, shots have been fired at a number of these confrontations, and on one occasion, in April 2002, Chávez was forced to abandon the presidential palace and take refuge at a military base. At present, Chávez remains in control, but the opposition is seeking to replace him through a recall petition and fresh elections; should this effort fail (as is likely), more extreme measures may be employed. Further roiling this incendiary mix, the Bush administration has provided funds to some of the antigovernment organizations in Venezuela and Chávez has threatened to retaliate by cutting off oil deliveries to the United States; whether this will lead to a more severe clash between the two countries cannot be foreseen, but it is hardly out of the question.[53]

Socioeconomic clashes of this sort have not erupted in the major Caspian Sea producers—yet. But many analysts looking at Azerbaijan and Kazakhstan see symptoms of the same oil-related pathology that is bedeviling Colombia and Nigeria. Both of these newly independent Caspian states are ruled by autocratic leaders—Ilham Aliyev in Azerbaijan, Nursultan Nazarbayev in Kazakhstan—and both have spawned wealthy elites with close ties to the oil industry and the government. These elites have profited enormously from the recent upturn in oil and gas production, while most ordinary citizens have seen both their income and social services plummet since the collapse of the Soviet Union in 1992.[54] "The reality of post-communist development [in the Caspian states] has . . . been an increase in corruption and a sharp drop in living standards once protected by a comprehensive safety net," Martha Brill Olcott of Colgate University observed in 1998. The growing poverty has "rendered the population more susceptible to the appeal of Islamic radicalism" and other extremist movements, making the region "a zone of instability and crisis."[55]

The potential for violence in the Caspian states was amply demonstrated in March 2004, when four days of bombings and gun violence left forty people dead and many others wounded in Uzbekistan, a major producer of natural gas. Some of the dead were said to be suicide bombers who detonated their charges in police stations and other public facilities. No group claimed responsibility for the attacks, but government officials blamed them on militant Islamic organizations in the country. Uzbekistan, like the other Central Asian republics, is governed by an authoritarian regime with zero tolerance for political dissent; with few legal channels available for the expression of opposing views, critics of the regime perceive no option but to engage in armed resistance. The result is a recurring cycle of violence, with public acts of defiance followed by massive government crackdowns and more outbreaks of fighting.[56]

Still other factors exacerbate the potential for conflict in the region. Like certain Persian Gulf producers, many of the former Soviet republics harbor ethnic and religious minorities that hate being incorporated in multiethnic states dominated by others and seek autonomy or independence for themselves—often in territories containing or adjoining major oil fields, refineries, or pipelines. Typically, these aspirations have existed for a very long time, often predating the discovery of oil; but they have gained increased momentum in recent years with the collapse of the Soviet Union and other political developments.

Russia is currently involved in one of the bloodiest of these struggles: the ongoing war in Chechnya. This largely Muslim territory was incorporated into the czarist Russian empire in the nineteenth century, after heavy and prolonged fighting, and then subsequently into the Soviet Union as a semiautonomous region of the Russian Republic. Following the breakup of the USSR in 1992, Chechen nationalists took control of the capital, Grozny, and proclaimed an independent state. Moscow ordered its troops to crush all resistance in Grozny in December 1994; then, after another bruising insurrection, Russian forces were forced out of the city in 1996. A new round of fighting began in 1999, following a series of clashes in nearby Dagestan, and has continued ever since. Most of Chechnya is now under Russian control, but there are still rebel forces in rural areas and on the outskirts of towns, conducting occasional ambushes and organizing terror attacks in key cities—including one in Grozny that killed Moscow's handpicked president of the republic, Akhmad Kadyrov. The Russian authorities periodically announce that they have prevailed in this bitter contest; nevertheless, the killing goes on.[57]

The war in Chechnya is usually described as a clash between hostile ethnic and religious forces, or as a power struggle between the central government in Moscow and an independence-seeking population on the periphery. But it also has an important geopolitical dimension: under Soviet rule, Grozny was a major center for oil refining and a critical transit point for pipelines carrying Caspian Sea energy to Russia, Ukraine, and eastern Europe. While it is impossible to say just how decisive oil-related factors have been in the repeated Russian crackdowns on the Chechen separatists, there is no doubt that Moscow is determined to retain its control over these strategic transit routes and to prevent Chechnya from becoming a base for sabotage and guerrilla attacks on its expanding energy interests in the Caspian basin.[58]

Severe ethnic conflicts have also flared in neighboring Georgia. The most acute threat to stability is the separatist movement in Abkhazia, a Muslim area on the Black Sea coast. When Georgia declared its independence in 1991, the Abkhazians established their own ethnic state and fought off the new Georgian army. A cease-fire has been in place since 1993, but there is no formal settlement and fighting erupts periodically along the de facto border between the two territories. Georgia has also faced periodic revolt by ethnic minorities in the Adzharian Autonomous Republic, on its southern border with Turkey. These, and other schisms pose a severe threat to the safety of the Baku-Tbilisi-Ceyhan pipeline, which will run the entire width of the country.[59]

So, too, in Azerbaijan: when that former Soviet republic became independent in 1991, the Armenian majority of Nagorno-Karabakh, a semi-autonomous district in the west, expunged all vestiges of Azerbaijani rule and established an independent state. A war followed, in which Azerbaijan lost control over one-fifth of its territory and some 750,000 people wound up in makeshift refugee camps (where many remain today). A cease-fire has been in effect since 1994 but, as in Abkhazia, there is no final settlement, and the fighting could resume at any time. Like the wars in Chechnya and Georgia, this conflict has a geopolitical dimension, since Nagorno-Karabakh lies within easy striking range of the BTC pipeline and so could become a base for attacks on it.

Ethnic and sectarian conflict also abounds in Africa. Angola was torn by war from the moment it gained its independence from Portugal in 1975. The fighting between the two main factions, the Popular Movement for the Liberation of Angola (MPLA) and the National Union for the Total Independence of Angola (UNITA), left behind a heavy toll in human lives. Most of the violence took place in central and western Angola, but it spilled over into the oil-rich enclave of Cabinda, separated from the rest of the country by a small strip of the Congo. Despite the repeated efforts by the United Nations, the fighting continued until the fall of 2002, when the UNITA leader, Jonas Savimbi, was killed by forces loyal to the MPLA. Although most of Angola is now enjoying a respite from war, separatist forces are still battling in Cabinda.

On top of all this, there is yet another source of conflict: disputes over energy-rich border zones and offshore areas. The most important of these is the five-nation quarrel over offshore territories in the Caspian Sea.[60] During the Soviet era, the Caspian was divided solely (and amicably) between the USSR and Iran; but with the breakup of the Soviet Union in 1992, three new nations—Azerbaijan, Kazakhstan, and Turkmenistan—staked their own claims to the Caspian. Even after a number of summits, the five nations involved are still wrangling over the ownership of the undersea oil.[61] In July 2001, Iran sent a gunboat into contested waters to harry an oil-company vessel operating in an offshore exploration zone claimed by Azerbaijan.[62] This and other such incidents have prompted the new Caspian nations to beef up their naval forces in preparation for future clashes.[63]

In short, *none* of Washington's hedge oil producers offer sanctuary from the disorder and strife of the Persian Gulf. The level of violence may, at any given time, be lower or higher, but over the long term *all* are likely to erupt in conflict. Clearly, the flow of energy from these suppliers to the United States and the rest of the world is no safer from disruption than the flow from the Gulf.

Extending the Carter Doctrine: U.S. Involvement in the Caspian

Faced with the threat of instability in its hedge oil suppliers, the United States has responded predictably: by ramping up its military capability. In a sense, this response represents the extension of the Carter Doctrine—whereby the overseas flow of oil is designated a matter of national security and so afforded American military protection—to new areas of the world. Although no American official has put it in so many words, it is clear from numerous statements and actions that there has been just such a policy extension. As if to symbolize the change, the U.S. Central Command—originally created expressly to implement the Carter Doctrine in the Gulf—was given command authority over the Central Asian states of the Caspian Sea basin on October 1, 1999.[64]

A new relationship between the United States and the Caspian republics began to take shape in the mid-1990s, just a few years after the region had become unyoked from the Soviet Union. As American energy firms concluded major oil deals with the governments of Azerbaijan and Kazakhstan, the Department of Defense established military ties with these post-Soviet states and U.S. aid began to flow to their armed forces. From there it was only a short step to the deployment of American military advisers, the sale of American arms, and the initiation of joint training operations[65]—an exact repetition of the Persian Gulf scenario.

President Bill Clinton was a vigorous advocate for American companies seeking drilling rights in the Caspian basin, and he explicitly designated the area's energy resources a matter of national security. "In a world of growing energy demand," he told President Heydar Aliyev of Azerbaijan at a White House meeting in August 1997, "our nation cannot afford to rely on any single region for our energy supplies." By helping Azerbaijan to develop its untapped oil reserves, "we not only help Azerbaijan to prosper, we also help diversify our energy supply and strengthen our nation's security."[66] Clinton reiterated this view in conversations with other officials from the region, including Presidents Nursultan Nazarbayev of Kazakhstan and Saparmurat Niyazov of Turkmenistan.[67]

These national-security concerns of the Clinton administration resulted in two important initiatives: first, the promotion of a new pipeline route for Caspian oil and natural gas; and, second, the establishment of close military ties with friendly Caspian states, especially Azerbaijan, Georgia, and Kazakhstan. The BTC pipeline through Azerbaijan, Georgia, and Turkey seemed to extricate U.S. policy makers rather nicely from a strategic quandary. All the existing pipelines in the region passed through Russia, a former adversary of the United States that could possibly become a future adversary. The most logical alternative route was through Iran to existing oil terminals on the Persian Gulf—but exporting via the Gulf would wreck the whole strategy of turning to the Caspian as an alternative. The beauty of the BTC scheme was that it bypassed Russia and Iran altogether.[68] Unfortunately, it also skirted several conflict zones—including Chechnya, Abkhazia, Adzharia, and Nagorno-Karabakh. The inevitable solution to this new set of problems was for Washington to step up its delivery of military aid to its new friends in the region.

The first country to benefit from this largesse was Georgia. Its pivotal location between the Caspian basin and the Black Sea, its vulnerability to

Caspian Sea Basin Showing Major Pipeline Routes

insurgent violence, and its pro-Western orientation combined to win it the largest allocation of U.S. aid to the Caspian states—a total of $302 million in 1998–2000 alone.[69] The aid was intended to bolster the government of President Eduard Shevardnadze, a former Soviet foreign minister considered close to the West, and to enhance its military capabilities. To underscore American support for Shevardnadze, Secretary of Defense William S. Cohen visited Tbilisi in 1999 to promise additional assistance. In a meeting with Cohen, Shevardnadze drew a clear connection between U.S. military aid and Georgia's critical role in protecting the BTC pipeline, claiming that "the transport of energy resources from Central Asia and the Caspian region to the West" would expose Georgia to greater peril and thus justify the increased assistance.[70]

The Clinton administration also stepped up its military support for the Aliyev regime in Azerbaijan at this time, as the BTC pipeline (along with all of the oil it would carry) originated in that country and crossed much of it before entering Georgia. But the Department of Defense was barred at that time from providing direct military aid to Azerbaijan by the Freedom Support Act (FSA) of 1992. Under pressure from Armenian-Americans angry at Aliyev's refusal to lift the economic blockade Azerbaijan had imposed on landlocked Armenia, Congress had added an amendment to the FSA prohibiting such military assistance.[71] To get around this impediment, the Pentagon simply cooperated with Azerbaijan's military in antiproliferation efforts—which Congress allowed—and included Azerbaijani forces in joint military exercises.[72] Additional military aid and training were provided to Azerbaijan by Turkey, a NATO member and Washington's strategic partner in the Caspian region.[73]

The administration viewed Kazakhstan, too, as a vital ally in the region, because of its strategic location on the eastern side of the Caspian and its huge supply of untapped oil, which American policy makers hoped would eventually be carried by a proposed pipeline beneath the Caspian Sea itself to the starting point of the BTC conduit in Baku.[74] Accordingly, the United States signed a military aid agreement with Kazakhstan in 1997 and began supplying its forces with arms, technical assistance, and advanced military training.[75]

Although Washington's primary aim at this point was to bolster the capacity of local forces to protect oil-related infrastructure, the Department of Defense was also beginning to prepare for the possible deployment of U.S. combat forces in the region. In the most visible expression of this effort, in September 1997, some five hundred paratroopers from the Army's elite 82nd Airborne Division were flown 7,700 miles, from Fort Bragg, North Carolina, to a remote area of southern Kazakhstan, to participate in combat maneuvers with Kazakh, Kyrgyz, and Uzbek forces.[76] Although described officially as a "peacekeeping" exercise, CENTRAZBAT '97, as it was known, was clearly a test of America's ability to project power into the Caspian basin in the event of a crisis. "There is no nation on the face of the earth that we cannot get to," said General Jack Sheehan, the commander in chief of the U.S. Atlantic Command and the highest-ranking officer to attend the exercise.[77] And, lest anyone doubted the nature of our interests in the region, a deputy assistant secretary of defense accompanying Sheehan, Catherine Kelleher, cited "the presence of enormous energy resources" as a justification for American military involvement.[78]

The 1997 operation was the first in an annual series of CENTRAZBAT exercises designed to test the speed with which Washington could deploy U.S.-based forces directly to the region and commence combat operations. Joining the American units involved were troops from our key partners there, including Azerbaijan, Georgia, Kazakhstan, Kyrgyzstan, Turkey, and Uzbekistan.[79] In 1999, moreover, the Department of Defense devised an elaborate computer model of the Caspian basin for use in testing possible scenarios for U.S. intervention in the region.[80]

All these initiatives were well under way on September 11, 2001, and gained added momentum in the months that followed. Within days of the terrorist attack, Azerbaijan, Georgia, and Kazakhstan had agreed to provide logistic support or overflight rights for the U.S. assault on Afghanistan, while Kyrgyzstan and Uzbekistan allowed American forces to establish temporary bases on their territory.[81] After the war in Afghanistan, the Bush administration put fresh emphasis on U.S. military ties with the Caspian states. "Our country is now linked with this region in ways we could never have imagined before September 11," Assistant Secretary of State A. Elizabeth Jones told the Senate Foreign Relations Committee in December 2001.[82] The administration stepped up visits by senior officials to leaders in the region and significantly increased the flow of military and economic aid to friendly governments.[83] All told, U.S. assistance to the greater Caspian Sea area (including Armenia, Azerbaijan, Georgia, Kazakhstan, Kyrgyzstan, Tajikistan, Turkmenistan, and Uzbekistan) was expected to top $1.5 billion in fiscal years 2002–4, a 50 percent increase over the preceding three-year period.[84]

In petitioning Congress for this aid, administration officials consistently stressed the importance of these countries in combating international terrorism. But it is clear from government documents that the war against terrorism intertwined with our Caspian oil policy. Thus, in proposing grants of $51.2 million to Azerbaijan in fiscal 2005, the State Department affirmed that "U.S. national interests in Azerbaijan center on our strong bilateral security and counterterrorism cooperation, the advancement of U.S. energy security, [and] progress in free-market and democratic reforms." It was further noted that "the involvement of U.S. firms in the development and export of Azerbaijani oil is key to our objectives of diversifying world oil supplies, providing a solid base for the regional economy, and promoting U.S. energy security. . . ." Likewise, in requesting $108.1 million for Georgia, the department noted that by housing the BTC pipeline the country would "become a key conduit through which Caspian Basin energy resources will flow to the West, facilitating diversification of energy sources for the United States and Europe."[85]

The integration of the administration's antiterrorism and energy-protection policies into a single strategic framework is vividly evident in Georgia, the leading recipient of U.S. aid in the region. According to the State Department, this aid is intended to help Georgian forces guard the border with Russia and other neighbors, to fight Chechen insurgents in the remote Pankisi Gorge, and to protect key pipeline routes. At the heart of the effort is a $64 million "train and equip" program designed to enhance the "counterinsurgency capabilities" of the Georgian army by training several battalions in modern combat techniques and providing them with a full panoply of modern military gear. Some 150 U.S. Special Operations Forces instructors, along with other military specialists, have been deployed in Georgia for this purpose.[86] In February 2003, the operation was expanded to incorporate an $11 million U.S. program to train a four-hundred-man "pipeline protection battalion" for the new Georgian Special Protection Service, an elite unit created by President Shevardnadze in early 2003 to guard the Georgian section of the BTC pipeline.[87]

When a popular revolt ousted Shevardnadze in November 2003, the Bush administration quickly endorsed the new pro-Western government that replaced him. Our intent is "to underscore America's very strong support for stability and security and the territorial integrity here in Georgia," Secretary of Defense Donald Rumsfeld declared after a meeting with acting president Nino Burdzhanadze in Tbilisi on December 5, just two weeks after the revolt, making it clear that the United States had every intention of continuing its relationship with the Georgian military.[88] This relationship is "strategically important," a high Pentagon official accompanying him explained, both for reasons relating to the war on terrorism and "in terms of energy," given the presence there of the BTC pipeline.[89] In yet another show of support for the new Georgian government, Secretary of State Colin Powell attended the inauguration of the newly elected president, Mikhail Saakashvili, on January 25, 2004.

Oil-security considerations also figure in the military aid programs for Azerbaijan and Kazakhstan. According to the State Department, some part of our $50 million package to Azerbaijan in fiscal 2004 will go toward enhancing the country's "maritime border security"; in response to a number of incursions by Iranian gunboats into sections of the Caspian that Azerbaijan claims, we are helping it establish a small naval force.[90] In Kazakhstan, U.S. assistance is being used to refurbish an old Soviet-era air base at Atyrau, on the Caspian's north coast, near the country's prolific Tengiz oil field; in conjunction with this effort, the United States is also helping to finance the establishment of a "rapid-reaction brigade" that is intended to "enhance Kazakhstan's capability to respond to major terrorist threats to oil platforms or borders."[91]

In a further show of support for the Caspian republics, Secretary of Defense Rumsfeld traveled to the region in February 2004 and met with local military officials. At his first stop, in Tashkent, he lauded "the excellent military-to-military relationship between Uzbekistan and the United States." This relationship, he continued, "is strong and has been growing stronger." Then, following a meeting with the Kazakh minister of defense in Astana, he told reporters that "we talked about the U.S. support for Kazakhstan's sovereignty and independence and our important military-to-military relationship." Asked to describe America's interests in the country, Rumsfeld replied, "it is Caspian security, the western portion of Kazakhstan [where most of the oil lies], which is important to this country."[92]

Increased military aid is not, moreover, the only expression of growing U.S. involvement in the Caspian basin: as it has been doing since the Clinton era, the Department of Defense is bolstering its capacity for direct military action in the region. The temporary bases established at Bishkek in Kyrgyzstan and at Khanabad in Uzbekistan to support American combat operations in Afghanistan during the war against the Taliban are now being converted into permanent installations. (See map on page 163.) Pentagon officials are also considering the acquisition of additional "forward operating bases" in Azerbaijan and Georgia to support future troop deployments in the region.[93] In addition, Washington is eyeing the refurbished airfield at Atyrau; according to the State Department, it is going to be used by U.S. and Kazakh troops for "joint training in the area of counter-terrorism"[94]—a possible first step toward its becoming a permanent home for American forces.

Any number of potential upheavals and crises could trigger direct American military involvement in the region: a new round of Iranian gunboat assaults on Azerbaijani oil vessels in the Caspian Sea, perhaps, or the outbreak of a civil war in Georgia. Exactly what form American intervention might take we cannot know. But one thing is certain: the Caspian harbors a witches' brew of unresolved rivalries and disputes, and Washington might easily view any full-scale war in the region as a severe enough threat to the nation's interests to justify the use of military force and the sacrifice of American lives.

Extending the Carter Doctrine: Latin America and West Africa

American worries about the security of oil supplies from the Andean region of Latin America and the west coast of Africa have also led to expanded military commitments there. Both these areas have experienced widespread violence that has forced them, on occasion, to curtail their oil deliveries to the United States. In response, Washington has lavished key countries with more and more military aid. And, as with the Gulf and the

Caspian basin, the procurement of additional oil from these regions has come to be seen as a matter of national security—and so, in line with the extended Carter Doctrine, a valid reason for expanding the level of U.S. military involvement.

The fighting in Colombia is a source of particular concern. Colombia was once one of our leading oil suppliers, and it has the potential to provide far larger volumes in the future. The Department of Energy estimates its current reserves at a relatively modest 1.8 billion barrels, but some geologists believe that huge untapped reservoirs lie awaiting discovery in the country's northeast, near some of Venezuela's largest fields.[95] However, the violence there has prevented any exploration, and in the meantime Colombia's output has dropped by 28 percent.[96]

For the past thirty years, Colombia has been lacerated by a four-way struggle between the central government, leftist guerrillas belonging to the FARC and ELN, right-wing paramilitary organizations, and heavily armed drug cartels.[97] The guerrillas want to overthrow the government and replace it with one governed by socialist or communist principles. The paramilitaries, largely grouped into the United Self-Defense Forces of Colombia (AUC), want to preserve the privileges of Colombia's large landowners. Both have financed their operations by either selling illegal drugs or serving as protection forces for the drug cartels and rural coca growers. The oil industry figures in this struggle as a critical source of income for the government and an inviting target for the guerrillas.

Contending that the violence has produced an atmosphere of lawlessness in which the illegal drug trade can flourish, the United States has long provided arms and other forms of military aid to the country's army and police forces. But while the guerrillas and the paramilitaries have both collaborated with the drug barons in their pursuit of operating revenues, Washington has channeled its support to the government exclusively for fighting the FARC and the ELN—groups characterized by American leaders as "narcoterrorist" organizations whose elimination is vital to our security. Meanwhile, Congress has sharply increased U.S. aid to the Colombian government—awarding $1.3 billion in 2000 under Plan Colombia, and a combined $1.1 billion in fiscal years 2003 and 2004.[98]

Though American support for Plan Colombia and associated programs usually stresses the perniciousness of the drug trade, in 2002 the Bush administration announced another objective: helping the Colombian government protect its oil pipelines from guerrilla attack. The White House requested an additional $98 million to bolster security along the Cano Limón–Coveñas pipeline, a highly vulnerable 480-mile-long conduit from Occidental Petroleum's fields in the embattled Arauca region in the northeast to Coveñas, on the Caribbean coast.[99] These funds (and another $147 million sought for fiscal year 2004) are to be used to train and equip two elite battalions of the Colombian army to guard the pipeline against the ELN and FARC.[100]

Ostensibly, the principal aim of this aid is to boost the Colombian government's export revenues. "Lost revenue from guerrilla attacks has severely hampered the GOC's [Government of Colombia's] ability to

Colombia: Cano Limón–Coveñas Pipeline

meet the country's social, political, and security needs," the State Department reported in 2002. By improving pipeline security, the United States will "enhance the GOC's ability to protect a vital part of its energy infrastructure."[101] But it is obvious that Washington is also concerned about the recent plunge in Colombia's oil exports to the United States—from a peak of 468,000 barrels per day in 1999 to 256,000 in 2002—and the reluctance of the major international oil companies to commit themselves to developing the country's untapped reserves.[102] By making the region safe for oil exploration, the administration hopes to increase Colombia's exports to this country.

It is in this larger, strategic context that the pipeline-protection project should be viewed. The Pentagon has deployed around seventy U.S. Army Special Forces instructors in Arauca city and the neighboring town of Saravena, to train units of the Colombian army's Eighteenth Brigade. Although the Americans are supposed to restrict their activities to training and advisory missions, U.S. News and World Report disclosed in 2003 that some of the training occurs "during actual military and intelligence-gathering missions,"[103] and it is widely believed that the Americans will fight when they are accompanying their Colombian trainees on patrols in the countryside around Saravena, a hotbed of guerrilla activity.[104]

Many analysts view this development as a major escalation of our long-standing stake in Colombia's civil war. Previously, American involvement was aimed primarily at curbing the flow of illicit drugs into this country; but now it is turning into something else. "For the first time, the Administration is proposing to cross the line from counter-narcotics to counterinsurgency," Senator Patrick J. Leahy of Vermont observed in 2002. "This is no longer about stopping drugs, it's about fighting the guerrillas."[105] More accurately, it's about protecting oil.[106] And while the White House may contend that our military presence in Colombia will stay small and inconspicuous, critics charge that our role is growing and that we are "slowly being drawn into a Vietnam-like morass."[107]

America's military involvement in West Africa is less advanced, but there, too, signs of creeping U.S. entanglement are easy to find. Military aid to the region is growing, and the Department of Defense is scouting locations for air and logistic bases. There are no American combat troops in this part of Africa—yet—but the growing American military presence in Djibouti, a former French colony on the Red Sea coast that is being used as a base for counterterror operations, provides an ominous precedent.[108]

As noted earlier, African oil plays a major role in the Bush administration's diversification strategy. "Along with Latin America," the *NEP* predicted in 2001, "West Africa is expected to be one of the fastest-growing sources of oil and gas for the American market."[109] To that end, U.S. officials have been busy trying to persuade local governments to make a push to attract foreign investment and to boost their petroleum output.[110] This was reportedly Secretary of State Colin Powell's message at meetings with leaders of several of the major oil-producing states in September 2002,[111] and Secretary of Energy Spencer Abraham has also repeatedly stressed the point to African energy officials.

If producers like Angola and Nigeria are to attract foreign investors and increase their output, however, they will have to address their endemic corruption, widespread crime, and recurring political disorder. Political and economic reform is only part of the solution; improving domestic security will also require investments in the military and the police far more costly and substantial than most of these states can even contemplate. And so the United States has stepped in with more security assistance and more military training—all under the auspices of the extended Carter Doctrine. "African oil is of national strategic interest to us," Assistant Secretary of State Walter Kansteiner said in 2002, "and it will increase and become more important as we go forward."[112]

The principal recipients of U.S. security assistance in West Africa are Angola and Nigeria. Total aid to these two countries in fiscal years 2002–4 amounted to $300 million, a significant increase over the previous three-year period. In fiscal 2004, they also became eligible to receive surplus U.S. arms under the Pentagon's Excess Defense Articles (EDA) program. In addition, they benefit from military instruction provided by the Department of Defense under the International Military Education and Training program (IMET), as do several of their oil-producing neighbors.[113]

In Africa, as in the Caspian, the United States would prefer to place the burden of regional security on local states; and so we have long forgone permanent military bases there. But that approach has begun to change. Acknowledging that American troops may someday be heading to Africa, the Department of Defense has begun searching out possible sites for forward operating bases like those in Kyrgyzstan and Uzbekistan. These installations do not have the elaborate, costly facilities of the permanent U.S. bases in Europe and the Asia-Pacific region; rather, they are spartan affairs, meant just to support the occasional deployment of helicopters, combat planes, and light infantry forces.[114]

Among the more attractive candidates for such a facility is São Tomé e Principe, a small cluster of Atlantic islands that gained their independence from Portugal only in 1975. São Tomé is close to the major West African oil-producing countries and yet, as a small island state, has largely escaped the violence and conflict that have plagued the mainland. The Department of Defense has not formally announced its intention to acquire a facility there, but General Carlton Fulford, the deputy commander in chief of the European Command (which oversees U.S. military operations in West Africa), visited the islands in July 2001 to look for possible base locations.[115]

To further enhance its forces' mobility, the Pentagon is also looking at sites for bare-bones facilities—essentially, unimproved airstrips—on the African mainland; among the potential candidates are Senegal, Ghana, Mali, Uganda, and Kenya.[116] Although officials tend to talk mainly about terrorism when explaining the need for such facilities, they have told Greg Jaffe of the *Wall Street Journal* that "a key mission for U.S. forces [in Africa] would be to ensure that Nigeria's oil fields, which in the future could account for as much as 25 percent of all U.S. oil imports, are secure."[117]

No doubt American leaders are reluctant to become as entangled in African conflicts as they have become in those of the Persian Gulf, the Caspian, and Colombia. No matter; the fact that Washington has begun to view African oil supplies as a national security concern will lead inexorably to increased military involvement in the region. Washington has already taken the first steps and shows no sign of reversing its direction.

As one indication of the Pentagon's growing interest in the region, NATO supreme commander General James Jones declared in May 2003 that the carrier battle groups under his command will shorten their future visits to the Mediterranean and "spend half the time going down the west coast of Africa."[118] When and under what circumstances we will see the actual deployment of American combat troops in West Africa is anyone's guess. But, if recent developments elsewhere are any indication, it will happen, as our reliance on African oil leads us into ever-increasing military involvement in the region's security affairs.

When President Bush was first announcing his energy plan, in May 2001, he asserted that the pursuit of energy from non-Gulf suppliers would enable us to escape the turmoil and supply disruptions that are inextricably bound to our deepening dependence on Persian Gulf oil; at the same time, it would allow us to keep increasing our year-to-year consumption of petroleum. It should be apparent by now that this is not the case. Import diversification can help us obtain additional oil, but not to anything like the extent required to reduce our reliance on the Gulf and certainly not in a trouble-free manner. There is no promised land where vast quantities of petroleum lie waiting for us to come take them, without any risk of our getting mired in protracted regional conflict.

The situation I have described is worrisome enough. But it will get worse. Other countries—including China and Russia—are seeking additional oil from many of the same suppliers and are just as willing as we are to meddle in local security affairs. Consequently, any eruption of ethnic or political violence in these areas could do more than entrap our forces there. It could lead—as we shall see—to a deadly confrontation between the world's major military powers.

6

Geopolitics Reborn:
The U.S.-Russian-Chinese Struggle
in the Persian Gulf and Caspian Basin

Regional conflict, civil war, insurgency, terrorism—these are the most persistent and widespread threats to the global flow of petroleum in the early twenty-first century. As I have shown, violent upheaval in one form or another has afflicted nearly every major oil-producing region, a circumstance that increases the likelihood of American military involvement. But there is yet another, and possibly greater, threat looming over these troubled regions: that the intense competition among the major powers for control over the possession and the distribution of energy will lead to a larger conflict. This competition is already aggravating tensions in several areas, including the Persian Gulf and Caspian Sea basins. And although the great powers will no doubt seek to avoid clashing directly, their deepening entanglement in local disputes is bound to fan the flames of regional conflicts and increase the potential for major conflagrations.

The great powers have always battled for control over important sources of wealth and advantage. European states fought over the resource-rich territories of the Americas and Africa; imperial Britain vied with Russia for control of Central Asia and with the Ottoman Turks for Egypt and the Levant. These rivalries often led to border skirmishes and local wars, usually at the outer edges of imperial expansion; but on occasion they led to epic conflicts, such as the Seven Years War, the Napoleonic wars, and World War I. Though the risk of such earth-shaking upheavals has subsided in recent decades, the imperial impulses behind them have by no means disappeared. And if there is a prize that could provoke great-power warfare on a grand scale today, it is the vast untapped energy reserves of the Persian Gulf and the Caspian Sea areas.

Right now, the United States, Russia, and China are competing for the energy riches of these areas. All three powers have a vital stake in the global flow of oil, and all three seek some degree of control over the political dynamics of the most important oil-producing regions. All three have deployed combat forces in these areas or established military ties with friendly local governments. And, as the global demand for petroleum rises and more countries begin to rely on these regions for their energy, we can expect all three to bolster their strategic positions and to try to curb the influence of their rivals.

In fact, it is already happening. The United States has long supplied arms and military training to friendly states in the Persian Gulf area; we are now extending such aid to prospective partners in the Caspian basin. Russia continues to arm the former Soviet republics of the Caucasus and Central Asia and has emerged as a major military supplier to Iran. China, a relative newcomer to this contest, provides arms and military technology to Iran and has conducted joint military exercises with Kyrgyzstan. Both the United States and Russia have established military bases in the Caspian, and both have deployed combat units and air squadrons there; all three powers, moreover, have sought to enlist local states in military alliances of one sort or another. These attempts began in the early 1990s, following the collapse of the Soviet Union, and have been intensified since the beginning of this century.

Competition of this sort comes under the rubric of *geopolitics*—that is, the struggle between rival powers for control over territory, natural resources, vital geographic features (harbors, rivers, oases), and other sources of economic and military advantage. Such competition governed the international behavior of the European powers from the fifteenth to early twentieth centuries and fueled the creation of their overseas empires—empires built, as former national security adviser Zbigniew

Brzezinski observed in 1997, "through the careful seizure and retention of vital geographic assets, such as Gibraltar and the Suez Canal and Singapore."[1] To accomplish their aims, the imperial powers assembled large navies and expeditionary armies and sent them wherever they sought to secure or retain geopolitical assets. These interimperial contests shaped much of the political and military history of the past several centuries.

Geopolitical competition also defined many of the engagements of the cold-war era, although ideological rivalry played its part as well. The United States and the Soviet Union vied for control over the resource-rich and strategically located countries of the Middle East and Africa. Not surprisingly, Soviet efforts to court states with large oil or mineral reserves set off alarm bells in Washington. "As one assesses the recent step-up of Soviet proxy activities in the Third World," soon-to-be secretary of state Alexander M. Haig testified in 1980, "then one can only conclude that the era of the 'resource war' has arrived."[2] This outlook led to U.S. intervention, direct or indirect, in a score of conflicts, including the civil wars in Angola, the Congo, Yemen, and Afghanistan.[3] But with the end of the cold war, geopolitical competition appeared to give way to ethnic and religious antagonism as the driving force in international security affairs.

Now geopolitical factors are once again shaping the strategic outlook of the major powers. Eurasia and the Middle East have become "the grand chessboard" on which "the struggle for global primacy continues to be played," as Brzezinski observed. For the United States to succeed in this contest, he asserted, "American foreign policy must remain concerned with the geopolitical dimension" of world affairs.[4] Such perceptions—however reminiscent they are of an earlier era—are strongly influencing current strategic thinking in the major capitals of the world.

Oil Geopolitics—Then and Now

The relationship between oil, military power, and geography goes back to the early years of the twentieth century, when Great Britain converted its naval fleet from coal to oil propulsion. Lacking any oil of its own, Britain found itself dependent on petroleum reserves in the Middle East, and so, when World War I broke out, protecting those reserves became crucial. The advent of the tank, the combat plane, and the diesel-powered submarine only intensified the importance of oil; by the end of the war, access to petroleum was a major factor in the strategic planning of the contending powers.[5]

And it continued to be so after the war. Great Britain—which by then had effective control over the oil fields of Persia—attempted to extend its sway to fields in Iraq and Kuwait. France sought a foothold in this area too. Japan set its sights on the Dutch East Indies, then a major producer. And the United States began its search for petroleum along the southern rim of the Persian Gulf. All these powers, as well as Germany and the Soviet Union, knew that access to oil would prove decisive in the next war[6]; thus, when World War II erupted, they all devoted substantial forces to acquiring it.

Imperial Japan provides a case in point of the risks they were willing to take for the sake of oil. Japan had next to no domestic petroleum, a vulnerability that Tokyo decided to address by seizing the prolific oil fields of the Dutch East Indies. Since it knew that such a move was sure to trigger an American response, Tokyo ordered a preemptive strike on the U.S. Pacific Fleet at Pearl Harbor in Hawaii—thus prompting the U.S. entry into the war.[7] Oil-supply considerations governed German strategy too. One of the reasons Germany invaded the Soviet Union in 1941 was to gain control over the vast oil reserves of the Caucasus region, in order to compensate for a scarcity of domestic petroleum. Foiled in that effort—the Wehrmacht came to within a few hundred miles of Baku but never succeeded in breaking the Soviet resistance there—the Germans were forced to curb their use of oil-powered vehicles, putting them at a severe disadvantage in their subsequent battles with the Allies.[8]

Postwar America understood that petroleum supply would be just as critical in future conflicts as it was in the two world wars, hence our keen interest in the Persian Gulf. As I explained in chapter 2, the Truman administration believed that Soviet gambits in Iran, Greece, and Turkey were ultimately aimed at oil fields farther south. Washington countered by sending arms and other forms of military aid to friendly states in the area and by establishing a permanent naval presence in the Gulf. To be sure, these and subsequent moves in the region were framed in ideological terms, as part of the global crusade against communism—but they rested on a classic geopolitical foundation.

The cold-war fixation on oil came to a head in 1979 with the Soviet occupation of Afghanistan. It was this action, following on the heels of the
Islamic seizure of power in Iran, that impelled Jimmy Carter to promul-
gate his famous doctrine in January 1980. But when the Soviet system collapsed in 1992, the traditional motives of geopolitical struggle—political
and economic rivalry among the major powers—seemed to disappear.
With no other superpower to cause it trouble, the United States saw no
reason to organize its security policy around the global competition for
strategic advantage. During the 1990s, American strategists focused on
other threats: regional conflict, "rogue" states, and ethnic unrest.

Not that classical geopolitics faded entirely from discussion: as the
1990s wore on, a group of strategists and defense intellectuals—many of
them associated with neoconservative journals and think tanks—began
to warn of the growing threat to our interests posed by aspiring powers,
notably Russia and China. Pointing to the large military forces Moscow
and Beijing were maintaining and their support for "rogue" states like
Iran and Iraq, these analysts argued that we should substantially boost
our military expenditures and vigorously defend our vital interests. As
Robert Kagan and William Kristol asserted in *Present Dangers*, "American statesmen today ought to recognize that their charge is not to await
the arrival of the next great threat, but rather to shape the international
environment to prevent such a threat from arising in the first place."[9]

Those who share this point of view tend to emphasize the centrality of
military power in major geopolitical contests.[10] But these strategists also
acknowledge the energy dimensions of such rivalries. "Geopolitics and
energy existed in a symbiotic relationship for most of the twentieth century," the Center for Strategic and International Studies energy group observed in 2000; "there is little doubt that this symbiosis will continue."[11]
As the group noted, all the major powers—and especially Russia, China,
and the United States—recognize the crucial importance of Persian Gulf
and other oil reserves and so have bolstered their political and military
ties with key suppliers and taken other steps to safeguard their access to
energy. These actions, in turn, have intensified their mutual suspicion
and set off a new round of geopolitical competition.

This competition touches practically every major oil-producing area

Persian Gulf / Caspian Sea Region

in one way or another, but it is in the Persian Gulf/Caspian Sea region that it will almost certainly assume its most explosive form. With some 70 percent of the world's known petroleum reserves and a vast portion of its natural gas reserves, the region is destined to become, in Brzezinski's term, the *grand chessboard* on which Washington, Moscow, and Beijing will play out their struggle for primacy.

The United States has every intention of prevailing in this contest.

Fully cognizant of our dependency dilemma, American leaders have long sought control over the Persian Gulf's oil, and they appear determined to extend this control far into the future. The same geopolitical chess game is now being played in the Caspian Sea basin and Central Asia as well. Any challenges to U.S. interests in these regions will be countered with the full weight of American military power.

By remaining the dominant power in these areas, the United States can achieve more than just the safety of its future oil supply. It can also exercise a degree of control over the energy supply of *other* oil-importing countries. To the extent that they rely on the greater Gulf/Caspian region to satisfy their own oil and gas requirements, the energy security of these countries has become tied to the presence of powerful American forces there—a situation that naturally provides Washington with a certain amount of political leverage. We can use it to extract political favors— for example, the provision of troops or funds for American military campaigns—or to bully recalcitrant allies into line.[12] In an extreme case, we could use our military dominance in these areas to cut off the flow of energy to a hostile power.

However, Russia and China are every bit as determined to enhance their own strategic positions in this part of the world. Though they lack our military clout, they bring other assets—geographic, historical, and political— to the contest. The Middle East and Central Asia are sites of wide-ranging internal division and conflict that any major player can exploit to gain an advantage or to obstruct its rivals. The relative fortunes of any power in this epic contest will rest on a combination of military strength, geographic advantage, economic might, strategic prowess, diplomatic cunning, and many other factors. I have already examined America's position; let us now turn to a similar investigation of Russia and China.

The Once and Future Challenger

The starting point for any assessment of Russia's strategic future is the recognition of just how enfeebled it has become—at least compared to the place it once held as the dominant core of the Soviet Union. Shorn of its vast empire in eastern Europe, the Caucasus, and Central Asia, Russia today is a pale shadow of the menacing superpower that once competed with the United States for global mastery. The country's economy has contracted substantially since 1990, and its military establishment has fallen into unremitting, systemic deterioration. "Russia enters the new decade amidst significantly lowered expectations," Eugene B. Rummer of the National Defense University observed in 2001. "Its domestic prospects look dim. Its prospects as a major player in the international arena are equally dim as a result of domestic weakness and inability to articulate, let alone implement a coherent foreign policy agenda."[13]

Yet Russia retains some of the characteristics of a great power. With a population of 146 million people and a territory stretching across eleven time zones, it remains a primary geopolitical actor in the heart of Eurasia. It possesses a large and potent nuclear arsenal—second only to that possessed by the United States—and hundreds of intercontinental ballistic missiles. It is still a major supplier of conventional arms and nuclear technology to other nations, including China, Iran, and India. And—what is most important in this context—it commands a vast supply of oil and natural gas, along with a substantial network of pipelines connecting the Caspian basin and Central Asia to eastern and western Europe.[14]

Faced with this jumble of strengths and weaknesses, Russian leaders have tried to stem the further loss of wealth and power and to regain some of the country's former greatness, focusing—especially since President Vladimir Putin came to power—on economic reform and modernization.[15] Not that Putin and his associates have no interest in foreign affairs, but they are careful to ensure that their diplomatic endeavors in no way undermine domestic revitalization. Within these limits, Russian officials have labored furiously to enhance Moscow's influence in the territory of the former Soviet Union and the areas immediately surrounding it—especially the greater Caspian Sea region.[16]

No longer able to bully neighboring countries with the threat of force, Moscow has had to advance its interests via other means—for example, the sale of arms and military technology to those states with the capacity (whether in hard currency or bartered commodities) to pay for them. But Moscow has also taken advantage of certain vestigial features of the former Soviet Union. The current Russian leadership—many of whose members, including Putin, were in the upper ranks of the KGB—enjoys close fraternal ties with many of the officials of the other former Soviet republics who likewise served in the Soviet *nomenklatura*. Similarly, the legacy of Soviet central planning, which bound the economies of Russia and the far-flung republics together, still gives Moscow some economic and political leverage over these countries. In a conspicuous exercise of this leverage, Russia cut off the flow of natural gas to Georgia in 2001, to signal its displeasure over certain policies of the latter.[17]

It is in the realm of energy policy, however, that Moscow has gone after international influence and advantage most fiercely. With oil and gas exports now providing the major share of Russia's foreign income—55 percent of export revenue and 40 percent of government income in 2002—Moscow is doing everything it can to boost energy production so that it can acquire the additional funds for economic and political revitalization.[18] Putin has also used energy exports as a means of firming up his country's ties with influential foreign consumers, including Germany, Japan, and the United States.[19] And not only has he tried to preserve Russia's near monopoly over the transport of Caspian Sea oil and gas to the West (via the Soviet-era pipeline system); he has also done his best to scuttle the development of any alternative transportation routes that would bypass Russia.[20]

This desire to dominate the transport of Caspian Sea energy has inevitably led to conflict with parallel U.S. ambitions in the region. This competition arose in the mid- and late 1990s, when Washington set out to establish political and military ties with the former Soviet republics of the Caucasus and Central Asia and thereby pave the way for investment by American energy firms. Moscow endeavored to strengthen its own political and military influence with the new nations in response.[21] From the very beginning, both sides perceived these diplomatic overtures as moves in a classical geopolitical contest. In 1997 Sheila Heslin of the National Security Council staff told a Senate investigating committee that American efforts to promote construction of new pipelines through the Caucasus to the Black Sea and Turkey were part of a larger campaign "to break Russia's monopoly of control over the transportation of oil from the region."[22] Not surprisingly, Russian leaders responded just as assertively.

"It hasn't been left unnoticed in Russia that certain outside interests are trying to weaken our position in the Caspian basin," Andrei Y. Urnov of the Russian Ministry of Foreign Affairs declared in May 2000. "No one should be perplexed that Russia is determined to resist the attempts to encroach on her interests."[23]

The struggle for control over the pipeline routes from the Caspian basin to international markets is no small matter. For Russia, not only are the pipelines a source of revenue, but they also provide Moscow with political leverage over the former Soviet republics to its south. That is precisely why the United States is so determined to diminish Russia's control over the flow of energy.[24] In Washington's eyes the alternative conduits—most notably the BTC pipeline through Georgia—are a matter of national security. "This is about America's energy security, which depends on diversifying our sources of oil and gas," Energy Secretary Bill Richardson affirmed in 1998. "It's also about preventing strategic inroads by those who don't share our values."[25]

Moscow's sensitivity on this issue, and especially its ostentatious power displays toward its neighbors, have provoked a serious and often rancorous debate in Washington as to Russia's motives. Some analysts regard Putin's principal goals as inoffensive and even beneficial: namely, promoting economic growth at home and restoring stability on the country's southern perimeter, particularly in the Muslim-majority areas of the Caucasus and Central Asia. Higher Russian oil output, they reason, is entirely in line with America's vital interests; so is Moscow's desire to quash terrorism, especially given that the Caspian basin has proved such a fertile ground for Al Qaeda and other terrorist groups.[26] But other analysts view Russian policy in a far more sinister light, as part of a concerted effort on Moscow's part to reassert its global prestige and to reimpose its sway over what was once the Russian/Soviet empire. This latter view is especially popular among neoconservatives, who have never quite abandoned their cold-war-hardened suspicions of the Russian leadership.[27]

The Bush administration has vacillated between these two outlooks. It entered office with an unmistakable bias toward the negative view of Russia. During his first months as president, George W. Bush made it clear that he would proceed with foreign-policy and military initiatives that were known to displease Moscow, including the eastward expansion of NATO, the abrogation of the Anti-Ballistic Missile (ABM) Treaty, and the establishment of a national missile defense system. After 9/11, however, the hostility appeared to abate. President Putin was among the first foreign leaders to telephone Bush after the attacks and to pledge his country's support in the war against terrorism. The Russians gave their tacit approval to American use of former Soviet bases in Central Asia as staging areas for operations against Al Qaeda in Afghanistan, and collaborated in the delivery of arms and logistic support to the anti-Taliban forces of the Northern Alliance.[28] These acts led to cooperation in other areas, including energy and arms control. Most significant, Washington and Moscow agreed in November 2001 to reduce the number of actively deployed warheads in their respective nuclear arsenals.[29]

But the spirit of cooperation did not last. By early 2002, the two sides had resumed their competition for power and influence in the greater Caspian area.[30] The ensuing debate over military intervention in Iraq—with the United States favoring the use of force to remove Saddam Hussein and destroy his WMD stockpiles, and Russia favoring diplomacy and UN inspections—made matters far worse. Despite earnest efforts to patch things up after the war, each side remains deeply suspicious of the other's long-term intentions and both continue to behave like geopolitical adversaries vis-à-vis the Persian Gulf and the Caspian Sea regions.[31] With the debate over Iraq largely concluded, other issues—the presence of American combat forces in the Caucasus and Central Asia, Russian military aid to Iran, the ongoing dispute over pipeline routes—have come to the fore, and the tension is likely to worsen in the years to come.[32]

A major irritant in this antagonism has been the conspicuous expansion of the American military presence in the Caspian area. When the Bush administration was seeking permission to station American forces in Kyrgyzstan and Uzbekistan for use in the war in Afghanistan, it explained that the deployments would last only as long as it took to defeat the Taliban and Al Qaeda.[33] But once we had prevailed and large-scale military operations had come to a close, American leaders received permission from Kyrgyzstan and Uzbekistan to retain U.S. forces there indefinitely. Russian leaders reacted angrily, charging that Washington had taken advantage of their good faith in order to bolster America's geopolitical position in the area.[34] As the Russian minister of defense, Sergei B. Ivanov, told a gathering of NATO officials in October 2003, "We have always been proceeding from the fact that those bases exist solely for the period required for the final, definitive stabilization of the situation in Afghanistan."[35]

Washington had already aroused Russian ire by sending American military instructors to Georgia in February 2002.[36] As previously noted, the stated aim of this operation was to enhance Georgia's ability to protect its borders and its infrastructure, including oil and gas pipelines. But many observers in Moscow view the American advisers as another sign of the American drive to supplant Russia as the dominant power in the Caspian basin.[37] The deployment of the instructors "could further aggravate the situation in the region," Russian foreign minister Igor S. Ivanov warned at the time.[38] President Putin subsequently stated that he had no objection to the Americans in Georgia so long as they confined their activities to antiterrorist operations. Other Russian leaders, though, have continued to seethe over the presence of American forces so close to Russia's southern boundary.[39]

The Russians have not, however, confined themselves to complaining. To the degree that its resources allow, Moscow has sought to counter America's expanded military presence with similar initiatives of its own. Most notably, in December 2002, it installed a squadron of combat planes and seven hundred support troops at a military base near Bishkek, Kyrgyzstan, not far from the U.S. base at Manas International Airport. Ostensibly, the Russians are there to provide air support for the joint rapid-reaction force authorized by leaders of Russia, Kazakhstan, Kyrgyzstan, and Tajikistan in May 2001 under the auspices of the Collective Security Treaty Organization, a loose association of several former Soviet republics. Most observers, however, viewed the move as an attempt to balance the growing American presence in Central Asia.[40] Moscow has also increased its troop strength in Tajikistan (where some fourteen thousand Russian soldiers patrol the extended border with Afghanistan) and beefed up its naval presence in the Caspian Sea proper.[41] And, in response to the growing American influence in the Caucasus, Moscow has reneged on an earlier promise to shut down its bases in Georgia and withdraw its forces.[42]

Russia is further bolstering its strategic position by providing arms and military assistance to friendly local powers, including Armenia, Kazakhstan, Kyrgyzstan, Tajikistan, Turkmenistan, and Uzbekistan. Although they are hardly substantial in dollar terms, these deliveries—typically involving small numbers of jets, helicopters, artillery, and troop carriers—are significant because the recipients generally lack the funds to buy modern weapons on the international market. They are usually packaged, moreover, with military training accords and deployments of Russian military advisers. In 2001, to cite one example, Moscow agreed to provide Uzbekistan with artillery systems, helicopters, and antiaircraft guns, and also to increase the number of Uzbek officers and pilots being trained at Russian military academies.[43] It has made similar agreements with the other former Soviet republics.[44]

Of course, one power's blandishments—an arms transfer, a deployment of advisers, a trade deal—require a commensurate response from the other. Consider the case of Georgia, the site of the soon-to-be-completed BTC pipeline. The United States has provided Georgia with more than $1.3 billion in aid over the past ten years—a relatively hefty amount for a country of only 5 million people—and is helping train and equip its military forces. Moscow, in turn, has refused to remove its own forces (most of which are based in the autonomous region of Adzharia) and is providing various forms of assistance to the secessionist regimes in Abkhazia and South Ossetia. The two powers temporarily suspended their rivalry to cooperate in the peaceful ouster of Eduard Shevardnadze from the Georgian presidency in November 2003—then quickly resumed it. Secretary of Defense Donald Rumsfeld reaffirmed U.S. support for the country in a hastily arranged meeting with Shevardnadze's successors in Tbilisi on December 5,[45] at about the same time that Moscow hosted a meeting of leaders from Georgia's secessionist enclaves and denounced American meddling.[46]

This sort of skirmishing—never building to an outright clash but always thwarting progress toward cooperation—originates in the struggle over energy. Although Moscow claims to have abandoned its opposition to the BTC pipeline, its determination to maintain some form of control over the flow of Caspian oil flow is obvious in its support for the secessionist regimes in Abkhazia and South Ossetia, both of which are within striking distance of the pipeline route, and its refusal to remove its forces from Georgia. The United States, for its part, is girding the Georgian army for the inevitable attacks on the pipeline. The same dynamic applies to the Azerbaijani section of the BTC: Russia betrays its hostility to the project by assisting Armenia—and, by extension, the secessionist Armenian enclave of Nagorno-Karabakh—while the United States aids Azerbaijan.[47]

Another pipeline contest is in the offing—this one in Kazakhstan and Turkmenistan on the Caspian's eastern shore. Kazakhstan has emerged as the major producer in the region, and Moscow and Washington both want to determine the routes by which Kazakh oil will flow to the West. Some of this petroleum now travels via Russia in a newly constructed pipeline between Kazakhstan's Tengiz field and Novorossiysk, on the Black Sea coast. In an effort to sideline Russia, American officials have urged the Kazakhs and the energy companies to build an oil and gas pipeline beneath the Caspian Sea to the BTC starting point in Baku. Predictably, Moscow has furiously resisted these initiatives.[48] In January 2002, President Putin proposed the establishment of a "Eurasian Gas Alliance" that would unite all Central Asian producers in an integrated transportation system that would rely, to a considerable extent, on lines crossing Russia to markets in the West.[49] (See map on page 134.)

Although the struggle for power and influence is most acute in the Caspian basin, no one would claim the United States and Russia exactly see eye to eye in that other geopolitical tinderbox, the Persian Gulf. The Soviets once wielded considerable influence there. Soviet officials were frequent visitors to Saddam Hussein's Baghdad, and the USSR provided Iraq with the lion's share of its military equipment. While Moscow honored the UN arms embargo on Iraq after its 1990 invasion of Kuwait, Russian energy firms stayed on in Baghdad, signing multibillion-dollar contracts to develop untapped Iraqi oil reserves. Moreover, once the 2003 war in Iraq (over which Russia and the United States disagreed so strenuously) had ended, Moscow insisted on the inviolability of its Hussein-era oil contracts and made it a condition for the forgiving of Iraq's gargantuan debt, a major objective of American policy makers.[50]

Moscow's links with Iran also grate on Washington. Although these relations are not as cordial as they were with the Baathist regime in Baghdad, Russia still supplies a great deal of conventional arms and nuclear technology to Iran and has resisted American efforts to punish the Iranians for their surreptitious WMD program.[51] Between 1994 and 2001, Russia provided Iran with $1.2 billion worth of conventional weapons—more than any other supplier.[52] Major deliveries included thirty MiG-29 and thirty Su-24 combat aircraft, some three hundred T-72 tanks, and three Kilo-class diesel submarines. Of these, the Kilo submarines have provoked the most concern in Washington, largely because of their potential use in obstructing oil shipping in the Persian Gulf and adjacent waters.[53]

Of far greater concern to the United States is Russia's sale of nuclear and missile technology to Iran. In 1995, Iran signed an $800 million contract with Russia for the completion of a one-thousand-megawatt reactor at Bushehr, a project originally undertaken by German firms but suspended in 1980 after the outbreak of the Iran-Iraq War. The Russians insist that because the Iranians will use the Bushehr reactor for civilian purposes only, the contract is entirely legitimate under the nuclear Non-Proliferation Treaty (NPT). Many in Washington suspect, however, that Iran hopes to use the reactor and its associated facilities to acquire equipment and know-how it can then apply to its secret nuclear weapons program.[54] American officials have accordingly put enormous pressure on Moscow to suspend the project—so far without success. After meeting with George W. Bush at Camp David in September 2003, President Putin told reporters, "We are ready to pursue" the Bushehr project, going on to say that Russia would urge the Iranians to abide by their NPT obligations but would not accede to American demands to stop work on the reactor.[55]

The United States has also had a hard time persuading Moscow to cut off assistance to Iran's ballistic missile program. According to the Congressional Research Service (CRS), Russian firms and institutes have provided these programs with "training, testing equipment, and components including specialty steels and alloys, tungsten-coated graphite, gyroscopes and other guidance technology, rocket engine and fuel technology, laser equipment, machine tools, and maintenance manuals."[56] Washington has responded to such reports by imposing economic sanctions on the Russian firms allegedly involved in these transactions and by entreating the Kremlin to crack down on any firms that violate the country's export regulations. But, promises of cooperation from Moscow notwithstanding, some Russian firms are apparently still involved in these missile projects.[57]

In spite of this simmering rivalry, officials in Washington and Moscow continue to insist that they have a good relationship and that any differences can still be resolved amicably. Since the United States is likely to become a significant consumer of Russian oil, there may indeed be prospects for more cooperation in the future. But nothing in the statements or behavior of the two powers suggests they have abandoned their struggle for geopolitical advantage in the Persian Gulf and Caspian Sea basins—quite the opposite. And as international demand for energy from these areas expands, the stakes in this contest will also grow—and so, too, will the determination of each player to emerge on top.

Enter China

Now a new actor must be added to the political and military contest in the greater Persian Gulf/Caspian Sea region: China wants to acquire a geopolitical stake of its own. Until very recently, China played a rather limited role in the area, confined largely to weapons sales and a certain amount of trade. It sold some arms and missile technology to Iran, Iraq, and Saudi Arabia, and established limited military ties with some of the Central Asian republics; it has not, however, acquired military bases or deployed any of its troops. But China is a rising power, and its surging economy is generating an ever-expanding thirst for imported energy. Not surprisingly, then, Beijing has begun to compete with Washington and Moscow for the same sort of strategic advantages in the region.

China's entry into the contest will pose a difficult challenge to both of the other major players. For the United States, China will become a major rival for new oil, and its pursuit of a larger share of the region's output may contribute to tighter supplies and higher prices.[58] Like its rivals, Beijing will no doubt cultivate closer economic and political ties with local producers—if need be, by stepping up its transfers of arms and military technology. This will inevitably accelerate local arms races and exacerbate regional tensions; it could even lead to conflict with Washington if the recipients are hostile regimes, like Iran. And Beijing's gains will come at the expense of Russia's influence in neighboring countries. What we are seeing, then, is the emergence of a three-way geopolitical struggle.[59]

Beijing's interests are at least in part inspired by national-security concerns. Like Russia, China faces a territorial threat from secessionist ethnic minorities. The nation's westernmost province, the Xinjiang Uighur Autonomous Region, projects directly into the heart of Central Asia and so is exposed to all the turmoil and discontent that plague that area. Of greatest concern to Beijing is the Uighur separatist movement in Xinjiang, a low-level insurgency waged by advocates of an independent Uighur state. Such a state existed briefly after World War II, and the Chinese authorities fear that the region's Turkic-speaking majority (of which the Uighurs form the largest component) will seek to resurrect some version of it. To keep this from happening, Beijing long ago imposed an authoritarian system of control in Xinjiang and, as in Tibet, has encouraged heavy immigration by Han Chinese. And because Uighur dissidents have cultivated ties with radical Islamist forces in the neighboring Central Asian republics, Beijing has sought to enhance its influence in those countries and to cooperate with their governments in suppressing extremist movements.[60]

Closely linked to China's concern over Xinjiang is its fear of encirclement by the United States. Although relations between Washington and Beijing are better now than they have been in decades—largely as a result of their mutual determination to stamp out terrorism—Chinese officials still bitterly recall the many years they suffered in international isolation thanks to the United States. It is hardly surprising, then, that they should be fearful of a fresh attempt by Washington to "encircle" and "contain" China. Beijing has long dreaded the likelihood of the United States' aiding Taiwan in its effort to establish an independent state, or, at the very least, preventing China from using force to restore control over

Western China and Central Asia

the island should it declare its independence. Now Beijing has a new worry: that the United States will establish a constellation of bases in Central Asia and thereby threaten China from the rear, where—particularly in Xinjiang—it feels most vulnerable. To stave off such encirclement, the Chinese have worked hard to develop close ties with the Central Asian republics and to dissuade them from allowing the Americans to establish a permanent military presence in their midst.[61]

The reason America has shown up at China's back door is—of course—the pursuit of energy. The same compulsion is now taking hold of China.

Most of China's energy comes from domestic coal, oil, natural gas, and hydropower; at present, imports constitute only a small share of the total supply. But China's economy is expanding so rapidly that its need for energy—especially oil and natural gas—is fast overwhelming domestic capacity. To quench its growing thirst for petroleum, China will have no choice but to turn to the same sources the United States has: the Persian Gulf, the Caspian Sea basin, and Africa. And because Beijing is no less concerned about the security of its imports from these areas than Washington is, it will likely pursue a similar policy of plying oil-producing regimes with arms, advisers, and military technology.

In Washington's eyes, Beijing's bid for greater influence in the Gulf/Caspian region is to some degree a natural consequence of China's surging economic growth. Insofar as Beijing's actions reflect understandable national-security concerns, Washington does not see them as a fundamental threat to American interests. But many American analysts, who foresee China growing into a major military rival, blanch at any sign of geopolitical initiative on Beijing's part.[62] The Bush administration remains ambivalent, viewing China as a potential partner in some areas, such as the war on terror, and as a potential adversary in others, such as Taiwan.[63] At present, the White House appears determined to pursue friendly relations; however, China's hunger for additional energy will pose a significant challenge in the future: not only will it drive up prices and, in some cases, produce tight supplies, but it will also firm up Chinese military ties with countries, like Iran, that Washington considers enemies. China's growing need for oil is the wild card in this contest, and so it deserves our close attention.

During much of the cold-war era, China produced enough oil, natural gas, and coal to satisfy its domestic needs. Energy self-sufficiency was, in fact, a major strategic priority in Beijing, which feared becoming dependent on outside powers (and thus beholden to them politically). The Chinese also sought to produce a surplus of coal and oil for export to neighboring countries, as a way to build diplomatic ties and acquire hard currency. All the effort they devoted to the exploitation of the country's known petroleum supplies and the search for new ones enabled them to stay self-sufficient in oil until 1993, when rising consumption finally overtook domestic production. Since then, China has had to rely more and more on imported oil.[64]

This growing reliance on imports is vividly evident in the latest Department of Energy projections. In 2001, China produced approximately 3.3 million barrels of oil per day and consumed 5.0 million barrels, generating a shortfall of 1.7 million barrels that had to be made up with imports. At 34 percent of total consumption, its level of dependency was considerably lower than America's import rate of 54 percent. But China's domestic oil output is expected to remain essentially flat over the coming decades, while demand is expected to grow by 4 percent per year, producing a corresponding increase in demand for imports. In 2025, the DoE predicts, China's net petroleum consumption will reach an estimated 12.8 million barrels of oil per day while output will remain at 3.4 million barrels, resulting in an import requirement of 9.4 million barrels per day—well over *five times* the 2001 amount.[65] (See figure 7.)

What explains this dramatic increase in China's need for imported oil? To begin with, there is the expected stagnation in domestic hydrocarbon production. The prolific fields at Daqing and Liaohe in the northeast, China's mainstay during the cold-war era, have by now been thoroughly exploited and will yield diminishing returns in the years ahead. Chinese authorities have tried to compensate by boosting output at other fields—notably in the Tarim Basin of Xinjiang province—and by drilling for oil offshore in the East and South China seas. Yet none of these efforts appear likely to raise China's net petroleum output much above the current rate of 3.3 million barrels per day, and so any increase in consumption beyond this level will have to be satisfied with imports.[66]

And it is the demand side of the equation that is the real motor driving imports. As the world's fastest-growing economy, China is going to need ever greater amounts of energy. According to the latest DoE projections, its total energy requirement is expanding by approximately 3.5 percent per year, from 40 quadrillion Btu in 2001 to 91 quadrillion Btu in 2025—by which time its net energy consumption will equal that of all the western European countries combined and will have surpassed that of every other individual country save the United States.[67] To satisfy this colossal increase in demand, China will have to (1) build hundreds of additional

Figure 7

OIL PRODUCTION, CONSUMPTION, AND IMPORTS IN CHINA, PROJECTIONS, 2000–2025

	2000	2005	2010	2015	2020	2025	Annual growth, 2001–2025 (percent)
Gross domestic product (billion 1997 dollars)	1,119	1,599	2,228	2,980	3,877	4,976	6.1
Population (millions)	1,275	1,321	1,365	1,402	1,429	1,445	0.5
Energy consumption (quadrillion Btu)	37.0	43.2	54.6	65.7	77.7	91.0	3.5
Domestic oil production (mbd)	3.3	3.5	3.6	3.5	3.5	3.4	0.0
Domestic oil consumption (mbd)	4.8	5.5	7.6	9.2	11.0	12.8	4.0
Oil imports (mbd)	1.5	2.0	4.0	5.7	7.5	9.4	7.6
Oil imports as a percentage of total consumption	31.3	36.4	52.6	62.0	68.2	73.4	

Source: U.S. Department of Energy, Energy Information Administration (DoE/EIA), *International Energy Outlook 2004* (Washington, D.C.: DoE/EIA, 2004), tables A1, A3, A4, A14, D4. Data for 2000 and 2005 from 2003 edition of this annual reference.

Abbreviations: Btu=British thermal units; mbd=Million barrels per day

electric power plants and expand every other component of its energy infrastructure, and (2) accelerate the production of every type of energy: oil, coal, natural gas, hydroelectric, and nuclear.

At present, coal supplies much more energy to China than oil does (62 percent vs. 28 percent). Still, petroleum plays a critical role, both in transportation and in the manufacture of petrochemicals—the source of the plastics and other materials used to fashion the cornucopia of consumer products that undergird the Chinese economy.[68] With private automobile ownership expected to grow by 10 to 20 percent per year and industrial output continuing its heady expansion, China can't help but consume more oil every year.[69] For China's communist leadership, which has always sought to maximize the country's economic self-reliance, this situation represents a profound political and economic challenge, in that China will not be able to sustain its high level of economic growth and personal enrichment—on which the government rests its continued claim to legitimacy—without obtaining additional petroleum.

This thirst for oil will become critical as the growing purchasing power of China's large and expanding middle class produces an appetite for consumer goods of all sorts, especially automobiles. According to some estimates, more than 300 million Chinese citizens now earn more than two thousand dollars per year—the level at which (measured in terms of purchasing-power parity) car buying has taken off in other developing countries.[70] And in China, as in other developing countries, "automobile ownership has assumed a symbolic importance as a measure of economic success and as a signal of the nation's material promise," Michael McElroy and Chris Nielson of Harvard University have observed.[71] The inevitable upshot: a soaring demand for gasoline, diesel fuel, and other petroleum products.[72]

But while Chinese leaders may be eager to satisfy the consumer cravings of the growing and politically significant middle class, they have good reason to worry that each increment of foreign oil only deepens the country's vulnerability to economic and political disruptions in the major oil-producing regions. Rising dependence on imports "will dramatically increase the supply-side risks of petroleum resources," Tian Fengshan, China's minister for state land and resources, observed in 2002, "and that will damage the country's capacity to ensure its oil resources as well as economic and political security."[73] For Chinese authorities, no less than their American counterparts, this kind of vulnerability is a constant concern.[74] So too is the stubborn fact that dependency on foreign oil means dependency on the Persian Gulf basin, the *one* major producing area with the capacity to satisfy the rising international demand. China would much prefer to rely on Indonesia and other suppliers in Southeast Asia, but production in these areas is declining and so the country will have no choice but to turn to the Gulf. Indeed, the share of China's crude-oil imports from Middle Eastern producers is expected to rise from 48 percent in 1997 to 81 percent in 2010—a development that, given all the turmoil and conflict in the Middle East, cannot fail to cause major anxiety in Beijing.[75]

Senior officials in Beijing no doubt worry about the same things that trouble American policy makers when it comes to dependence on Middle Eastern oil, but they have another cause for concern, too. "China's leaders are uncomfortable with the fact that the United States is the preeminent power in the Middle East, the region that provides China with the bulk of its oil imports," says Erica Downs of the Rand Corporation. The area is saturated with American bases, troops, and naval squadrons, and while the Chinese know that the U.S. forces are largely there to safeguard the outflow of oil (thus benefiting China, along with other nations), Beijing fears that the United States might someday cut off China's flow of oil (say, in response to a fresh crisis in Taiwan) and cripple its economy. "China currently does not possess the naval capabilities necessary to defend its sea shipments of oil," Downs wrote, "and, consequently, regards their passage through waters dominated by the U.S. Navy . . . as a key strategic vulnerability."[76]

In seeking to minimize their country's strategic vulnerabilities, China's leaders have acted much like their American counterparts, declaring the procurement of foreign oil a matter of national security and drawing on the full resources of the state to search for safe and adequate supplies. As Philip Andrews-Speed and his colleagues at the University of Dundee have suggested, these Chinese actions "conform to an energy security policy which is dominated by strategic measures and where the government is willing to assume considerable potential costs to achieve its energy security objectives."[77] Key decisions on oil-related matters— the development of new fields, the allocation of overseas investments, the routing of major pipelines, and so on—are made at the highest government levels and integrated into the country's overall foreign policy.[78]

In their quest for energy security, the Chinese have come up with a multilayered strategy aimed at increasing the country's access to foreign supplies while minimizing its vulnerability to overseas supply disruptions and trade embargoes. This strategy calls on Beijing to establish a significant presence in many producing regions, to develop close political and military ties with its major providers abroad, and to diversify both the sources of its imported energy and the transportation routes by which it flows into the country.[79] These are, of course, the very sort of policies that American officials have long favored, but they entail an unprecedented level of Chinese involvement in the oil politics of the Middle East and other key producing regions. "China is rapidly becoming a force to reckon with in the global energy system," the International Energy Agency observed in 2000. "Other players must make room for it. China is not a marginal player but a powerful new force in the international energy market."[80]

The most obvious sign of China's entry into the global energy system is its investments in or trade arrangements with foreign energy firms in the key producing areas, especially the Persian Gulf, North Africa, and the Caspian Sea basin. In forging these arrangements, Beijing has relied on its three large state-owned oil companies: the China National Petroleum Corporation (CNPC), the China National Petrochemical Corporation (Sinopec), and the China National Offshore Oil Corporation (CNOOC). In many respects, these firms act as arms of the government, establishing a conspicuous presence in producing countries and implementing official policy.[81] "China's energy security is the first concern," a top CNPC official acknowledged in December 2003. "The company's interests are second."[82] As of 2003, these firms had secured important ties with energy enterprises in more than a dozen countries, including Angola, Burma (Myanmar), Ecuador, Egypt, Indonesia, Iran, Iraq, Kazakhstan, Kuwait, Libya, Nigeria, Oman, Peru, Russia, Saudi Arabia, Sudan, Thailand, Venezuela, and Yemen.[83] Many of these arrangements can make sense in purely economic terms—as part of a global quest for crude petroleum—but they also reflect the strategic orientation of Chinese energy policy.[84]

This strategic approach is clearly visible in China's most important overseas energy endeavors, notably those in Kazakhstan, Iran, and Sudan.

Kazakhstan has played an especially critical role in China's foreign energy policy, and it has received some of the largest Chinese investments—the most significant of which is CNPC's majority share in Aktobemuniagaz, a formerly state-owned enterprise that controls several large fields in the Aktobinsk area. CNPC paid a reported $4.3 billion for a 63 percent stake in Aktobemuniagaz and promised to make additional investments in infrastructure, including a 3,700-mile pipeline from the Aktobinsk fields to coastal China.[85] CNPC also owns an interest in Uzen, Kazakhstan's second-largest oil field, and is seeking additional investment opportunities in the country, along with other Chinese firms. "At the moment, we are producing about four million tons of oil in Kazakhstan, but that is not nearly enough for us," a senior CNPC official told Lutz Kleveman, the author of *The New Great Game.* "In coming years, we want to acquire many more fields in Central Asia."[86]

Kazakhstan is attractive because it borders China and provides a land bridge between the Caspian Sea and East Asia—a geopolitical blessing that allows for the transport of Caspian oil and gas to China on interior routes that avoid the (U.S.-dominated) Persian Gulf. Chinese officials take this advantage so seriously that they have committed to building a pipeline from the Aktobinsk fields to coastal China, at an estimated cost of $10 billion. In purely economic terms, it would make more sense for Beijing to ship its Kazakh oil to consumers in Europe via existing Russian pipelines and satisfy its own energy needs by buying cheaper crude from the Persian Gulf. The proposed pipeline to China, however, would enable Beijing to strengthen its bonds with Kazakhstan and to free itself, to some degree, from reliance on the Gulf.[87] So it is hardly surprising that in his first trip abroad as China's president, Hu Jintao traveled to Kazakhstan in June 2003 and renewed the commitment to this pipeline—"an important sign," he told reporters, "that China places great attention and importance on developing friendly relations with Kazakhstan."[88]

Of almost as much interest to China in terms of energy are Iran and Sudan. Iran already supplies a major portion of China's imports with crude from its own fields, and Beijing is also eager to enlist Tehran as a partner in the transport of Caspian Sea oil to China. Because of the difficulty of moving Caspian energy directly to eastern Asia, China has begun to deliver Kazakh oil to refineries in northern Iran, near the Caspian coast, in exchange for equal amounts of Iranian crude from fields in the south, which can be shipped to China from ports on the Persian Gulf. To facilitate such petroleum "swaps," Sinopec and CNPC are collaborating on the construction of a 240-mile pipeline from Iran's Caspian Sea port of Neka to refineries in the Tehran area; Sinopec is also helping to upgrade Iranian refineries, in order to process the heavier crude coming in from Kazakhstan.[89] As China's need for oil grows, Iran is slated to play an even greater role in Beijing's energy strategy.

Sudan, strategically located in the northeast corner of Africa, with access to the Red Sea, has become another factor in China's overseas energy plans. Shunned by the United States and other Western powers for its ties to radical Islamist movements, its egregious human rights record, and its brutal war against secessionist forces in the south, Sudan has had considerable difficulty attracting foreign partners for the development of its considerable oil reserves—thus providing Chinese firms with an opening they could not find anywhere else.[90] After Chevron abandoned its exploration operations in the Bentiu region of the south, China stepped in and helped establish the Greater Nile Petroleum Operating Company to develop promising fields in the area. (CNPC owns 40 percent of the consortium, Petronas of Malaysia 30 percent, the Canadian independent Arakis Energy 25 percent, and the Sudanese state firm Sudapet 5 percent.) To move this oil to international markets, CNPC oversaw the construction of a 930-mile pipeline from Bentiu to Suakin, on the Red Sea coast. In yet another giant project, CNPC helped to build a new refinery at Jayli, thirty miles north of the capital city of Khartoum. In no other country does China play such a prominent role in the energy field.[91]

China's investments in Kazakhstan, Iran, and Sudan represent its most elaborate efforts to establish ties with major foreign suppliers, but by no means its only ones. During the past few years, Chinese firms have acquired development rights to or part ownership of major fields in Ecuador, Indonesia, Russia, Venezuela, and elsewhere. In almost every case, CNPC, CNOOC, and Sinopec outbid Western firms—often

by substantial amounts—suggesting a concerted effort by China to expand its foreign energy holdings and diversify its sources of supply.
And Beijing shows every sign of accelerating such endeavors in the
years ahead.[92]

Following the lead of other oil-importing countries, China is courting
as many oil producers as it can. But it is not putting its faith in diversification alone. Like the United States, China is bolstering its ties with its suppliers by providing them with arms, weapons technology, and other forms
of military assistance. Although its largesse in this regard has not been
nearly as elaborate or conspicuous as Washington's or Moscow's, Beijing is
just getting started. In most cases, the aid it has provided has consisted of
arms and equipment suitable for internal security and border protection:
prefabricated border posts and communications gear for Kyrgyzstan;
sniper rifles and night-vision goggles for Uzbekistan; police equipment
for Kazakhstan; and assorted military gear for Tajikistan. China also provides training to the militaries and police of these countries and shares
intelligence with them on the activities of insurgent and separatist
groups.[93] In a particularly striking development, Chinese troops joined
with Kyrgyz forces in October 2002 to conduct a joint counterinsurgency
exercise on Kyrgyzstan's side of their mutual border—the first such joint
training exercise on foreign territory that Chinese forces are known to
have engaged in.[94]

Even more strikingly, China has established formal security ties with
states in the greater Gulf/Caspian area and helped form a new regional
security institution to legitimize and facilitate its expanding military involvement in Central Asia.[95] This treaty organization was created at a
1996 meeting in Shanghai of China, Russia, Kazakhstan, Kyrgyzstan, and
Tajikistan—the Shanghai Five, as they came to be called. The resulting
accord, the "Agreement on Confidence-Building in the Military Field
Along the Border Areas," is aimed at averting border clashes and promoting
military-to-military cooperation. At a subsequent meeting, in August
1999, the Shanghai Five agreed to hold regular consultations for their senior military officers and to establish a joint antiterrorism center in
Bishkek, Kyrgyzstan. Prodded by Beijing, the group added Uzbekistan to
their ranks in 2001 and agreed to formalize the alliance as the Shanghai

Cooperation Organization (SCO). A charter was then drawn up and formally adopted at the SCO summit in Moscow, in May 2003.[96]

Although Russia is a charter member of the SCO and has supported its expansion, China has been the driving force. Not only did China convene the first meeting, but it wooed Uzbekistan into the fold with a commitment to establish a second antiterrorism center in Tashkent, the Uzbek capital. China has also promised to house the secretariat of the SCO and to pay many of the organization's bills.[97] "China's steady expansion of regional involvement within the Shanghai Five, and subsequently the Shanghai Cooperation Organization, is a geopolitical watershed," Zbigniew Brzezinski declared in 2003. "China, in effect, is [entering] the region as a major player."[98] And while this role is formally defined in political and economic terms, it may soon add a military dimension: according to some reports, the as yet unpublished charter of the SCO envisions the use of Chinese troops in Central Asia, if requested, to fight Islamic militants.[99] It is in this light that the Chinese-Kyrgyz exercise of October 2002 is most telling; although historically China has been more hesitant than either Russia or the United States to deploy its military forces in the region, it has now begun to prepare for such action in the years ahead.

To what extent Beijing may be willing to arm its new friends is not yet clear. However, the record to date—especially China's sale of missiles and arms technology to Iran—is not very comforting to Washington. According to the Congressional Research Service, Beijing has supplied Iran with advanced C-802 antiship missiles and C-801K air-to-surface missiles, along with older-model SA-2 surface-to-air missiles. The Chinese are also believed to have provided technological assistance and specialized equipment to Iran's Shahab ballistic missile program.[100] In response to these and other weapons sales, the United States has imposed economic sanctions on selected Chinese firms and pressured Beijing to sever its military ties with Tehran; this, reportedly, has produced a slowdown in Chinese missile-technology transfers to Iran, but not their cessation.[101]

China has also become a major military supplier to the Sudanese government, providing Khartoum with a wide variety of basic combat systems, including J-5, J-6, and F-7 combat planes (the Chinese versions of

Soviet MiG-17, -19, and -21 aircraft), Type-59 and -62 tanks, and Type-59 artillery pieces.[102] Although relatively unsophisticated compared to the arms that the United States supplies to such favorites as Israel, Saudi Arabia, and Kuwait, these weapons have given the Sudanese government a strong advantage in its combat with the insurgent forces in the south; many human rights advocates believe that the Sudanese have used them in a deliberate scorched-earth policy aimed at driving hostile tribes from oil-producing zones in the Bentiu area.[103]

China is also believed to be seeking a closer military relationship with Saudi Arabia. Beijing has provided arms to the Saudis in the past—most notably a 1988 delivery of several dozen CSS-2 "East Wind" intermediate-range ballistic missiles—but has not been a major military supplier in recent years.[104] However, with both countries seeking new strategic partners in an effort to balance American dominance in the Gulf, Riyadh and Beijing are believed to have discussed a new round of arms transactions. The Saudis are already planning to build a large refinery in China, and this project could set the stage for a reciprocal arrangement in the military field.[105]

In all these endeavors, China appears to have learned from Russia and the United States the value of using arms transfers to establish close ties and gain strategic advantage in oil-producing areas. In a sense, Beijing's behavior is an effort to catch up in a game in which it is far back in third place. Its net arms exports to the Middle East—a mere $1.6 billion worth between 1995 and 2002—barely show up next to the United States' $46.7 billion.[106] (See figure 8.) Nevertheless, some Washington analysts view these arms deliveries with rising alarm. It is particularly unnerving "that China has been securing [arms-]supplier relationships with many of the world's most odious governments," Frank Gaffney of the conservative Center for Security Policy observed in 2002, referring to Iran, Libya, and Sudan. "Needless to say, these transactions are also likely to have significant repercussions for U.S. security interests."[107]

To what extent this outlook will influence policy making in Washington is hard to predict. Right now, China's military role in the greater Gulf/Caspian area is still too small to trouble most American analysts.

But Beijing's unmistakable intention to expand its presence is a matter of enormous concern to everyone who foresees China as a challenger to American primacy there. As Bates Gill and Matthew Oresman of the Center for Strategic and International Studies have suggested, "Washington and Beijing could find themselves competing for influence in this region as their regional priorities move beyond immediate security concerns to encompass such fundamental questions as great power influence . . . and economic development and energy extraction."[108]

The stakes are high, and the risks are great. The United States faces a significant challenge to its dominance in the Persian Gulf and to its growing role in the Caspian. For China, increased influence in the region is essential to its long-term energy security. Both sides are resolute. Indeed, the U.S. invasion of Iraq, though it was driven by a number of factors, can be seen as part of a long-term drive to perpetuate America's dominance in this vital area; it can also be read (and, in Beijing, no doubt was) as a demonstration of our determination to retain control over the spigot of the Persian Gulf oil stream. China may be facing a long uphill struggle, but, given its urgent need for imported energy, it cannot afford to withdraw from the contest. And so the struggle for geopolitical advantage in the region will almost certainly intensify in the years ahead, becoming one of the main sources of friction and crisis in Sino-American relations.

When Great Powers Collide

One of the great unknowns in this evolving contest is the degree to which the three contending powers will view one another as rivals or as allies—or as some combination of both. Washington has cooperated with Moscow and Beijing in some areas and opposed them in others. Russia and China have claimed common interests in the region, but have pursued them more in word than in deed. The nightmare scenario for conservative analysts in Washington is a Sino-Russian alliance aimed at undermining American interests in the region. But it is just as easy to envision an American-Russian alliance designed to contain China, or an American-Chinese alliance against a reinvigorated Russia. Any of these

Figure 8
ARMS DELIVERIES TO THE MIDDLE EAST
BY MAJOR SUPPLIER, 1995–2002
(In millions of current U.S. dollars)

Recipient country	Supplier					
	United States	Russia	China	European	All others	Total
Algeria	0	700	200	700	300	1,900
Bahrain	900	0	0	0	0	900
Egypt	8,300	700	100	400	100	9,600
Iran	0	1,200	800	500	300	2,800
Iraq	0	0	0	100	0	100
Israel	5,900	0	0	1,000	300	7,200
Jordan	500	0	0	100	200	800
Kuwait	4,100	900	200	2,000	100	7,300
Lebanon	100	0	0	0	0	100
Libya	0	100	0	100	200	400
Morocco	100	0	0	600	100	800
Oman	0	0	0	800	300	1,100
Qatar	0	0	0	1,900	0	1,900
Saudi Arabia	25,700	0	0	38,900	0	64,600
Syria	100	200	0	300	200	800
Tunisia	100	0	0	100	0	200
U.A.E.	900	500	0	7,200	100	8,700

Recipient country	Supplier					
	United States	Russia	China	European	All others	Total
Yemen	0	300	300	600	100	1,300
Totals	46,700	4,600	1,600	55,300	2,300	110,500

Source: Richard Grimmett, *Conventional Arms Transfers to Developing Nations, 1995–2002* (Washington, D.C.: Library of Congress, Congressional Research Service, 2003), p. 59.

combinations—or a no-holds-barred competition among all three— would threaten at least one of these powers, perhaps enough to push it into harsh and dangerous countermoves.

The Sino-Russian relationship is especially unpredictable. China and Russia have cooperated in the development of the Shanghai Cooperation Organization and have collaborated in fighting Muslim extremists in Central Asia. Russia is also China's major supplier of arms and military technology—providing $1.3 billion worth between 1997 and 1999[109]— and the two countries established a "strategic partnership" in July 2000.[110] At the same time, Moscow has frustrated Chinese efforts to obtain more energy from Russia, most notably by refusing to permit the construction of a long-promised pipeline from Angarsk, in Siberia, to Daqing, in northern China.[111] As some Western analysts point out, Moscow and Beijing have little to offer each other outside the security arena, and so, in the economic realm, have favored trade with the West rather than with each other.[112]

In this precarious environment, the United States—like the other two players—will pursue every strategic advantage it can. Driven by the distorted logic of the dependency dilemma, Washington will strive to extend its influence to all corners of the Gulf/Caspian region and to eliminate every obstacle to the accelerated outflow of petroleum. In most cases, this will mean applying economic and political pressure, but it will also involve military alliances and the occasional use of force. Unable to compete on equal terms with Washington in the military arena, Moscow and

Beijing will no doubt seek to avoid direct confrontations with the United States; but they, too, will form alliances with local powers and use any means that come to hand to bolster their strategic positions. At times they may align with Washington on a particular issue; at others they may work together against American interests. None of these arrangements is likely to prove lasting. Instead, it is possible to imagine a constantly shifting set of alliances and antagonisms, much like the three-way competition between Oceania, Eurasia, and Eastasia that George Orwell portrayed in the novel *1984*. The three players may occasionally agree on such issues as terrorism and drug trafficking, but more often their interests will clash. This competitive system is inherently unstable, since all three seek advantages that can come only at the expense of one or both of the others.

All this will have enormous implications for international peace and stability. Nowhere else on earth do the vital interests of the major powers collide in this fashion, and nowhere are there so many potential sources of friction and crisis. The region is a powder keg of ethnic and religious conflicts, territorial disputes, and local power struggles. While the three main players may perceive a common interest in maintaining stability, the temptation to exploit these divisions in order to gain tactical advantage over one or the other may prove irresistible. And because all three are determined to prevail, the risks are high for a succession of the kind of crises and confrontations that rattled the Balkans prior to World War I.

In the worst possible case, this dynamic could lead to a direct confrontation between the forces of the United States and Russia or China. Unlikely as such a clash may seem, it could result from the escalation of a local struggle in which two powers support opposing sides—if, for example, American troops assisting government forces in Georgia were to come under fire from Russian-backed insurgents from the breakaway enclaves of Abkhazia or Adzharia. The scenario is improbable, but not inconceivable, given the rising level of American and Russian involvement in the Georgian civil war. And the possibilities multiply through every country suffering ethnic and religious unrest, every territorial dispute between local powers.

Not that every local flare-up will risk touching off a great-power confrontation. In some cases, the three will choose to remain neutral or allow one or two to back one side without fear of reprisal. But so long as all three great powers seek to control the world's preeminent source of petroleum, they will vie for strategic advantages. With luck, the contest will not end in a conflagration. But minor blowups and conflicts are inevitable, and with the United States, Russia, and China providing more and more arms to the belligerents, their luck could very well run out.

Escaping the Dilemma:
A Strategy for Energy Autonomy and Integrity

As a natural substance, petroleum exists in many forms. In its most desirable state, it is a free-flowing liquid material you can pump from the ground, transport over long distances, and refine into fuels and commodities. This is the petroleum that propelled the rise of modern industrial society, that exists in the popular imagination as a source of mobility, agility, and freedom: the winged stallion of the old Mobil emblem, the leaping tiger of Exxon. But petroleum can also take the form of a dense, dark, viscous material, as it does in the famous tar pits of La Brea, in central Los Angeles. In this form, it is the very opposite of freedom: it can entrap you, engulf you, kill you. For decades, the United States enjoyed all the benefits of free-flowing petroleum. But now and for the foreseeable future, we struggle under its other aspect as American forces become mired in one oil-related conflict after another.

The increasing involvement of American troops in these conflicts is an unavoidable consequence of the dependency dilemma: the reality that we need more and more imported petroleum every day to sustain a way of life that was born and established when the United States was largely self-sufficient in energy. Because most of our overseas sources of petroleum are unstable or unfriendly or both, we will continue to have to fight—

literally—to ensure our access to oil. And unlike earlier wars, in which we could withdraw our forces once the hostilities had come to an end, these encounters will require the *permanent* presence of American soldiers—for as long, that is, as we remain dependent on these sources for a significant share of our energy.

Wherever we look, American soldiers are stuck in ever-widening tar pits of oil-related conflict. The biggest contingent of these forces, of course, is trapped in the Persian Gulf area. The Bush administration would like us to believe that the invasion of Iraq and the capture of Saddam Hussein have *finally*, after all the fighting of the past, made the Gulf safe for the unhindered extraction of petroleum. Anyone who watches the nightly news knows better: the occupation of Iraq has only initiated a new phase in the decades-old struggle to control the region. Even former NSC official Kenneth Pollack—one of the most ardent and oft-cited advocates of invading Iraq—has acknowledged that the United States now confronts a security challenge in the Gulf every bit as daunting as the one it faced before. "With Saddam Hussein gone," he wrote in July 2003 in *Foreign Affairs*, "a broad rethinking of U.S. strategy toward the region is necessary, because in some ways the security problems of the Persian Gulf are now likely to get more challenging instead of less."[1] Recent events in Iraq have certainly borne this out.

The Caspian Sea is another potential quagmire. Hailed by White House officials and American oil companies as a bountiful alternative to the Persian Gulf, this region is just as volatile. Most of the post-Soviet states are governed by despots and oligarchs whose misrule invites the rebellion of all those excluded from the power and wealth that oil can bring. Ethnic and religious antagonisms sustain the ever-present perils of terrorism, sabotage, and insurgency. The United States has sought to get around these dangers by allying itself with local strongmen, like Nursultan Nazarbayev of Kazakhstan and Islam Karimov of Uzbekistan—alliances that can only deepen the risk of our getting pulled into future insurrections and civil wars.

The Gulf and the Caspian regions have yet another time bomb in common: the potential for conflicts among the great powers, arising from their competitive pursuit of strategic advantage. Such a conflagration is not likely to be deliberately ignited, but could erupt on its own when one power or another escalates a local conflict a little too carelessly. The danger is greatest right now in the former Soviet republic of Georgia, but it lies latent in other deeply divided states; the fact that the United States, Russia, and China are all deploying troops and/or military advisers in these areas deepens it that much more.

The picture is not much brighter elsewhere. Nigeria and Angola, the two most promising sources of West African oil, are embroiled in political and ethnic strife that show little sign of letting up. No American troops are stationed in the region yet, but the Department of Defense, anticipating the inevitable, has begun to search for operating bases in neighboring countries. In Colombia, U.S. military involvement is well under way, with American combat instructors helping to protect the strategic Cano Limón pipeline; as in other oil-producing states that currently harbor American forces, there are few prospects for an early withdrawal.

The United States does have some friends in these areas. Many local elites would applaud the use of American soldiers to protect the flow of oil—along with their privileged way of life. But these regions also harbor disenfranchised ethnic and political factions—in some cases, the bulk of the population—who despise the elites and hate the American forces that shore them up. So any expansion of our presence in these areas will provoke even more hostility and violence and prompt, in turn, the commitment of even bigger contingents, for even longer stays.

This deployment of American combat forces around the globe is going to place an enormous drain on our economic, military, and political resources. The bill—including the cost of keeping troops in Iraq and the Gulf, the Caspian basin, and Colombia, along with their supporting elements at home—will easily exceed $150 billion per year.[2] Given the enormity of the federal deficit and the attendant need to rein in government spending, we can sustain these expenditures only by pinching pennies at home—notably on domestic infrastructure and services, including, of course, health care and education. And then there will be the vast sums we send abroad to pay for imported petroleum, an estimated $3.5 trillion between 2001 and 2025.[3] With the American trade deficit already at precarious levels, spending on this scale will deliver a substantial blow to the American economy.

Politically and morally, the price will be just as steep. To retain our access to oil and to secure permission to deploy our troops where we deem them necessary, in such oil-rich states as Saudi Arabia, Oman, Qatar, Azerbaijan, Kazakhstan, and Uzbekistan, we will have to crawl into bed with some of the world's most corrupt and despotic leaders—plying them with ever more arms, military training, technical assistance, diplomatic support, and White House access while ignoring their contempt for democracy and their egregious human rights violations. And the numerous victims of these regimes will come to view America not as a standard-bearer of democracy but as a greedy prop of dictatorship.

These are the circumstances that breed terrorism. While anger at American support for Israel is a central source of Arab and Muslim rage, it is, as Kenneth Pollack has explained, our backing of corrupt and authoritarian governments that supplies the major impetus to rebellion. "Terrorism and internal instability in the Persian Gulf are ultimately fueled by the political, economic, and social stagnation of the local Arab states," he wrote in 2003. "Too many [ordinary people] feel powerless and humiliated by despotic governments that do less and less for them while preventing them from having any say in their own governance."[4] Militants direct their anger first at the regime in power, but, because they regard the United States—not unreasonably—as a major factor in the regime's survival, they extend their fury, and their vengeance, to American forces.

Ultimately, the cost of oil will be measured in blood: the blood of American soldiers who die in combat, and the blood of the many other casualties of oil-related violence, including the victims of terrorism. How high will it climb? No one can predict, but it will not be small. Already more than seven-hundred American soldiers have lost their lives in the invasion and occupation of Iraq, and thousands more have been wounded. The toll from oil-related terrorism, including 9/11, is even greater. A future conflict with Iran, or a protracted counterinsurgency war in Colombia or in the Caspian, would produce many, many more casualties.

Is *any* level of blood sacrifice in the protection of overseas petroleum morally justifiable? "Realist" thinkers contend, along with the members of the study group on national energy policy convened by the Center for

Strategic and International Studies, that the United States, as the world's only superpower, "must accept its special responsibilities for preserving access to worldwide energy supplies."[5] But this is not a defensible position—not when so many lives are at stake and alternatives are available.

And, in any case, not even the staunchest proponents of force can guarantee that the sacrifice of lives will actually protect the global flow of oil. As of this writing, the United States and its allies have approximately 150,000 ground troops in Iraq, yet this vast force was not able to prevent eighty-five damaging attacks on the country's major pipeline between the end of the war and the beginning of 2004.[6] Iraq's pipelines and pumping stations, like those of other large producers, are too spread out and too costly to guard on a round-the-clock basis to ever be secured from sabotage, no matter how many troops we send in. Moreover, the very *presence* of American troops makes things worse, embittering the populace and sending a steady influx of volunteers into the insurgent groups—and so escalating the threat to vital facilities even more.

It is still too early to say for sure whether, as some analysts contend, world petroleum output has indeed reached its peak level and is about to start declining. But there is no doubt at all that the day of peak production is coming, and that thereafter oil supplies will prove increasingly scarce. Two early-warning signs of such depletion materialized in early 2004, when Royal Dutch/Shell lowered its estimate of its proven reserves by 20 percent and oil-industry experts concluded that Saudi Arabia was exhausting its reserves at a faster rate than had previously been assumed.[7] True, the development of remote and previously unprofitable reserves in northern Siberia and the deep Atlantic, along with greater reliance on such unconventional sources of petroleum liquids as tar sands and shale oil, could postpone the eventual falloff in production, but they cannot prevent it. Whether this decline begins in the first or the second decade of the twenty-first century is immaterial in the long run. The point is that the world community will soon face the need for a full-scale transition from a petroleum-based economy to one powered by other sources of energy.

A great deal has been written about the impending decline in petroleum output.[8] The inevitable economic dislocation and personal hardship, no matter how wrenching and pervasive they may be, are not the worst we have to fear. As the oil supply begins to dry up, the competition for what remains will intensify, and the outbreak of conflicts over it will multiply. Any upheaval in a major producing area will provoke deep alarm in Washington and, more and more frequently, a military response. In other words, ensuring a continued supply of foreign petroleum will require an ever-increasing payment in American blood.

Is it really worth it? Will the advantages of abundant petroleum outweigh economic, military, political, and moral costs? For some Americans, the answer is no doubt yes. This, indeed, is the essence of the Bush administration's energy policy, which calls for maximizing our petroleum supply at any price. But for those who believe that fundamental values—and the safety of our young men and women in uniform—take precedence over material advantage, the only answer is no. A strategy that relies on the use of military force to slake our thirst for cheap petroleum is a strategy we cannot afford.

From Dependency to Autonomy and Integrity

What, then, is the alternative? How do we find our way out of this trap?

One approach that many politicians like to promote is energy "independence"—that is, a strategy aimed at reducing our reliance on *foreign* petroleum by increasing the exploitation of our *domestic* resources, such as oil in protected areas, coal, nuclear power, and alternatives like wind and solar energy. The concept of independence has an appealing ring for Americans. But it does not address the urgent need to prepare for the transition from a petroleum-based to a postpetroleum economy. Instead, it suggests that we can escape this inevitability by permitting the exploitation—and destruction—of America's prime wilderness areas. As I noted earlier, the untapped oil in the Arctic National Wildlife Refuge and similar sites is simply not sufficient to make up for even a small percentage of our intake of foreign petroleum, and so energy independence, as our politicians expounded it, is a travesty, a mask for our continuing *dependence* on imported energy. No amount of drilling in ANWR can stave off the day when the United States will have to commence the shift to a new energy system based on alternatives to oil.

Let me propose an alternative approach, one that has a chance of freeing us from our deepening dependency, from dangerous and immoral foreign commitments, and from the deceptive promise of independence: a national energy strategy of autonomy and integrity.

By *autonomy* I mean a situation in which we have acquired the self-reliance and freedom of action to extricate ourselves from the pernicious effects of petroleum dependency. We would not have to cease petroleum imports altogether. But we *would* have to find the will to say no to any conditions—whether in the form of diplomatic or security obligations—that come attached to the oil we want to buy. If a foreign producer were willing to sell American refiners petroleum at an affordable price and with no strings attached, they should be free to buy it. But any transaction that entailed an American security guarantee or any other political favor would be strictly off-limits.

By *integrity* I mean a state of affairs in which we make decisions on energy policy in accordance with fundamental American values and with a view to the nation's long-term interests. At the very least, integrity would require us to repudiate any arrangement with a foreign oil provider that obliged us to collude in despotism or the denial of basic human rights. It would also demand that we base any major decisions on national energy strategy on a transparent assessment of the relative advantages and disadvantages of all the available options—not the kind of secretive, industry-weighted process the Bush-Cheney administration used to come up with the *National Energy Policy* of May 2001.

Integrity also entails respect for the environment and, much more important, for the needs of future generations. While we certainly have to reduce our reliance on foreign oil producers, we're not doing ourselves, or our posterity, any favors by defacing our few remaining wilderness areas in the pursuit of an insignificant, short-term increase in domestic crude production. Nor are we promoting our nation's long-term interests by gorging ourselves on cheap oil at the expense of our children's and our grandchildren's welfare. Recognizing the obvious—that petroleum is a finite resource and that our successors are going to have to rely on other sources of energy—we have an obligation to lighten their burden by taking steps *now* to ease the way.

What would it take to implement such a strategy? In my view, achieving energy autonomy and integrity requires major progress in three areas: first, divorcing our energy purchases from our overseas security commitments; second, reducing our reliance on imported oil; and third, preparing the way for the inevitable transition to a postpetroleum economy. Before significant progress can be made on any of these fronts, however, we will have to adopt a new attitude toward petroleum—a conscious decision to place basic values and the good of the country ahead of immediate personal convenience.

Toward a "Paradigm Shift" on Energy

"Americans love energy," Secretary of Energy Spencer Abraham declared in July 2001.[9] In particular, Americans love the cheap and convenient energy provided by unending streams of liquid petroleum. Every year, the citizens of this country consume more oil than the year before, and their appetite for the stuff shows no sign of abating. Convincing people to consume *less*, and to begin preparing for the day of petroleum scarcity, will no doubt prove a formidable task. Consider, for example, that automakers reported an increase in sales of large, gas-guzzling pickup trucks and SUVs in early 2004, despite record-high gasoline prices.

Secretary Abraham also said, "The American people know that we are too dependent on foreign oil."[10] This is true as well. Most Americans understand, on some gut level, that we rely far too much on petroleum from the Middle East, and that we are destined to pay an ever-increasing price in blood to acquire it. We also know, in our heart of hearts, that the only way to reduce our consumption of imported petroleum is to reduce our consumption of oil, period. But we are not likely to change our fundamental behavior—to start relying less on conventional automobiles and other oil-powered devices—unless there is a dramatic change in national attitudes about individual and societal energy behavior. We need, in short, to undergo what sociologists call a *paradigm shift*—a complete rethinking of our basic outlook on this critical issue.

Americans have experienced paradigm shifts before. Not so very long ago, few people saw anything reprehensible about tobacco smoking in public; today, most Americans support legislation to ban smoking in public places. So we are perfectly capable of major alterations in our thinking. But such transformations do not occur by themselves: they require vigorous effort on the part of both national leaders and grassroots activists to convince us of the need for dramatic change. Remember, it was the repeated appeals of Surgeon General Dr. C. Everett Koop and other medical professionals that finally convinced Congress to impose the earliest restrictions on smoking. Persuading us to consume less petroleum will necessitate an even greater effort—but it must, and can, be done.

As the tobacco experience demonstrates, a fundamental shift in values requires dedicated leadership at both the national and local levels. But whereas we can see the emergence of grassroots leadership on the petroleum issue, there is still no national leadership. Small but influential groups of clergy, for example, have begun to portray the profligate consumption of petroleum as an offense to God's creation. "What Would Jesus Drive?" is the message affixed to placards carried by a coalition of Christian and Jewish religious leaders who have been lobbying officials of the Big Three automakers to boost the fuel-efficiency of their vehicles.[11] On a personal level, tens of thousands of Americans have turned in their old gas-guzzlers for hybrid vehicles, and more are joining them all the time; other people have begun biking to work or have lobbied for improved public transportation.[12] These, and other such initiatives, suggest that support for change is growing. In the absence of parallel efforts at the national level, however, a genuine transformation in our energy behavior is unlikely to occur.

Eventually, circumstances will *force us* to change our ways—the days of petroleum plenty will not last forever. But the sooner we begin this process, the fewer the lives that will be sacrificed in the pursuit of foreign oil and the greater the eventual rewards for our children and grandchildren. Hence, every effort must be made to persuade our leaders at every level to commence the process of transformation. Once *this* has been accomplished, we will be able to move quickly to implement the principal features of an alternative strategy, as sketched out below.

Separating Energy Policy
from Our Overseas Security Commitments

The first step is to detach our pursuit of energy from any commitments to foreign governments for military protection and security assistance. I certainly do not mean that the United States should forswear alliances and security arrangements with like-minded democratic states for defending against a mutual threat, on the order of NATO during the cold-war era. But, as I have shown in these pages, we have repeatedly armed and otherwise protected repugnant, undemocratic regimes for the sole purpose of getting our hands on their oil. Such arrangements have cost us untold hundreds of billions of dollars, thousands of American lives, and a good deal of our moral integrity. Now they threaten to entangle us in one protracted oil war after another in some of the world's most punishing and hostile areas.

In other words, the U.S. government needs to impose a blanket proscription on any security commitment whose primary purpose is to ensure our access to a country's energy deposits. Again, I am not ruling out military alliances with friendly nations for legitimate reasons. And I do not oppose purchasing a nation's exportable energy through ordinary commercial channels. But the United States must no longer agree to help defend any foreign state or regime *as a condition* of access to oil.

It is important here to distinguish between diplomatic relations and security commitments. We can and should maintain diplomatic ties with a wide variety of foreign governments. But that is very different from promising to come to their assistance should they find themselves under attack. Banning such commitments would in no way preclude our rushing to the aid of victims of armed aggression, in accordance with the UN Charter. What it *would* preclude is oil-for-protection agreements between the United States and our overseas petroleum suppliers.

While eschewing new arrangements of this sort, we must also extricate ourselves from those we have already agreed to. The most significant of these is our unseemly alliance with Saudi Arabia, which, from the very beginning, has rested on the understanding that the United States would defend the House of Saud against both foreign and domestic enemies in return for privileged access to Saudi oil. This arrangement must now be terminated. We cannot and should not bear the ultimate responsibility for the royal family's survival.

I am not suggesting, of course, that the United States sever its security relationship with Saudi Arabia overnight. But Washington could easily commit itself to helping Riyadh build up its self-defense capabilities during a designated transition period—say, two to three years. At the end of this period, all American military advisers would be withdrawn from the kingdom and all existing security guaranties nullified. If a democratic government should someday come to power—the country would no longer be "Saudi Arabia" at that point, since that name designates the Saud family's ownership of the country—the United States could offer it the same sort of cooperative military ties it has established with other democratic nations.

Likewise for the other Persian Gulf oil kingdoms: any agreement, formal or otherwise, by the United States to automatically defend these countries and their feudal regimes against internal or external attack should come to an end. Instead, Washington can assist them in improving their own self-defense forces while encouraging them to bolster the joint defense capabilities of the Gulf Cooperation Council (GCC), the mutual-assistance organization that Bahrain, Kuwait, Oman, Qatar, Saudi Arabia, and the United Arab Emirates established in 1981. These countries all rely on oil for their economic survival, and so *they* should assume the primary responsibility for its uninterrupted flow. The United States can assist them—for example, by helping them set up a joint air-defense network or a tanker protection fleet. But we should make no promises of military intervention on their behalf.

Iraq poses a more challenging situation, but essentially a similar one. Right now, the United States and its coalition partners are obligated by international law to provide both internal and external security for the Iraqi people. But Washington should turn over the primary responsibility for internal security to an Iraqi-led force, with American forces remaining in a rapidly diminishing supporting role under United Nations oversight. Once a legitimate, democratically chosen government has assumed power, our military role should be confined to participation in UN-mandated efforts to prevent the restoration of Iraq's WMD capabilities.

With all this in mind, it is time for the United States to begin dismantling the elaborate military infrastructure it has established in the greater Gulf area. The Central Command maintains dozens of bases and storage facilities in Bahrain, Iraq, Kuwait, Oman, Qatar, Saudi Arabia, and the United Arab Emirates, and has deposited immense quantities of arms and military systems in them. They cost the American public many billions of dollars a year—a hidden tax on the price of gasoline that few politicians mention—and vastly increase the temptation to use military force in any regional crisis. They should now be closed.

What about the risk that one of the Gulf states—Iran, say—might take advantage of our withdrawal to gain a strategic advantage by impeding the flow of oil through the Persian Gulf? Realistically speaking, such a scenario is implausible, since every one of these countries, Iran included, relies on the sale of oil to keep its economy afloat; a move of this nature would be the equivalent of committing economic suicide. That said, the GCC countries certainly need to establish a joint naval escort fleet to deter or respond to any such a threat. In an emergency, the United States might contribute ships to a multilateral force under the auspices of the United Nations and the GCC; but the initial burden of defense should fall on the Gulf states themselves.

The same approach should govern our behavior in the Caspian Sea basin. We are just now establishing a substantial infrastructure there, with new bases in Uzbekistan and Kyrgyzstan and growing military ties with Azerbaijan, Georgia, and Kazakhstan. To the degree that these arrangements counter the threat of Al Qaeda, we should retain them—on a temporary basis. But we should disavow anything more, and particularly any defense of the energy flow. We should encourage these states, too, to develop mutual security mechanisms for their common defense, possibly in conjunction with NATO and the Shanghai Cooperation Organization. We could also assist in the development of a multilateral Caspian Sea naval force to defend the region against terrorism, illicit arms trafficking, and drug smuggling. But we absolutely must not—and make it clear that we *will* not—assume responsibility for the survival of the region's authoritarian rulers.

The same basic logic should apply to major oil suppliers in other regions: Washington must refuse to provide military support in return for access to oil, but could assist these states, as appropriate, in enhancing their self-defense capabilities and forming regional cooperative security arrangements. In no case should we provide troops for the protection of refineries and pipelines or deploy military instructors along pipeline routes in active combat zones like the Arauca region of Colombia. And we must abide by our own human rights legislation and deny military aid to any government guilty of egregious violations.

Most important of all, we must disavow the notion that, as the world's sole superpower, we bear special responsibilities for preserving access to worldwide energy supplies. Since all countries—sellers as well as buyers—benefit from the unimpeded commerce in energy, all countries should assist to some degree in defending major international passageways from piracy and armed attack. We might choose to participate in such efforts on a cooperative basis with other nations—for example, in the establishment of a multilateral oil-tanker escort fleet—but we should neither assume the paramount responsibility for managing such activities nor conduct them on our own.

Together, these steps would greatly diminish the risk of our becoming militarily enmeshed in any overseas conflict that is of no other concern to the United States than its impact on the regional flow of petroleum. Not only would this approach save the lives of many American soldiers; it would roll back military expenditures and allow the Pentagon to concentrate on its primary job of providing for the nation's defense. Given that so much of the hatred for our country stems from Washington's support for oil-besotted potentates like the Saudi royal family, such a strategy would also diminish our vulnerability to international terrorism. Admittedly, it would not provide absolute protection against all dangers. No strategy would. But it offers the best prospect of eliminating the terrible risk that American forces will become ensnared in one bloody oil conflict after another.

Reducing Our Dependence on Imported Oil

The next step is to overcome our addiction to foreign petroleum. We do not have to cease importing foreign oil altogether. But we do have to get to a position of sufficient self-reliance that we can say no to unacceptable oil-for-protection deals without fearing terrible economic consequences. The goal is to reach the point where our national security and well-being are no longer tied to the survival of the Saudi royal family or any other petro-regime in the developing world. Energy autonomy is a prerequisite for freedom of action in the international political arena.

And the sole way to become less dependent on imported petroleum is to practice energy self-restraint. Because we cannot possibly compensate for diminished imports by increasing production at home (even if we *do* tear up our last protected wilderness areas), the only sure way to reduce our oil imports is to reduce our consumption of oil. There is simply no other way to achieve greater self-reliance in the energy sphere.[13]

Reining in our consumption of petroleum would benefit both the economy and the environment. If by 2010 we were to reduce our oil imports to the 1990 level—approximately 7.2 million barrels per day—we would save approximately $90 billion per year (unless the cost of oil were to stay above $35 per barrel, in which case we would save even more) and much larger amounts in following years.[14] Moreover, we would release 174 million *fewer* metric tons of carbon dioxide into the atmosphere, radically slowing the accumulation of greenhouse gases and thus reducing the severity of global climate change.[15]

Transportation accounts for approximately two-thirds of America's net oil consumption; it also happens to be the easiest type of petroleum use to control. (Other modes of oil consumption, notably industrial uses, petro-chemicals, and home heating, are likely to prove far more resistant to restriction.) The key here is light-duty vehicles—automobiles, minivans, SUVs, and pickup trucks—which together account for approximately 60 percent of all transportation-related petroleum consumption in this country.[16] Improvements in the fuel efficiency of heavy trucks, buses, and aircraft are important, too, but real progress toward energy self-sufficiency will have to begin with America's mammoth fleets of light-duty vehicles.

Reducing their oil consumption has been the focus of a great deal of research in recent years, and the results can be grouped into four basic approaches: first, improvement in the fuel efficiency of existing vehicles; second, the introduction of nonpetroleum fuels (especially ethanol) for existing engines; third, new and improved forms of automobile propulsion, especially hybrid (gas/electric) engines and hydrogen-powered fuel cells; and, fourth, the far more widespread use of mass transit.[17]

The United States has already mandated some improvements in the fuel efficiency of its light vehicles, thanks to the Energy Policy and Conservation Act of 1975, which set Corporate Average Fuel Efficiency (CAFE) standards. Essentially, CAFE standards require that manufacturers meet efficiency goals, as measured in miles traveled per gallon of gasoline consumed (mpg) and averaged for the entire fleet they produce. (A manufacturer may sell some vehicles with low mpg ratings if it sells enough high-mpg vehicles to raise the fleet-wide average above the minimum CAFE standard.) The 1975 act also assigned different rating systems to conventional automobiles and "light trucks," a category that includes SUVs and pickup trucks. In 2003, the fleet-wide average minimum requirement was 27.5 mpg for automobiles and 20.7 mpg for light trucks.[18]

The CAFE standards have been an extraordinarily effective tool for reducing our petroleum consumption. According to the National Research Council, manufacturer compliance with CAFE standards saved the United States an estimated 2.8 million barrels of oil per day in 2001.[19] Since approximately 55 percent—or about 1.5 million barrels—of that oil would have had to come from abroad, we reduced our consumption of imports by nearly 550 million barrels in that one year. So far so good. But there is a joker in the CAFE deck: the legal distinction between automobiles and light trucks. In 1975, when the standards were adopted, light trucks accounted for a relatively small share of the market—SUVs had not yet been introduced. By 2001, they accounted for more than half of light-vehicle sales in the United States; and because they have lower average mpg requirements than do automobiles, the average fuel efficiency of America's light-vehicle fleet has *fallen* in recent years.[20]

Obviously, the CAFE standards need to be strengthened. Even more important, the distinction between automobiles and light trucks must be eliminated or at least modified enough so that light-truck mpg requirements more fairly resemble those for automobiles. In addition, the minimum fuel-efficiency requirements for the combined light-vehicle fleet must be elevated. There are any number of ways to make vehicles more gasoline-efficient: improved engines, better aerodynamics, lighter materials, and so on.[21] How to increase efficiency is something for the manufacturers to decide, but the ultimate goal should be to *double* our fuel savings—thereby reducing our total petroleum usage by an estimated 5 million barrels per day, or 1.8 billion barrels per year.[22]

A second way of reducing our oil dependence is by substituting alternative fuels, including ethanol, for gasoline in existing types of vehicles.[23] Ethanol, or ethyl alcohol, is the colorless liquid produced by the fermentation of sugar or starch; it is the primary ingredient of most alcoholic beverages. American automobile engineers learned early on that ethanol could power internal-combustion engines, but gasoline largely displaced it because crude petroleum was easier and cheaper to convert into gasoline than corn and other grains into alcohol. A great deal of research must still be conducted as to how to bring down both the cost and the amount of energy it takes to manufacture ethanol.[24*]

Another part of the solution is the development and introduction of new types of vehicles and vehicle propulsion, especially hybrids, fuel-efficient diesel engines, and hydrogen-powered fuel cells. Hybrid vehicles combine a small, highly efficient gasoline engine with a battery-driven electric motor; the motor propels the car at low speeds and provides additional thrust at higher speeds. The heat energy generated when the vehicle breaks recharges the batteries, which—unlike those in battery-only electrical vehicles—do not require an external electrical source for this

---

*At present, most ethanol comes from the fermentation of corn, a process that consumes up to seven gallons of oil for every eight gallons of alcohol it creates. Clearly, this is not a viable solution to America's energy dilemma. Proponents of ethanol claim that with the development of genetically engineered microorganisms for use as biocatalysts, virtually any plant ("biomass") could serve as the raw material for the manufacture of ethanol. This (still unproven) technology would reduce the cost of manufacturing large quantities of ethanol so prodigiously that it should be given careful consideration and, if it proves viable, public support.

purpose. These vehicles consume far less petroleum than conventional automobiles do; the Toyota Prius, for example, can travel more than fifty miles on a single gallon of gasoline.[25] Road-ready hybrids are already available from Toyota and Honda; Ford and General Motors plan to introduce their own models as early as 2004.[26] Public policy should promote these vehicles first by providing tax breaks to consumers who buy them, and second, by lowering the allowable carbon-dioxide emissions level for *all* cars and trucks.

Fuel-efficient diesel engines hold nearly as much promise. Modern diesel-powered vehicles in Europe—where they make up about 40 percent of the new cars on the road—are one-third more fuel efficient than comparable gasoline models, and they produce far fewer pollutants than older diesels. They will need to produce even fewer before they can satisfy the United States' clean-air laws, but if they can manage to do so, their introduction here could significantly reduce our petroleum consumption.[27]

The widespread introduction of hydrogen-powered fuel cells may achieve even larger reductions in petroleum use. Like ordinary batteries, fuel cells generate electricity through a chemical reaction; but where traditional batteries stop generating electricity once their chemical reagents run out, fuel cells can keep operating for almost as long as their chemical fuel source—in most cases, hydrogen—is renewed; and since hydrogen is the most plentiful element in the known universe, its supply is limitless. The existing designs are still too heavy and cumbersome to be used in automobiles, but lighter and more efficient versions could very well power the cars of tomorrow.[28] (Because hydrogen is likely to play such a critical role in the transition to a postpetroleum economy, I will return to this subject in the next section.)

Finally, and most obviously: we urgently need to be using mass transit for routine commuting and for travel between cities as well. Americans' devotion to their private automobiles is well known, and yet experience has shown that people are willing to switch to rail and bus systems for their daily commute—*if* these systems are made efficient, comfortable, attractive, and affordable. Some cities, notably Washington, D.C., and

Portland, Oregon, have made real progress in this regard, but it is going to take much more effort and investment to attract enough commuters for mass transit to make much of a dent in our petroleum use. Likewise, ultrafast rail lines need to be constructed as an alternative to cars and planes for long-distance travel. Amtrak's Acela service in the northeastern United States has been successful and should be extended to other parts of the country, along with even faster trains, like the 186-mile-per-hour TGV already in use in France.

None of these approaches by itself has the capacity to diminish our petroleum consumption to the point of true energy autonomy. Some of them are going to take years of development to achieve their full promise (if they ever do). But they all offer potential paths to autonomy, and therefore deserve sustained public support. And if, at some future point, technological innovation leads to a significant breakthrough in one or another of these approaches, it should receive that much more backing.

Hastening the Transition to a Postpetroleum Economy

Both of these broad efforts—the separation of our energy policy from our foreign policy and the reduction of our day-to-day consumption of oil—are part of a larger and most urgent enterprise: the beginnings of the transition to the postpetroleum economy we are going to have to embrace in the not too distant future. By *postpetroleum economy*, I do not mean one in which oil will completely disappear from our lives. But the global petroleum supply will eventually dwindle, and, on top of that, the environmental consequences of unrestrained petroleum use—higher temperatures, rising sea levels, and punishing storms—will eventually become unbearable. That an energy transition *will* occur in the decades ahead is no longer a matter of debate at all. Even President Bush, in his 2003 State of the Union address, acknowledged that the United States must take steps now to prepare for the eventual switch from petroleum to hydrogen as our major source of transportation energy.[29] But Bush proposed spending a mere $1.2 billion on the development of hydrogen propulsion—far, far less than what researchers and innovators will require to effect a transition of this magnitude. We now need to invest much greater amounts in the development of new fuels and to speed up the introduction of alternative transportation systems.

What we need most at this point, though, is a comprehensive blueprint for the postpetroleum era—which is exactly what Vice President Cheney and his cronies on the NEPDG *should* have produced, instead of their dangerous and deluded plan for more of the same. Fortunately, many scientists and engineers are working hard to fill this need.[30] One particularly impressive project is the ten-point plan of the Apollo Alliance—a coalition of labor, environmental, and civic groups—which, emphasizing big investment in hybrids, alternative energy, and hydrogen generation, offers a credible road map for future development.[31] (Many of these proposals were also endorsed by Senator John Kerry, the 2004 Democratic Party presidential candidate.) The planning for a hydrogen economy being conducted by Amory Lovins at the Rocky Mountain Institute of Snowmass, Colorado, is also encouraging.[32] It will be some years before the best features of these plans are brought together in one integrated blueprint, but we can already make out its essential components: the development of hydrogen fuel; increased reliance on wind, solar, biomass, and other renewable sources of energy; and the development of new construction methods, transportation systems, and land-use patterns.

I cannot elaborate in detail here on all of these points. But let me say a few words about each of them.

First, on the potential of hydrogen. It probably holds the most promise for replacing oil with an abundant, affordable, and nonpolluting source of energy,[33] and ambitious efforts are now under way around the world to explore its use in a wide variety of applications.[34] The U.S. Department of Energy, for example, has embarked on a $1.7 billion "FreedomCAR"—Cooperative Automotive Research—and fuel initiative aimed at developing hydrogen-powered fuel cells, hydrogen production and delivery infrastructure, and advanced automotive technologies.[35] Hydrogen is the principal energy source for vehicular fuel cells; most of the major automobile companies have announced plans to manufacture cars, vans, and buses powered by these cells, and some test vehicles are already on the road.[36] Conceivably, fuel-cell cars could begin to replace gasoline-powered ones in another decade or so.[37] But although there are plenty of reasons to be optimistic about hydrogen-powered fuel cells, they are still very much in the experimental stage. Hydrogen is expensive to generate; it does not exist in a pure state in nature, so it has to be extracted from other materials, such as coal or water. It cannot be stored or transported through the existing oil-industry infrastructure, including America's roughly 180,000 service stations. And producing hydrogen may require large amounts of fossil fuels, either as raw material or as a source of energy for the process itself—thereby defeating the whole purpose.[38] Meeting these challenges is going to take very substantial public investment.

Renewable sources of energy, including wind, solar, and biomass, all have their advantages and disadvantages. Wind power is commercially viable in areas where the winds are steady and giant windmills do not interfere with other activities or land uses; but the most eligible locations lie in the extreme north, far from population and industrial centers. Solar energy is plentiful, and the technology to capture it is well developed—but the price is high. Biomass may be the most promising renewable energy source. Agriculture produces large amounts of waste that can be burned or converted into liquid fuel (such as ethanol), and virgin or fallow lands could be used to grow crops for this purpose. Devoting large agricultural tracts to fuel crops, however, could undermine global food production, especially as the world's population balloons. It is going to take much more effort to bring down the costs of these approaches and to deal with the problems they entail, but we have no choice: these renewable sources of energy will be essential components of the postpetroleum economy.[39]

Energy experts and industry officials will no doubt also advocate more controversial sources of energy for this transition—especially nuclear power and liquid fuels derived from coal. Both have their proponents and, needless to say, their detractors. Environmentalists condemn nuclear power because it produces highly poisonous wastes that are difficult (some say impossible) to store safely; they condemn coal because, despite its abundance in the United States, it produces vast amounts of carbon residues that will accumulate in the atmosphere unless someone finds some practical way of storing, or "sequestering," them. Proponents of both argue that we can safely deal with the wastes and by-products. This is not the place to evaluate the competing claims—except to say that we would be foolhardy to rely too extensively on either nuclear power or coal until we have made far more progress in neutralizing their drawbacks.[40]

And, finally, the American political establishment will have to change its attitude toward transportation and land-use planning. Without government-sponsored research, incentives, and mandates, the transition to a postpetroleum economy will never get off the ground. Hydrogen-powered buses, urban light-rail systems, and intercity rail connections—to cite just a few examples—are not going to pay off in the short run, whatever they may promise for the long run. In other words, they are not going to happen unless the government puts certain systems and rules into place. To begin with, it will have to devise new zoning ordinances and land-use regulations to discourage low-density sprawl and promote clustered development around light-rail stations and major transportation hubs—a settlement pattern that will also facilitate the construction of the kinds of civic linkages and services that dispersed suburban settings usually lack.[41]

Change on this scale costs money—lots of it. The price tag on developing new fuels and propulsion systems and constructing a high-speed rail system will run into the hundreds of billions of dollars. Where is all of this money going to come from? There is a simple, if stringent, solution: a surtax on gasoline consumption. I propose the establishment of a tax—the National Energy Security Enhancement Tax—on every gallon of oil consumed for ground transportation in this country. Such a tax, beginning at perhaps twenty-five cents per gallon and eventually reaching several times that amount, would finance virtually all the improvements needed to reduce this country's dependence on foreign petroleum. It would provide the funds for research on new engines and transportation systems. The increased expense of gasoline would force automobile owners to drive less and rely more on alternative means of getting around—leading to a decrease in imports of foreign petroleum (and of the outflow of dollars to foreign oil producers), and a concomitant curb on the buildup of carbon dioxide in the atmosphere. The higher taxes would, no doubt, produce serious economic hardship for some citizens; those who would suffer disproportionately—notably farmers and long-distance truckers—would have to be afforded adequate relief, possibly through a special credit on their income taxes. But the overall benefits would be huge, and let us never forget: every decline in our consumption of imported petroleum will bring with it a reduction in the blood tax we will otherwise have to pay for the protection of all that oil.

To share the burden of the transition, the United States needs to encourage international cooperation in the development of alternative fuels and transportation systems. In particular, we should invite other wealthy nations to join us in the development of hybrid vehicles, hydrogen fuel cells, ultrafast rail systems, and other promising technologies. Europe and Japan are particularly well positioned to work with us in these areas; but we should also reach out to China, the most economically dynamic nation in the world today. By collaborating with China, we can both share the expense of progress in the development of energy-saving technologies *and* reduce the risk of oil-related conflict between us: a win-win situation.

Soon enough, the world will begin to suffer severe and persistent shortages of conventional petroleum. It may not happen for ten, fifteen, or twenty years—but it will happen. We can spend the intervening years gorging ourselves on our own dwindling petroleum and fighting over what remains abroad. Or we can work with other countries to develop alternative energy systems and to devise contingency plans for allocating the available oil supply in the approaching era of crisis and scarcity. Increased international cooperation is thus a critical—an indispensable—component in the strategy of autonomy and integrity.

Beyond the Dependency Dilemma

The Bush administration commenced its spring 2001 review of energy policy at a critical juncture in American history. We had just passed the 50 percent mark in our reliance on imported petroleum and were headed toward even greater dependence in the future. And although 9/11 was still several months away, it was obvious to anyone who looked that resentment of America's conspicuous presence in the oil-producing regions of the Middle East was building toward an explosion. The administration's

National Energy Policy Development Group fully acknowledged these ominous trends. But when the moment of truth finally arrived, the group took the coward's way out, clinging to the status quo rather than accepting responsibility for leading the nation in a new and, undeniably, challenging direction. As a result, we have become even *more* deeply entangled in overseas oil conflicts and have lost precious time in devising a forward-looking energy strategy.

Despite this serious setback, we can still move beyond the worst, most self-deluded features of the Bush-Cheney plan and take the necessary steps to ensure our future safety and well-being. As I have argued, the best strategy for achieving this goal is one that seeks to reduce American dependence on imported oil and to sever the links between our energy behavior and our overseas security commitments. This strategy of autonomy and integrity will allow us to satisfy our basic energy requirements without spilling the blood of our soldiers in the ultimately futile protection of overseas petro-regimes and pipelines. It will also speed the development of the new fuels and transportation technologies that we can rely on once the world's supply of conventional petroleum begins to contract.

The way ahead is clear. We must repudiate the false promise of the Bush-Cheney energy plan and select the path of autonomy, self-restraint, and innovation. If we strengthen our resolve, accept a degree of self-discipline, and embrace the new technologies, we will escape the trap of dependency and establish a secure, sustainable, and responsible energy system; if we fail to do these things, we will condemn ourselves to rising bloodshed abroad and hardship at home. The choice is ours. The time of decision is now. It is not too late to abandon our allegiance to oil at any cost and embark on a new energy path. But it might soon be.

NOTES

1: THE DEPENDENCY DILEMMA

1. For background on Centcom and the other regional commands, see Dana Priest, *The Mission* (New York: Norton, 2003).

2. For background on these events, see Michael A. Palmer, *Guardians of the Gulf* (New York: Free Press, 1992), pp. 101–11.

3. For background on Centcom, see Jay E. Hines, "History of U.S. Central Command," U.S. Central Command, electronic document accessed at www.centcom.mil/aboutus/history1.htm on November 21, 2003.

4. J. H. Binford Peay, "Promoting Peace and Stability in the Central Region," report to the House Appropriations Committee Subcommittee on National Security, March 17, 1997, electronic document accessed at www.centcom.mil/execsum.html on August 6, 1997.

5. From an official announcement delivered by Assistant Secretary of State Richard W. Murphy, as cited in Palmer, *Guardians of the Gulf*, p. 123. For background on these events, see ibid., pp. 128–49.

6. From the transcript of Bush's address in the *New York Times*, August 9, 1991.

7. For background on these developments, see Hines, "History of U.S. Central Command"; Palmer, *Guardians of the Gulf*, pp. 228–42.

8. See chapter 4.

9. See Eric Watkins, "U.S. to Deploy Airborne Snipers to Protect Iraqi Pipelines," *Oil and Gas Journal*, October 13, 2003, p. 37.

10. See chapter 5.

11. Edward L. Morse, "A New Political Economy of Oil?" *Journal of International Affairs* 53, no. 1 (Fall 1999): 2.

12. U.S. Department of Energy, Energy Information Administration (DoE/EIA), *Annual Energy Outlook 2004* (Washington, D.C.: DoE/EIA, 2004), tables A1, A2, pp. 133, 135. (Hereinafter cited as DoE/EIA, *AEO 2004*.)

13. Ibid., table A1, p. 133.

14. The best single history on the rise of the U.S. petroleum industry and its impact on the nation's economy remains Daniel Yergin's *The Prize* (New York: Simon and Schuster, 1993).

15. Again, I am indebted to Yergin's *The Prize* for his vivid portrait of the "Hydrocarbon Age" (pp. 389–560).

16. For background on the relationship between oil and military power, see David S. Painter, "Oil," in Alexander DeConde, Richard Dean Burns, and Frederik Logevall, editors, *Encyclopedia of American Foreign Policy*, 2nd ed., vol. 3 (New York: Charles Scribner's Sons, 2002), pp. 1–20.

17. Robert E. Ebel, "The Geopolitics of Energy into the 21st Century," remarks to the open forum, U.S. Department of State, Washington, D.C., April 30, 2002, electronic document accessed at www.state.gov/s/p/of/proc/tr/10187.htm on July 1, 2002.

18. For background and discussion, see Yergin, *The Prize*, pp. 303–88; Painter, "Oil," pp. 3–4.

19. Spencer Abraham, remarks before the American Petroleum Institute, Dallas, Texas, n.d. (June 2002), electronic document accessed at www.energy.gov/HQDocs/speeches/2002/junss/AmericanPetroleumInstitute_v.html on August 6, 2002.

20. U.S. Department of Energy, Energy Information Administration (DoE/EIA), "Annual Energy Review 2000," electronic document accessed at www.eia.doe.gov/emeu/aer/txt on September 17, 2002.

21. U.S. Department of Energy, Energy Information Administration (DoE/EIA), *International Energy Outlook 2003* (Washington, D.C.: DoE/EIA, 2003), tables A4 and D4, pp. 185, 238. (Hereinafter cited as DoE/EIA, *IEO 2003*.)

22. DoE/EIA, *AEO 2004*, table A11, p. 150.

23. For a discussion and assessment of these dangers, see Robert E. Ebel, project director, *The Geopolitics of Energy into the 21st Century*, a report of the CSIS Strategic Energy Initiative, vols. 1 and 3 (Washington, D.C.: Center for Strategic and International Studies, 2002).

24. Spencer Abraham, comments before the House International Relations Committee, Washington, D.C., June 20, 2002, electronic document accessed at www.house.gov/international_relations/abra0620.htm on June 28, 2002.

25. For background, see David S. Painter, *Oil and the American Century* (Baltimore: Johns Hopkins University Press, 1986), pp. 37–51; Michael B. Stoff, *Oil, War, and American Security* (New Haven: Yale University Press, 1980).

26. For background on these developments, see Painter, *Oil and the American Century*, pp. 75–127; Palmer, *Guardians of the Gulf*, pp. 40–84.

27. See chapter 2 for further explication of this point.

28. DoE/EIA, "Annual Energy Review 2000."

29. For a compendium of diverse views on this topic, see "Fueling the 21st Century: The New Political Economy of Energy," a special issue of the *Journal of International Affairs* 53, no. 1 (Fall 1999).

30. See, for example, Sarah A. Emerson, "Resource Plenty," *Harvard International Review*, Summer 1997, pp. 12–15, 64–65.

31. For a thorough airing of the choices facing the United States at this time, see Independent Task Force on Strategic Energy Policy, *Strategic Energy Policy: Challenges for the Twenty-first Century* (Houston: James A. Baker III Institute for Public Policy, Rice University, 2001).

32. Headed by former secretary of defense James R. Schlesinger and former senator Sam Nunn, the task force placed special emphasis on the need to use force if necessary to ensure "open access" to the Persian Gulf. Ebel, *The Geopolitics of Energy into the 21st Century*, vol. 1, pp. 24, 30.

33. "Remarks by the President in Photo Opportunity After Meeting with National Energy Policy Development Groups," Washington, D.C., March 19, 2001, electronic document accessed at www.whitehouse.gov on March 5, 2003.

34. Remarks by President George W. Bush to Capital City Partnership, River Centre Convention Center, St. Paul, Minn., May 17, 2001, electronic document accessed at www.whitehouse.gov on May 17, 2001.

35. All data from DoE/EIA, *AEO 2004*, table A11, p. 150.

36. The 345-billion-barrel estimate, which includes 171 billion barrels already consumed between 1859 and 1995 plus 32 billion barrels in known reserves, 76 billion barrels in anticipated additions to known fields, and 66 billion barrels in anticipated new discoveries, is found in U.S. Geological Survey (USGS), *USGS World Petroleum Assessment 2000*, electronic document accessed at greenwood.er.usgs.gov/energy/World_Energy/DDS-60/index.html on July 8, 2002.

37. For background and discussion, see Kenneth S. Deffeyes, *Hubbert's Peak: The Impending World Oil Shortage* (Princeton: Princeton University Press, 2001).

38. DoE/EIA, *AEO 2004*, tables A7 and A11, pp. 144, 150.

39. Ibid., table A7, p. 144; DoE/EIA, *IEO 2003*, table A4, p. 185.

40. Testimony of Stuart E. Eizenstat before the House Committee on International Relations (HCIR), Washington, D.C., June 20, 2002, electronic document accessed at www.house.gov/international_relations/eize0620.htm on June 28, 2002.

41. DoE/EIA, *AEO 2004*, table A11, p. 150.

42. For background and discussion, see International Energy Agency (IEA), *World Energy Outlook 2002* (Paris: IEA, 2002), pp. 69–73, 89–102. (Hereinafter cited as IEA, *World Energy Outlook 2002*.)

43. Testimony of Eizenstat before the HCIR, June 20, 2002.

44. Ebel, *The Geopolitics of Energy into the 21st Century*, vol. 3, p. 37.

45. On the May 1, 2004, Saudi attack, which occurred in the oil-production hub of Yanbu, see Neil MacFarquhar, "After Attack, Company's Staff Plans to Leave Saudi Arabia," *New York Times*, May 3, 2004. See also chapter 4 for further discussion of this point.

46. For discussion of these effects, see Terry Lynn Karl, *The Paradox of Plenty* (Berkeley: University of California Press, 1997).

47. Ebel, *The Geopolitics of Energy into the 21st Century*, vol. 1, p. 11. The term *petro-states* is taken from Karl, *The Paradox of Plenty*.

48. U.S. Department of Energy, Energy Information Administration (DoE/EIA), *International Energy Outlook 2004* (Washington, D.C.: DoE/EIA, 2004), table A4, p. 167. (Hereinafter cited as DoE/EIA, *IEO 2004*.)

49. For discussion of peak oil and its harsh consequences, see Colin J. Campbell and Jean H. Laherrère, "The End of Cheap Oil," *Scientific American*, March 1998, pp. 78–83; Deffeyes, *Hubbert's Peak*; David Goodstein, *Out of Gas* (New York: Norton, 2004); Richard Heinberg, *The Party's Over* (Gabriola Island, British Columbia: New Society, 2003); Paul Roberts, *The End of Oil* (Boston: Houghton Mifflin, 2004). For a more optimistic scenario, see "Oil Resources in the 21st Century: What Shortage?" in U.S. Department of Energy, Energy Information Administration (DoE/EIA), *International Energy Outlook 2002* (Washington, D.C.: DoE/EIA, 2002), pp. 25–26; Emerson, "Resource Plenty," pp. 12–15, 64–65.

50. For discussion, see Klare, "Arms Transfers to Iran and Iraq During the Iran-Iraq War of 1980–88 and the Origins of the Gulf War," in Andrew J. Bacevich and Efraim Inbar, editors, *The Gulf War of 1991 Reconsidered* (London: Frank Cass, 2003), pp. 3–24.

2: LETHAL EMBRACE

1. BP, *Statistical Review of World Energy 2003* (London: BP, 2003), p. 4.

2. Stoff, *Oil, War, and American Security*, p, 209.

3. Data from ibid., p. 73.

4. Harold F. Williamson, Ralph L. Andreano, Arnold R. Daum, and Gilbert C. Klose, *The American Petroleum Industry: The Age of Energy, 1899–1950* (Evanston, Ill.: Northwestern University Press, 1959), p. 748.

5. Painter, *Oil and the American Century*, pp. 34–35, 96–98. See also Stoff, *Oil, War, and American Security*, pp. 70–72.

6. For background, see Aaron Dean Miller, *Search for Security* (Chapel Hill: University of North Carolina Press, 1980), pp. 54–57, 62–63, 74–77.

7. Andrew F. Carter to Frank Knox, January 17, 1944, cited in Stoff, *Oil, War, and American Security*, p. 72.

8. Herbert Feis, "Three International Episodes Seen from E.A.," 1946, as cited in ibid., p. 73.

9. Walter Ferris to Max Thornburg, "Project for a Study of U.S. Foreign Oil Policy," November 24, 1941, as cited in ibid., p. 67. See also discussion in Miller, *Search for Security*, p. 49.

10. U.S. Department of State, Inter-Divisional Petroleum Committee, *Foreign Petroleum Policy of the United States*, April 11, 1944, in *Foreign Relations of the United States 1944*, vol. 5, pp. 27–33.

11. For background, see Yergin, *The Prize*, pp. 204–5, 298–301; Painter, *Oil and the American Century*, pp. 4–8; Stoff, *Oil, War, and American Security*, pp. 18–21.

12. For background, see Miller, *Search for Security*, pp. 19–20; Stoff, *Oil, War, and American Security*, pp. 35–39.

13. Painter, *Oil and the American Century*, appendix, pp. 172, 175.

14. For background, see Stoff, *Oil, War, and American Security*, pp. 38–39, 57–61.

15. Gordon Merriam, "Draft Memorandum to President Truman," undated (August 1945), in *Foreign Relations of the United States 1945*, vol. 8, p. 45.

16. In this case, Ickes was referring to plans for the Petroleum Resources Corporation, the proposed government-owned oil company. See *Arabian Oil Hearings*, pp. 25240–41, as cited in Stoff, *Oil, War, and American Security*, p. 86. For discussion of this point, see ibid., pp. 62–88.

17. For background on this matter, see Stoff, *Oil, War, and American Security*, pp. 48–51, 58–59.

18. For background on these developments, see ibid., pp. 70–80.

19. William Bullitt to Franklin D. Roosevelt, June 1943, as cited in Miller, *Search for Security*, p. 76. Emphasis in the original.

20. Stoff, *Oil, War, and American Security*, pp. 78–79.

21. Ibid., pp. 80–87. On the postwar development of Aramco, see Yergin, *The Prize*, pp. 410–20.

22. Painter, *Oil and the American Century*, p. 1. For a similar analysis, see Stoff, *Oil, War, and American Security*, pp. 178–208.

23. Indeed, part of the point of the PRC proposal was to establish a rationale for such a role: while Congress and the public might balk at the idea of shedding blood in the defense of a private firm's oil holdings, it was argued, they would be far less wary if U.S. government assets were at risk—especially if they thought those assets were vital to national security. See also, Stoff, *Oil, War, and American Security*, pp. 86–87, 137.

24. For a description of this event, see Miller, *Search for Security*, pp. 128–31; Yergin, *The Prize*, pp. 403–5.

25. See Miller, *Search for Security*, pp. 128–31.

26. See Alexi Vassiliev, *The History of Saudi Arabia* (New York: New York University Press, 2000), pp. 326–27.

27. See, for example, the analysis in Vassiliev, ibid., pp. 326–27, and Miller, *Search for Security*, pp. 130–31.

28. For example, David E. Long, then a member of the State Department's policy planning staff, reported in 1985, "In the 1950s and 1960s, briefing books for senior U.S. official visitors to the kingdom regularly included lists of statements reaffirming the U.S. commitments to the security of Saudi Arabia in chronological order, usually beginning with President Roosevelt's pledge to King Abd al-Aziz aboard the USS *Quincy* in 1945." David E. Long, *The United States and Saudi Arabia* (Boulder, Colo.: Westview Press, 1985), p. 117.

29. Senate Committee on Armed Services (SASC), *Crisis in the Persian Gulf Region: U.S. Policy Options and Implications*, hearings, 101st Cong., 2d sess., 1990, p. 10.

30. Department of State to State-War-Navy Coordinating Committee, June 14, 1945, as cited in Palmer, *Guardians of the Gulf*, p. 28.

31. For background and discussion, see Painter, *Oil and the American Century*, pp. 153–71; Palmer, *Guardians of the Gulf*, pp. 40–51.

32. For background and discussion, see Thomas L. McNaugher, *Arms and Oil: U.S. Military Strategy in the Persian Gulf* (Washington, D.C.: Brookings Institution, 1985).

33. As cited in Walter Pincus, "Secret Presidential Pledges over the Years Erected U.S. Shield for Saudis," *Washington Post*, February 9, 1992. Significantly, the telegram indicates that this message was given personally to Crown Prince Saud by President Truman during a meeting in Washington in January 1947.

34. For background and discussion, see Palmer, *Guardians of the Gulf*, pp. 52–84.

35. For background on this episode, see ibid., pp. 29–35.

36. For additional background and analysis, see Painter, *Oil and the American Century*, pp. 112–13; Chester J. Patch Jr., *Arming the Free World: The Origins of*

the United States Military Assistance Program, 1945–1950 (Chapel Hill: University of North Carolina Press, 1991), pp. 102–4.

37. Truman, *Memoirs*, vol. 1, as cited in Painter, *Oil and the American Century*, p. 112.

38. Joint Chiefs of Staff memo to U.S. Department of State, October 12, 1946, in *Foreign Relations of the United States, 1946*, vol. 7, pp. 529–32.

39. For background on the events leading up to the Truman Doctrine speech, see Patch, *Arming the Free World*, pp. 88–129.

40. For background and discussion, see Irene L. Gendzier, *Notes from the Minefield: United States Intervention in Lebanon and the Middle East, 1945–1958* (Boulder, Colo.: Westview Press, 1999), pp. 26–32.

41. For background on these developments, see Long, *The United States and Saudi Arabia*, pp. 33–36.

42. For background, see ibid., pp. 35–50.

43. For background on the Suez crisis and Eisenhower's response, see Keith Kyle, *Suez* (New York: St. Martin's, 1991).

44. For background, see Gendzier, *Notes from the Minefield*, pp. 151–52, 158–59, 215–16; Palmer, *Guardians of the Gulf*, pp. 78–79; Long, *The United States and Saudi Arabia*, pp. 38–39, 111–13.

45. Long, *The United States and Saudi Arabia*, pp. 38–40, 51.

46. Ibid., pp. 51–53.

47. For background and discussion of this episode, see Gendzier, *Notes from the Minefield*, pp. 229–363.

48. See Long, *The United States and Saudi Arabia*, pp. 44–45.

49. Richard Nixon, *U.S. Foreign Policy in the 1970s*, report to the Congress, February 18, 1970 (Washington, D.C.: U.S. Government Printing Office, 1970), pp. 55–56.

50. For background on this review, see Michael T. Klare, *American Arms Supermarket* (Austin: University of Texas Press, 1985), pp. 112–15. See also James H. Noyes, *The Clouded Lens* (Stanford, Calif.: Hoover Institution Press, 1979), pp. 53–59.

51. House Committee on Foreign Affairs, Subcommittee on the Near East and South Asia, *New Perspectives on the Persian Gulf*, hearings, 93rd Cong., 1st sess., 1973, p. 39.

52. For background and discussion, see House Committee on International Relations (HCIR), *United States Arms Policies in the Persian Gulf and Red Sea Areas: Past, Present, and Future*, report of a staff survey mission to Ethiopia, Iran, and the Arabian Peninsula, 95th Cong., 1st sess., 1977, pp. 5–15.

53. International Institute for Strategic Studies (IISS), *The Military Balance, 1979–1980* (London: IISS, 1979), pp. 39, 44.

54. HCIR, *United States Arms Policies in the Persian Gulf and Red Sea Areas,* pp. 28–32.

55. Ibid., p. 11.

56. The shah, Mohammad Reza Pahlavi, had fled the country in 1953 when Iran's independent-minded prime minister, Mohammed Mossadegh, nationalized the Iraqi oil industry and instituted a range of other reforms. Fearful of the precedent set by Mossadegh, the United States orchestrated a coup d'état that resulted in his ouster and the return to power of the shah, who now assumed near-dictatorial powers. See Stephen Kinzer, *All the Shah's Men* (New York: Wiley, 2003).

57. For background and discussion, see Klare, *American Arms Supermarket,* pp. 115–21.

58. HCIR, *United States Arms Policies in the Persian Gulf and Red Sea Areas,* p. 20.

59. See Glenn Frankel, "U.S. Mulled Seizing Oil Fields in '73," *Washington Post,* January 1, 2004; Lizetta Alvarez, "Britain Says U.S. Planned to Seize Oil in '73 Crisis," *New York Times,* January 2, 2004.

60. See Yergin, *The Prize,* pp. 651–52.

61. For background and discussion of these events, see George Ball, "What Brought the Shah Down," *Washington Star,* March 14, 1979; Klare, *American Arms Supermarket,* pp. 121–26; Abdul Kasim Mansur (a pseudonym), "The Crisis in Iran," *Armed Forces Journal,* January 1979, pp. 28–29; Theodore H. Moran, "Iranian Defense Expenditures and the Social Crisis," *International Security* 3 (Winter 1978–79): 178–92.

62. See Palmer, *Guardians of the Gulf,* pp. 106–11.

63. "Western industrialized societies are largely dependent on the oil resources of the Middle East region, and a threat to access of that oil would constitute a grave threat to the vital national interest," Secretary of State Alexander Haig affirmed in March 1981. Such a threat "must be dealt with; and that does not exclude the use of force." From an interview in *Time,* March 5, 1981, as cited in Palmer, *Guardians of the Gulf,* p. 113.

64. See Hines, "History of U.S. Central Command."

65. For background on this episode, see Klare, *American Arms Supermarket,* pp. 150–54; Long, *The United States and Saudi Arabia,* pp. 64–66. See also John M. Goshko, "Reagan Will Press AWACS for Saudis Despite Opposition," *Washington Post,* April 22, 1981; John M. Goshko and Michael Getler, "The Flak over AWACS," *Washington Post,* April 26, 1981; Lee Lescaze, "Reagan Launches Blitz for Saudi AWACS," *Washington Post,* August 6, 1981.

66. See Michael T. Klare, "Subterranean Alliances: America's Global Proxy Network," *Journal of International Affairs* 43, no. 1 (Summer–Fall 1989): 99–106, 115; Bob Woodward, *Veil: The Secret Wars of the CIA, 1981–1987* (New York: Pocket Books, 1987), p. 582.

67. Ahmed Rashid, *Taliban* (New Haven: Yale University Press, 2001), pp. 128–33.

68. As quoted in the *New York Times,* October 2, 1981.

69. The letter to Fahd was never made public, but people who had seen the letter told Don Oberdorfer of the *Washington Post* that it "reaffirmed U.S. support for Saudi Arabia and for freedom of navigation in the Persian Gulf and indicated that the United States would back this up with military power if requested to do so." Oberdorfer, "President Vows Aid for Saudis," *Washington Post,* May 22, 1984.

70. For background and specifics, see Joyce Battle, editor, *Iraqgate: Saddam Hussein, U.S. Policy, and the Prelude to the Persian Gulf War* (Washington. D.C.: National Security Archive, 1995). See also Alan Friedman, *Spider's Web: The Secret History of How the White House Illegally Armed Iraq* (New York: Bantam, 1993).

71. Statement before the Subcommittee on Near Eastern and South Asian Affairs of the House Foreign Affairs Committee, September 26, 1983, as cited in Palmer, *Guardians of the Gulf,* p. 288.

72. For background on this episode, see ibid., pp. 128–49.

73. For background on the war and Iran's decision making, see Anthony H. Cordesman and Abraham R. Wagner, *The Lessons of Modern War,* vol. 2, *The Iran-Iraq War* (Boulder, Colo.: Westview Press, 1990).

74. On the White House reaction to the Iraqi invasion of Kuwait and the decision to respond with military force, see Bob Woodward, *The Commanders* (New York: Simon and Schuster, 1991), pp. 224–73. See also U.S. Department of Defense, *Conduct of the Persian Gulf War,* final report to Congress (Washington, D.C.: U.S. Government Printing Office, 1992), pp. 19–20, 32–33.

75. From the transcript of Bush's address in the *New York Times,* August 9, 1990.

76. SASC, *Crisis in the Persian Gulf Region,* p. 11.

77. Woodward, *The Commanders,* pp. 225–26, 230, 236–37.

78. See ibid., pp. 236–39, 247–54.

79. William A. Eddy to Secretary of State Byrnes, July 8, 1945, *in Foreign Relations of the United States 1945,* vol 8, p. 925.

80. Fahd's initial reluctance is recounted in Woodward, *The Commanders,* pp. 253–56, 258–61. See also Lawrence Freedman and Efraim Karsh, *The Gulf Conflict, 1990–1991* (Princeton: Princeton University Press, 1993), pp. 86–90.

81. The Cheney-Fahd meeting is recounted in Woodward, *The Commanders,* pp. 263–73. See also Freedman and Karsh, *The Gulf Conflict, 1990–1991,* pp. 92–93; Palmer, *Guardians of the Gulf,* p. 167.

82. Woodward, *The Commanders,* p. 273.

83. U.S. Department of Defense (DoD), *Conduct of the Persian Gulf Conflict,* an interim report to Congress (Washington, D.C.: DoD, 1991), chap. 3, pp. 1–2. See also Palmer, *Guardians of the Gulf,* p. 168.

84. See Rashid, *Taliban,* pp. 128–33. See also Phil Hirschkorn, Rohan Gunaratna, Ed Blanche, and Stefan Leader, " 'Blowback,' " *Jane's Intelligence Review,* August 2001, pp. 42–45.

85. Rashid, *Taliban,* p. 131.

86. Ibid., pp. 133–34.

87. For a detailed account of Operation Desert Storm, see Freedman and Karsh, *The Gulf Conflict, 1990–1991,* pp. 299–409; Palmer, *Guardians of the Gulf,* pp. 213–42.

88. For a discussion of this matter, see Freedman and Karsh, *The Gulf Conflict, 1990–1991,* pp. 411–17.

89. Testimony of General Anthony C. Zinni before the Senate Committee on Armed Services, Washington, D.C., February 29, 2000, from transcript prepared by the Federal News Service and accessed at http://web.lexis-nexis.com on June 6, 2000.

90. For background on the U.S. military presence in the Gulf at this time, see David C. Morrison, "Gathering Storm," *National Review,* August 20, 1994; Dana Priest and John Lancaster, "Slimming Elsewhere, U.S. Builds Muscle in Gulf," *Washington Post,* November 18, 1995.

91. U.S. Department of Defense, Security Cooperation Agency (SCA), *Foreign Military Sales, Foreign Military Construction Sales, and Military Assistance Facts, as of September 30, 1999* (Washington, D.C.: SCA, n.d.), pp. 3, 13. For background and discussion, see Morrison, "Gathering Storm."

92. Rashid, *Taliban,* pp. 133–35.

93. From bin Laden's 1998 fatwa calling for a jihad against the United States, as published by *Al-Quds Al-Arabic* in London on February 23, 1998, electronic document accessed at www.emergency.com on May 30, 2002.

94. In fairness to Professor Huntington, it should be noted that he added a question mark to the title of his essay. Samuel P. Huntington, "The Clash of Civilizations?" *Foreign Affairs* 72, no. 1 (Summer 1993): 22–49.

3: CHOOSING DEPENDENCY

1. "Remarks by the President While Touring Youth Entertainment Academy," Grace Episcopal Church, Plainfield, N.J., March 14, 2001, electronic document accessed at www.whitehouse.com on September 19, 2003.

2. "Remarks by the President in Photo Opportunity After Meeting with National Energy Policy Development Group," the White House, March 19, 2001, electronic document accessed at www.whitehouse.gov on March 5, 2003.

3. National Energy Policy Development Group (NEPDG), *National Energy Policy* (Washington, D.C.: White House, May 17, 2001), p. x. (Hereinafter cited as NEPDG, *NEP 2001.*)

4. For background on the issues facing the NEPDG, see Robert L. Bamberger, *Energy Policy: Setting the Stage for the Current Debate*, issue brief for Congress (Washington, D.C.: Library of Congress, Congressional Research Service, August 13, 2001).

5. On ties between Enron and the White House, see Kevin Phillips, "The Company Presidency," *Los Angeles Times*, February 10, 2002; Jim Yardley, "Letters Show Bush and Lay Shared Much," *New York Times*, February 16, 2002.

6. See Don Van Natta Jr. and Neela Banerjee, "Top G.O.P. Donors in Energy Industry Met Cheney Panel," *New York Times*, March 1, 2001; Van Natta and Banerjee, "Documents Show Energy Officials Met Only with Industry Leaders," *New York Times*, March 27, 2002. See also Jim VandeHei, "Democrats Take Aim at Bush Weak Spot: Administration's Ties to Energy Industry," *Wall Street Journal*, May 16, 2001.

7. As cited in Joseph Kahn, "Cheney Promotes Increasing Supply as Energy Policy," *New York Times*, May 1, 2001. See also Jim VandeHei, "Cheney Sees Little Role for Conservation in Energy Plan Aimed at Boosting Supply," *Wall Street Journal*, May 1, 2001.

8. Quoted in ibid. See also VandeHei, "Democrats Take Aim at Bush Weak Spot."

9. For discussion, see David E. Sanger, "Bush Shows His Green Side to Sell Agenda," *New York Times*, May 19, 2001.

10. From the transcript of Bush's speech at River Centre Convention Center, St. Paul, Minn., May 17, 2001, as published in the *New York Times*, May 18, 2001.

11. Ibid.

12. As quoted in Sanger, "Bush Shows His Green Side to Sell Agenda."

13. From remarks by Secretary of Energy Spencer Abraham at the National Press Club, Washington, D.C., July 25, 2001, electronic document accessed from the U.S. Department of Energy, www.energy.gov on August 17, 2001.

14. DoE/EIA, *AEO 2003*, p. 27.

15. NEPDG, *NEP 2001*, chap. 8, pp. 1, 3–4.

16. Ibid., figure 2, p. x.

17. For background and discussion, see Painter, *Oil and the American Century*, esp. pp. 1–10, 199–209.

18. NEPDG, *NEP 2001*, chap. 8, p. 6.

19. Ibid., chap. 8, p. 4.

20. DoE/EIA, *IEO 2003*, table D1, p. 235.

21. For discussion of this point, see Ebel, *The Geopolitics of Energy into the 21st Century*, vol. 1, pp. 21–22.

22. NEPDG, *NEP 2001*, chap. 8, p. 5.

23. Seven of the *NEP*'s 105 recommendations are directed to this matter, more than to almost every other issue. See ibid., chap. 8, pp. 16–17.

24. Ibid., chap. 8, pp. 6–7.

25. Ibid., chap. 8, pp. 9–10.

26. Ibid., chap. 8, pp. 12–14.

27. Ibid., chap. 8, p. 11.

28. Ibid., chap. 8, pp. 11–12.

29. From leaked sections of the document published in the *New York Times*, March 8, 1992. For background and discussion, see James Mann, *Rise of the Vulcans* (New York: Viking, 2004), pp. 209–15.

30. Quoted in Melissa Healy, "Global Role: Planning Document Outlines Strategy for Facing Challenges to American Influence," *Los Angeles Times*, March 9, 1992. See also Peter Grier, "Hot Debate over U.S. Strategic Role," *Christian Science Monitor*, March 16, 1992.

31. See Barton Gellman, "6-Year Plan Softens Earlier Tone on Allies," *Washington Post*, May 24, 1992.

32. Project for the New American Century (PNAC), *Rebuilding America's Defenses: Strategy, Forces and Resources for a New Century* (Washington, D.C.: PNAC, 2000). For more on the views of these figures, see Mann, *Rise of the Vulcans*.

33. Speech by Governor George W. Bush at the Citadel, Charleston, S.C., September 23, 1999, electronic document accessed at www.georgewbush.com on December 2, 1999.

34. Ibid.

35. Remarks by President George W. Bush at Norfolk Naval Air Station, Norfolk, Va., February 13, 2001, electronic document accessed at www.whitehouse.gov on February 15, 2001.

36. Jane Mayer, "Contract Sport," *New Yorker*, February 16 and 23, 2004, pp. 80–91.

37. Dick Cheney, prepared statement before the House Foreign Affairs Committee, Washington, D.C., March 19, 1991, p. 7.

38. U.S. Department of Defense, *Quadrennial Defense Review Report* (Washington, D.C.: DoD, September 30, 2001), pp. 4, 43.

39. From General Franks's prepared statement to the House Armed Services Committee during hearings on U.S. military posture, February 27, 2002, electronic document accessed at www.centcom.mil on September 15, 2003.

40. On the Malacca initiative, see John Burton and Shawn Donnan, "U.S. Plan to Guard Strait of Malacca Not Welcome," *Financial Times*, April 6, 2004. See also chapter 5 for further discussion of this point.

41. The author first argued this point in Klare, "Les Vrais Desseins de M. George Bush," *Le Monde Diplomatique*, November 2002, pp. 1, 16–17.

42. Spencer Abraham, comments before the House International Relations Committee, Washington, D.C., June 20, 2002, electronic document accessed at www.house.gov/international_relations/abra0620.htm on June 28, 2002.

4: TRAPPED IN THE GULF

1. BP, *BP Statistical Review of World Energy, 2003* (London: BP, 2003), p. 4.

2. For elaboration of this point and additional data, see Anthony H. Cordesman, *Middle Eastern Energy After the Iraq War: Current and Projected Trends* (Washington, D.C.: Center for Strategic and International Studies, January 30, 2004).

3. DoE/EIA, *IEO 2003*, table D1, p. 235.

4. Data provided by the International Energy Agency (IEA) and cited in Jeff Gerth, "Report Sees Vast Needs for Energy Capital," *New York Times*, November 5, 2003.

5. Data from DoE/EIA, *IEO 2003*, tables A4, D1, pp. 185, 235.

6. For elaboration of this point, see Cordesman, *Middle Eastern Energy After the Iraq War*, pp. 8–9.

7. Data from DoE/EIA, *IEO 2003*, tables A4, D1, pp. 185, 235.

8. Ibid.

9. BP, *BP Statistical Review of World Energy 2003*, p. 18; IEA, *World Energy Outlook 2002*, p. 107. Both sources refer to "Middle East" (rather than "Persian Gulf") exports and include Syria in their tallies; but because Syria accounts for such a tiny fraction of the region's total output, this is essentially analogous to Persian Gulf oil. For discussion, see Cordesman, *Middle Eastern Energy After the Iraq War*, pp. 11–15.

10. For discussion of this point, see Ebel, *The Geopolitics of Energy into the 21st Century*, vol. 1, pp. 19–26.

11. NEPDG, *NEP 2001*, chap. 8, p. 5.

12. U.S. Department of Energy, Energy Information Administration (DoE/EIA), *International Energy Outlook 2001* (Washington, D.C.: DoE/EIA, 2001), table D6, p. 240. (Hereinafter cited as DoE/EIA, *IEO 2001*.)

13. Ibid.

14. Data provided by the International Energy Agency and cited in Doris Leblond, "IEA: $16 Trillion in Energy Investment Needed by 2030," *Oil and Gas Journal*, November 10, 2003, p. 37.

15. DoE/EIA, *IEO 2001*, tables D1, D6, pp. 235, 240.

16. For background on Saudi Arabia's production capacity and the regime's stance on foreign investment in upstream activities, see DoE/EIA, "Saudi Arabia," country analysis brief, January 2002, electronic document accessed at www.eia.doe.gov on February 8, 2002. See also earlier editions of this document.

17. For background, see DoE/EIA, "Kuwait," March 2003, country analysis brief, electronic document accessed at www.eia.doe.gov/cabs/kuwait.html on October 9, 2003. See also earlier editions of this document.

18. For background, see DoE/EIA, "Qatar," November 2003, country analysis brief, electronic document accessed at www.eia.doe.gov/cabs/qatar.html on February 5, 2004; DoE/EIA, "United Arab Emirates," December 2002, country analysis brief, electronic document accessed at www.eia.doe.gov/cabs/uae.html on February 5, 2004.

19. For background, see DoE/EIA, "Iraq," country analysis brief, September 2001, electronic document accessed at www.eia.doe.gov on September 28, 2001; DoE/EIA, "Iran," country analysis brief, September 2000, electronic document accessed at www.eia.doe.gov/cabs/iran.html on September 25, 2000.

20. General Anthony C. Zinni, prepared testimony before the Senate Committee on Armed Services, February 29, 2000, electronic document accessed at www.lexis-nexis.com on June 6, 2000.

21. For background on the Iraqi threat in 2001–2, see Anthony H. Cordesman, *Iraq: A Dynamic Net Assessment* (Washington, D.C.: Center for Strategic and International Studies, July 12, 2002).

22. "Iran's ambitions to be the dominant regional power remain undiminished," Zinni testified in 2000. Of particular concern to Centcom was that "Iran has put in place a multi-layered framework composed of conventional and asymmetrical subsurface, surface, and airborne systems that can impact access to [Persian] Gulf shipping lanes." Zinni, prepared testimony before the Senate Committee on Armed Services, February 29, 2000.

23. The author first articulated this argument in Klare, "The Deadly Nexus: Oil, Terrorism, and America's National Security," *Current History,* December 2002, pp. 409–13.

24. Spencer Abraham, remarks before the Council on Foreign Relations Conference on U.S.-Saudi Relations, Washington, D.C., April 22, 2002, electronic document accessed at www.energy.gov/HQDocs/speeches/2002 on August 6, 2002.

25. See Thomas E. Ricks, "Briefing Depicting Saudis as Enemies; Ultimatum Urged to Pentagon Board," *Washington Post,* August 6, 2002. For Washington's reaction, see Ricks, "Views Aired in Briefing on Saudis Disavowed," *Washington Post,* August 7, 2002. For discussion of this episode, see Alfred B. Prados, *Saudi Arabia: Current Issues and U.S. Relations,* issue brief for Congress

(Washington, D.C.: Library of Congress, Congressional Research Service, April 3, 2003), p. 3.

26. Ralph Peters, "The Saudi Threat," *Wall Street Journal*, January 4, 2002.

27. See, for example, Simon Henderson, "Saudi Arabia: Friend or Foe?" *Wall Street Journal*, October 22, 2001; Henderson, "The Saudi Way," *Wall Street Journal*, August 12, 2002; William McGurn, "An 'Ally's' Contempt for America," *Wall Street Journal*, September 3, 2003. For discussion, see Carola Hoyos, "Public Harmony Hides U.S.-Saudi Tensions," *Financial Times*, August 8, 2002.

28. "State's Reeker Says U.S. Ties with Saudi Arabia are 'Excellent,' " U.S. Diplomatic Mission to Pakistan, August 8, 2002, electronic document accessed at usembassy.state.gov/islamabad on October 10, 2003.

29. "Bush, Rice Meet with Saudi Arabia's Ambassador to U.S.," U.S. Diplomatic Mission to Pakistan, August 28, 2002, electronic document accessed at usembassy.state.gov/islamabad on October 10, 2003.

30. See Elaine Sciolino, "Ally's Future: U.S. Pondering Saudis' Vulnerability," *New York Times*, November 4, 2001; Seymour M. Hersh, "King's Ransom," *New Yorker*, October 22, 2001, electronic document accessed at www.newyorker .com on October 14, 2003. Evidence of official concern is also apparent in a contemporaneous publication of the Institute for National Strategy Studies of the National Defense University, Joseph McMillan, *U.S.-Saudi Relations, Rebuilding the Strategic Consensus*, Strategic Forum no. 186, November 2001, electronic document accessed at www.ndu.edu/inss on March 11, 2003.

31. Sciolino, "Ally's Future."

32. For a summary of these concerns, see McMillan, *U.S.-Saudi Relations*. See also Anthony H. Cordesman, *Saudi Security and the War on Terrorism: Internal Security Operations, Internal Threats, and the Need for Change* (Washington, D.C.: Center for Strategic and International Studies, April 22, 2002); Michael Scott Doran, "The Saudi Paradox," *Foreign Affairs* 83, no. 1 (January–February 2004): 35–51.

33. World Resources Institute (WRI), *World Resources 2002–2004* (Washington, D.C.: WRI, 2003), table 12, p. 278. Data for 1950 from WRI, *World Resources 2000–2001* (Washington, D.C.: WRI, 2000), p. 296.

34. For data, background, and discussion see Sciolino, "Ally's Future"; Eric Rouleau, "Trouble in the Kingdom," *Foreign Affairs* 81, no. 4 (July–August 2002): 75–89; Neil MacFarquhar, "Leisure Class to Working Class in Saudi Arabia," *New York Times*, August 26, 2001; Daniel Pearl, "Rising Poverty Is New Concern for Saudis," *Wall Street Journal*, June 26, 2000. Per capita income figures have been adjusted for inflation.

35. See Cordesman, *Saudi Security and the War on Terrorism,* pp. 16–20. See also entry for Saudi Arabia in U.S. Department of State, *Country Reports on Human Rights Practices,* various editions.

36. Gwenn Okruhlik, "Networks of Dissent: Islamism and Reform in Saudi Arabia," *Current History,* January 2002, p. 22.

37. Rouleau, "Trouble in the Kingdom," p. 77. The hostility provoked by the presence of U.S. forces is also discussed in Elaine Sciolino and Eric Schmitt, "U.S. Rethinks Its Role in Saudi Arabia," *New York Times,* March 10, 2002, and McMillan, *U.S.-Saudi Relations.*

38. Rouleau, "Trouble in the Kingdom," pp. 75–76. For further discussion, see McMillan, *U.S.-Saudi Relations.*

39. See Hersh, "King's Ransom." See also Neil MacFarquhar, "Profligate Princes Stir Succession Questions and Threaten Reform," *New York Times,* November 18, 2001.

40. Okruhlik, "Networks of Dissent," pp. 24–25. For discussion of charges laid against the royal family by dissident clerics, see Cordesman, *Saudi Security and the War on Terrorism,* pp. 20–22; James M. Dorsey, "Saudi Cleric Aims Decree at Royal Family," *Wall Street Journal,* October 15, 2001; Hugh Pope, "The Islamic Thorn in the Side of Saudi Arabia's Monarch," *Wall Street Journal,* January 7, 2002.

41. For background and discussion, see Doran, "The Saudi Paradox"; Okruhlik, "Networks of Dissent," pp. 23–25; Cordesman, *Saudi Security and the War on Terrorism,* pp. 1–3, 24–25, 31–32. See also Neil MacFarquhar, "Anti-Western and Extremist Views Pervade Saudi Schools," *New York Times,* October 19, 2001; MacFarquhar, "Mixed Views of bin Laden in Homeland," *New York Times,* October 5, 2001; Neela Banerjee, "The High, Hidden Cost of Saudi Arabian Oil," *New York Times,* October 21, 2001.

42. Banerjee, "The High, Hidden Cost of Saudi Arabian Oil."

43. Hersh, "King's Ransom."

44. In particular, the secretive, multibillion-dollar Carlyle Group. Carlyle has an estimated $12.5 billion invested in U.S. aerospace, defense, health care, and telecommunications firms. Senior officers and advisers include former president Bush, former secretary of state Baker, and former secretary of defense Carlucci. Prominent Saudi investors include Prince Bandar and his father, Prince Sultan, the defense minister. For background, see Tim Shorrock, "Crony Capitalism Goes Global," *Nation,* April 1, 2002, pp. 11–16; Mark Fineman, "Arms Buildup Is a Boon to Firm Run by Big Guns," *Los Angeles Times,* January 10, 2002. For more on ties between senior Republicans and the Saudi royal family, see Craig Unger, *House of Bush, House of Saud* (New York: Scribner, 2004).

45. For a discussion of the views of radical Saudi dissidents, see Okruhlik, "Networks of Dissent," pp. 22–28; Rouleau, "Trouble in the Kingdom," pp. 75–89; MacFarquhar, "Anti-Western and Extremist Views Pervade Saudi Schools."

46. "Ever since the Gulf War [of 1991] ended, we've been working to try to minimize the amount of time and size of the footprint that U.S. forces have in Saudi Arabia," Andrew H. Card Jr., the White House chief of staff, said in January 2002. Cited in Sciolino and Schmitt, "U.S. Rethinks Its Role in Saudi Arabia."

47. As quoted in Eric Schmitt, "U.S. to Withdraw All Combat Units from Saudi Arabia," *New York Times*, April 30, 2003.

48. Don Van Natta Jr., "Last American Combat Troops Quit Saudi Arabia," *New York Times*, September 22, 2003.

49. See Sciolino and Schmitt, "U.S. Rethinks Its Role in Saudi Arabia"; Craig S. Smith, "A Tiny Gulf Kingdom Bets Its Stability on Support for U.S.," *New York Times*, October 24, 2002; Mark Fineman, "U.S., Qatar Sign Air Base Accord," *Los Angeles Times*, December 12, 2002; Michael R. Gordon and Eric Schmitt, "U.S. Will Move Air Operations to Qatar Base," *New York Times*, April 28, 2003.

50. For background and discussion, see Robert G. Kaiser and David B. Ottaway, "Shoring Up a Shaky Alliance," *Washington Post National Weekly Edition*, February 18–24, 2002.

51. In April 2002, for example, Bush met with Crown Prince Abdullah at his Crawford ranch and assured him of his commitment to a compromise solution. "He knows my position," Bush said of his conversation with Abdullah. "He also knows that I will work for peace, I will bring the parties along." Quoted in Elisabeth Bumiller, "Saudi Tells Bush U.S. Must Temper Backing of Israel," *New York Times*, April 26, 2002.

52. In June 2003, Bush flew to Jordan to preside at a ceremony in which Ariel Sharon and Mahmoud Abbas, then the Palestinian prime minister, agreed to abide by the tenets of the road map. See Elisabeth Bumiller, "Israel and Palestinians Say They Will Take First Steps in Quest for Mideast Peace," *New York Times*, June 5, 2003.

53. See James M. Dorsey, "Saudi Prince Tries to Reshape Kingdom," *Wall Street Journal*, February 5, 2002; "A Man with a Plan," *Economist*, March 23, 2002, p. 44; "Palpitations at the Kingdom's Heart," *Economist*, August 24, 2002, pp. 35–36. Regarding opposition to Abdullah's proposed reforms, see Doran, "The Saudi Paradox"; Hersh, "King's Ransom"; William Safire, "The Split in the Saudi Royal Family," *New York Times*, September 12, 2002.

54. For background and discussion, see Doran, "The Saudi Paradox"; Banerjee, "The High, Hidden Cost of Saudi Arabian Oil"; "Second Thoughts on Two Islamic States," *Economist*, November 10, 2001, pp. 19–20.

55. For background on this issue, see Prados, *Saudi Arabia: Current Issues and U.S. Relations*, pp. 1–3. See also: Glenn R. Simpson, "Saudi Arabia Has Yet to Join

U.S. Drive to Block Assets Tied to Terrorist Groups," *Wall Street Journal,* October 31, 2001; Douglas Jehl, "Saudis Balk at Request on Accounts," *New York Times,* November 27, 2001; Neil MacFarquhar, "New Challenge to Saudis: Royal Family's Resolve Against Terrorism Questioned," *New York Times,* May 14, 2003.

56. See James M. Dorsey, "Saudis Take Steps Against Terror Funding," *Wall Street Journal,* February 4, 2002; David E. Sanger, "Bush Officials Praise Saudis for Aiding Terror Fight," *New York Times,* November 27, 2002; David S. Cloud, "Saudi Arabia Aims to Halt Flow of Terror Funding," *Wall Street Journal,* December 4, 2002.

57. On the attacks, which occurred on May 12, 2003, see Steven R. Weisman, "Bush Condemns Saudi Blasts; 7 Americans Are Dead," *New York Times,* May 14, 2003. On the Saudi response, see Neil MacFarquhar, "A Bombing Shatters the Saudi Art of Denial," *New York Times,* May 18, 2003; Douglas Jehl, "Saudis Triple Bomb Inquiry; Vow Joint Antiterror Effort," *New York Times,* May 17, 2003; Michael Schroeder, "U.S., Saudis Set Effort to Fight Terror Financing," *Wall Street Journal,* August 26, 2003.

58. DoE/EIA, *IEO 2003,* table D1, p. 235. Includes sub-Saharan Africa only.

59. See John M. Biers, "Analysts Question Role of Saudi Oil Reserves," *Wall Street Journal,* February 3, 2004; Jeff Gerth, "Forecast of Rising Oil Demand Challenges Tired Saudi Fields," *New York Times,* February 24, 2004.

60. For background on the sanctions, see Kenneth Katzman, *Iraq: Oil-for-Food Program, International Sanctions, and Illicit Trade,* report for Congress (Washington, D.C.: Library of Congress, Congressional Research Service, April 2, 2003), pp. 1–5.

61. On the death of children, see ibid., p. 8.

62. See Karl Mueller and John Mueller, "Sanctions of Mass Destruction," *Foreign Affairs,* May–June 1999, pp. 43–47; Sidharth Puram, "U.S. Sanctions on Iraq: The Persistence of a Failed Policy," *Breakthroughs* (Massachusetts Institute of Technology, Center for International Studies), Spring 2002, pp. 37–44.

63. Colin Powell, testimony before the Senate Foreign Relations Committee, Washington, D.C., March 8, 2001, transcript provided by Federal News Service, electronic document accessed at www.lexis-nexus.com, October 30, 2003.

64. John F. Burns, "10 Years Later, Hussein Is Firmly in Control," *New York Times,* February 26, 2001.

65. On Iraq's illicit oil sales, see Katzman, *Iraq: Oil-for-Food Program, International Sanctions, and Illicit Trade,* pp. 12–15. It was later discovered that the Hussein regime received billions of dollars in bribes and kickbacks on transactions associated with the oil-for-food program, some of which reportedly was used to buy influence in key foreign countries. See Glenn R. Simpson,

"Hussein Allegedly Made Payoffs for Support in U.N.," *Wall Street Journal,* April 22, 2004.

66. See DoE/EIA, "Iraq," September 2001.

67. Colin Powell, testimony before the Senate Foreign Relations Committee, March 8, 2001.

68. "From the very beginning, there was a conviction [in the White House] that Saddam Hussein was a bad person and that he needed to go," former Treasury secretary Paul H. O'Neill commented in 2004. Quoted in *New York Times,* January 12, 2004. O'Neill's observation was seconded by Richard A. Clarke, the former White House counterterrorism chief, in his explosive account of this period, *Against All Enemies* (New York: Free Press, 2004). For further background on the White House debate over Iraq, see Seymour Hersh, "The Iraq Hawks," *New Yorker,* December 24, 2001, pp. 58–63; Bob Woodward, *Plan of Attack* (New York: Simon and Schuster, 2004).

69. See Michael Elliott and James Carney, "First Stop, Iraq," *Time,* March 31, 2003, electronic document accessed at www.time.com on March 31, 2003.

70. For background on this plan, see Katzman, *Iraq: Oil-for-Food Program, International Sanctions, and Illicit Trade,* pp. 9–10.

71. Colin Powell, testimony before the Senate Foreign Relations Committee, March 8, 2001.

72. Neil King Jr., "U.S. Fails to Win Speedy U.N. Vote on Iraq in Setback for Bush's Foreign Policy Aims," *Wall Street Journal,* June 1, 2001.

73. Ibid. See also Katzman, *Iraq: Oil-for-Food Program, International Sanctions, and Illicit Trade,* p. 10.

74. See Alfred B. Prados and Kenneth Katzman, *Iraq-U.S. Confrontation,* issue brief for Congress (Washington, D.C., Library of Congress, Congressional Research Service, February 20, 2002), p. 8.

75. See Elliott and Carney, "First Stop, Iraq." See also Bill Keller, "The World According to Powell," *New York Times Magazine,* November 25, 2001, electronic document accessed at www.nytimes.com on October 30, 2003.

76. For an overview of the White House discussions on war with Iraq, see Bob Woodward, *Bush at War* (New York: Simon and Schuster, 2002). See also Elliott and Carney, "First Stop, Iraq"; Hersh, "The Iraq Hawks"; Seymour Hersh, "The Debate Within," *New Yorker,* March 11, 2002, pp. 34–39.

77. For discussion, see Kenneth Katzman, *Iraq: U.S. Regime Change Efforts, the Iraqi Opposition, and Post-War Iraq,* issue brief for Congress (Washington, D.C.: Library of Congress, Congressional Research Service, March 17, 2003); Prados and Katzman, *Iraq-U.S. Confrontation*; Jeffrey Record, "The Bush Doctrine and the War with Iraq," *Parameters* (U.S. Army War College), Spring 2003, pp. 4–21.

78. A similar analysis was offered by Daniel Yergin, author of *The Prize*. "While this crisis is focused on overall security," he wrote in late 2002, "there is a clear energy dimension to the confrontation: the security and stability of the Persian Gulf region, from which flows almost a quarter of the world's oil." Yergin, "A Crude View of the Crisis in Iraq," *Washington Post*, December 6, 2002.

79. On Cheney's pivotal role, see James Harding, "The Figure in the White House Shadows Who Urged the President to War in Iraq," *Financial Times*, March 22/23, 2003.

80. From the transcript of Cheney's address in the *New York Times*, August 26, 2002.

81. For background, see David Rieff, "Blueprint for a Mess," *New York Times Magazine*, November 2, 2003, pp. 31–33.

82. As the *Wall Street Journal* put it, "A State Department-sponsored panel of expatriate Iraqi oil experts is recommending opening the country's vast fields to foreign investment should U.S. military action topple Saddam Hussein and provide political stability in the country." Chip Cummins, "Expatriate Iraqis Say Oil Fields Should Be Opened," *Wall Street Journal*, March 3, 2003. On the working group and its proceedings, see U.S. Department of State, Office of the Spokesman, "Future of Iraq, Oil and Energy Working Group Meeting," notice to the press, Washington, D.C., December 19, 2002, electronic document accessed at www.state.gov on December 19, 2001. See also Warren Vieth, "Report Favors Giving Iraqis, Not U.S., Control of Oil," *Los Angeles Times*, December 19, 2002; Vieth, "Privatization of Oil Suggested for Iraq," *Los Angeles Times*, February 21, 2003.

83. For background on Ahmed Chalabi, see Rieff, "Blueprint for a Mess," pp. 30–31. See also Robert Dreyfuss, "Tinker, Banker, NeoCon, Spy," *American Prospect*, November 18, 2002, electronic document accessed at www.prospect.org on November 14, 2002.

84. Quoted in Dan Morgan and David B. Ottaway, "In Iraq War Scenario, Oil Is Key," *Washington Post*, September 15, 2002.

85. See Dreyfuss, "Tinker, Banker, NeoCon, Spy"; Peter Beaumont and Faisal Islam, "Carve-Up of Oil Riches Begins," *Observer* (London), November 3, 2002.

86. As Lord Browne, BP's chief executive, put it, "We would like to make sure, if Iraq changes its regime, that there should be a level playing-field for the selection of oil companies to go in there." Quoted in Anthony Sampson, "Oilmen Don't Want Another Suez," *Observer* (London), December 22, 2002.

87. U.S. Department of Defense (DoD), "Background Briefing on Oil as a Weapon of Terror," DoD news briefing by senior defense official, Washington, D.C., January 24, 2003, electronic document accessed at www.defenselink.mil on January 27, 2003.

88. See Chip Cummins, "Oil Companies Aid Military Planners," *Wall Street Journal*, March 27, 2003.

89. See Chip Cummins and Thaddeus Herrick, "Halliburton Units Tapped to Oversee Oil Fields in Iraq," *Wall Street Journal*, March 7, 2003.

90. James Dao, "Navy Seals Easily Seize 2 Oil Sites," *New York Times*, March 22, 2003.

91. The Oil Ministry building "was virtually the only government building to emerge from the war unscathed and was heavily guarded by American troops." Sabrina Tavernise, "Iraqis Anxiously Await Decisions About the Operation and Control of the Oil Industry," *New York Times*, April 28, 2003.

92. Quoted in C. J. Chivers, "Oil Fields in a Sorry State, Stripped Even of the Toilets," *New York Times*, April 20, 2003. See also Neela Banerjee, "Widespread Looting Leaves Iraq's Oil Fields in Ruins," *New York Times*, June 10, 2003; Chip Cummins, "Chaos Stunts Revival of Iraqi Oil Flow," *Wall Street Journal*, April 14, 2003.

93. Neela Banerjee, "In an Oil-Rich Land, Power Shortages Defy Solution," *New York Times*, January 8, 2004.

94. See Neela Banerjee, "Bush Seeks $2.1 Billion More for Iraqi Oil Industry," *New York Times*, September 13, 2001; Chip Cummins, "For Iraq Oil, Signs of Progress Mix with a Glut of Problems," *Wall Street Journal*, August 11, 2003; Eric Watkins, "Iraqi Oil Exports Hampered by Pipeline Saboteurs," *Oil and Gas Journal*, August 25, 2003, p. 48; Watkins, "Iraq Oil Exports Face Delays after Pipeline Sabotage," *Oil and Gas Journal*, November 10, 2003, p. 33.

95. Richard W. Stevenson, "The Struggle for Iraq: U.S. Budget," *New York Times*, September 9, 2003; Banerjee, "Bush Seeks $2.1 Billion More for Iraqi Oil Industry."

96. Eric Watkins, "U.S. to Deploy Airborne Snipers to Protect Iraqi Pipelines," *Oil and Gas Journal*, October 13, 2003, p. 37.

97. Ibid.

98. Neela Banerjee, "An American and 2 Iraqis to Assume Key Oil Posts," *New York Times*, May 3, 2003; Banerjee, "3 Get Top Posts to Revive Iraqi Oil Flow," *New York Times*, May 4, 2003.

99. See "For Iraqi Oil, a U.S. Corporate Mold," *Wall Street Journal*, April 25, 2003.

100. See Cummins, "For Iraq Oil, Signs of Progress Mix with a Glut of Problems."

101. Chip Cummins, "Iraq Invites Foreign Oil-Firm Offers," *Wall Street Journal*, September 25, 2003. See also Neela Banerjee, "A Revival for Iraq's Oil Industry as Output Nears Prewar Levels," *New York Times*, March 1, 2004.

102. For background, see DoE/EIA, "Iraq," country analysis brief, August 2003, electronic document accessed at www.eia.doe.gov/cabs/iraq.html on November 8, 2003. See also Serge Schmemann, "Controlling Iraq's Oil Wouldn't Be Simple," *New York Times*, November 3, 2002; Yergin, "A Crude View of the Crisis in Iraq."

103. Chip Cummins, "State-Run Oil Company Is Being Weighed for Iraq," *Wall Street Journal,* January 7, 2004.

104. Quoted in Cummins, "Iraq Invites Foreign Oil-Firm Offers."

105. See DoE/EIA, "Iraq," August 2003.

106. For background and discussion, see Deutsche Bank, *Baghdad Bazaar: Big Oil in Iraq?* (London: Deutsche Bank, October 21, 2002).

107. Cummins, "State-Run Oil Company Is Being Weighed for Iraq."

108. See Deutsche Bank, *Baghdad Bazaar: Big Oil in Iraq?*

109. DoE/EIA, "Iraq," August 2003.

110. For an inventory of these plans, see International Energy Agency (IEA), *World Energy Outlook 2001* (Paris: IEA, 2001), p. 107.

111. See "Disputes Flare Anew over Iraqi E&D Contracts," *Oil and Gas Journal Online,* May 28, 2003, electronic document accessed at www.ogjonline.com on May 30, 2003; Andrew Jack, "Lukoil Restarts Work in Iraq Despite Contract Dispute," *Financial Times,* June 7/8, 2003.

112. For discussion, see Warren Vieth and Elizabeth Douglass, "Gauging Promise of Iraqi Oil," *Los Angeles Times,* March 12, 2003.

113. Quoted in Neela Banerjee, "Iraq Is Strategic Issue for Oil Giants, Too," *New York Times,* February 22, 2003. See also "Don't Mention the O-Word," *Economist,* September 14, 2002, pp. 25–27.

114. See Yochi J. Dreazen and Christopher Cooper, "Behind the Scenes, U.S. Tightens Grip on Iraq's Future," *Wall Street Journal,* May 13, 2004.

115. Quoted in Serge Schmemann, "Controlling Iraq's Oil Wouldn't Be Simple," *New York Times,* November 3, 2002.

116. For discussion of the administration's options with regard to Iran, see David S. Cloud, "U.S., Iran Stall on Road to Rapprochement," *Wall Street Journal,* May 12, 2003; Michael Dobbs, "Pressure Builds for President to Declare Strategy on Iran," *Washington Post,* June 14, 2003.

117. In Bush's words: "States like these, and their terrorist allies, constitute an axis of evil, arming to threaten the peace of the world. By seeking weapons of mass destruction, these regimes pose a grave and growing danger. They could provide these arms to terrorists, giving them the means to match their hatred. They could attack our allies or attempt to blackmail the United States. In any of these cases, the price of indifference would be catastrophic."

118. Quoted in Neil MacFarquhar, "Young Iranians Are Chafing Under Aging Clerics' Edicts," *New York Times,* June 16, 2003.

119. Quoted in David E. Sanger, "Bush Says U.S. Will Not Tolerate Building of Nuclear Arms by Iran," *New York Times,* June 19, 2003.

120. For background, see Kenneth Katzman, *Iran: Current Developments and U.S. Policy,* issue brief for Congress (Washington, D.C.: Library of Congress, Congressional Research Service, March 13, 2003), pp. 3–6.

121. Ibid., pp. 3–4.

122. See Steven R. Weisman, "U.S. Demands That Iran Turn Over Qaeda Agents and Join Saudi Inquiry," *New York Times,* May 26, 2003; Douglas Jehl, "U.S. Asks Iran to Crack Down on Qaeda Leaders Believed Active There," *New York Times,* May 22, 2003; David S. Cloud, "U.S. Officials to Discuss Iran as Tensions Rise," *Wall Street Journal,* May 27, 2003.

123. "Iran remains a serious concern because of its across-the-board pursuit of WMD and missile capabilities," CIA director George J. Tenet testified in February 2002. "Tehran may be able to indigenously produce enough fissile material for a nuclear weapon by late this decade." George J. Tenet, "Worldwide Threat—Converging Dangers in a Post-9/11 World," testimony before the Senate Select Committee on Intelligence, February 6, 2002, electronic document accessed at www.cia.gov on November 9, 2003. See also Katzman, *Iran: Current Developments and U.S. Policy,* June 3, 2003, pp. 3–4.

124. The installation at Natanz is expected to be used for the production of highly enriched uranium (HEU); that at Arak is intended for the manufacture of heavy water for a new reactor that will be capable of producing plutonium. Iranian officials subsequently admitted the existence of the two facilities but insisted that they were designed for peaceful uses only and were not tied to a secret weapons program. See Sharon Squassoni, *Iran's Nuclear Program: Recent Developments,* report for Congress (Washington, D.C.: Library of Congress, Congressional Research Service, August 15, 2003). See also David Albright and Corey Hinderstein, "Iran: Player or Rogue?" *Bulletin of the Atomic Scientists,* September–October 2003, electronic document accessed at www.thebulletin.org on September 8, 2003; Douglas Frantz, "Iran Closes In on Ability to Build a Nuclear Bomb," *Los Angeles Times,* August 4, 2003; Paul Kerr, "IAEA Report Highlights Inconsistencies in Iranian Statements About Its Nuclear Programs," *Arms Control Today,* September 2003, pp. 30–31.

125. Elaine Sciolino, "Iran Will Allow U.N. Inspections of Nuclear Sites," *New York Times,* October 22, 2003.

126. See DoE/EIA, "Iran," country analysis brief, April 2003, electronic document accessed at www.eia.doe.gov/ on April 16, 2003.

127. For background, see A. E. Alhajji, "Oil Production Capacity Rebuilding Experience Has Implications for Iraq," *Oil and Gas Journal,* November 3, 2003, pp. 20–21.

128. See Katzman, *Iran: Current Developments and U.S. Policy,* June 3, 2003, pp. 10–12; DoE/EIA, "Iran," April 2003.

129. See ibid., pp. 12–13.

130. DoE/EIA, "Persian Gulf Oil and Gas Exports Fact Sheet," country analysis brief, March 2002, electronic document accessed at www.eia.doe.gov/cabs/pgulf2.html on March 22, 2002.

131. The Gulf possesses approximately 68 percent of the world's known oil and gas reserves, "more than 40 percent of which pass through the Strait of Hormuz," General Tommy R. Franks of Centcom testified in 2001. "And so one of our responsibilities—in fact, one of our objectives—is to maintain access to these energy resources." Quoted in Jim Garamone, "Franks Lists Threats Facing Central Command," American Forces Information Service, April 13, 2001, electronic document accessed at www.defenselink.mil on April 25, 2001.

132. For description and analysis of Iran's missile strength and war-fighting capabilities, see Anthony H. Cordesman, "Iranian Military Capabilities and 'Dual Containment,' " in Gary C. Sick and Lawrence G. Potter, editors, *The Persian Gulf at the Millennium* (New York: St. Martin's Press, 1997), pp. 189–229.

133. For a parallel assessment, see "Next on the List?" *Economist*, June 14, 2003, pp. 22–24.

134. For the text of Zalmay Khalilzad's speech, see U.S. Department of State, "Senior U.S. Official Spells Out Dual-Track U.S. Policy Toward Iran," August 2, 2002, electronic document accessed at usinfo.state.gov/regional/nea/text/0802klzd.htm on November 9, 2003.

135. Ibid.

136. Ibid.

137. For background and discussion, see Dobbs, "Pressure Builds for President to Declare Strategy on Iran."

138. See Glenn Kessler, "U.S. Eyes Pressing Uprising in Iran," *Washington Post*, May 24, 2003. See also "Next on the List?"

139. Richard Bernstein, "Europeans Criticize Iran's Plan to Start Up Enrichment Plant," *New York Times*, April 1, 2004.

140. Marilyn Radler, "Worldwide Reserves Grow; Oil Production Climbs in 2003," *Oil and Gas Journal*, December 22, 2003, pp. 43–44, 46.

141. Quoted in John F. Burns, "General Vows to Intensify U.S. Response to Attackers," *New York Times*, November 12, 2003.

142. For discussion, see Patrick E. Tyler, "Attacks in Saudi Arabia Aim to Rattle a Dynasty," *New York Times*, November 10, 2003.

5: NO SAFE HAVENS

1. From the transcript of Bush's speech at River Centre Convention Center, St. Paul, Minn., May 17, 2001, as published in the *New York Times*, May 18, 2001.

2. NEPDG, *NEP 2001*, chap. 8, pp. 6–7.

3. Ibid., chap. 8, pp. 9–14.

4. BP, *Statistical Review of World Energy, 2003*, p. 4.

5. DoE/EIA, "Caspian Sea Region," country analysis brief, July 2002, electronic document accessed at www.eia.doe.gov/cabs/caspian.html on July 7, 2003.

6. BP, *Statistical Review of World Energy 2003*, p. 6.

7. This includes approximately 450,000 barrels per day (b/d) from Angola, 280,000 b/d from Colombia, 1.5 million b/d from Mexico, 875 b/d from Nigeria, and 1.5 million b/d from Venezuela. DoE/EIA, country analysis briefs for Angola (November 2002), Colombia (May 2002), Mexico (February 2003), Nigeria (January 2002), and Venezuela (April 2002), electronic documents accessed at www.eia.doe.gov on December 2, 2002, February 15, 2003, February 10, 2003, October 21, 2002, and April 4, 2002, respectively.

8. Tim Weiner, "Bush Due to Visit Mexico to Discuss Exporting Energy," *New York Times*, February 13, 2001. Secretary of State Colin Powell also discussed oil in meetings with leaders from Angola and Gabon during a September 2002 trip to Africa. See James Dao, "In West African Visits, Powell Seeks to Prime Oil Pumps," *New York Times*, September 6, 2002.

9. White House Press Office, "President Bush, President Putin Announce New Energy Dialogue," May 24, 2002, electronic document accessed at www.white house.gov on August 6, 2002.

10. "Remarks before the Kazakhstan International Oil and Gas Exposition," Almati, Kazakhstan, October 4, 2002, electronic document accessed at www.state.gov on July 1, 2002.

11. "Remarks by Energy Secretary Spencer Abraham, U.S.-Russia Commercial Energy Summit," Houston, Texas, October 1, 2002, electronic document accessed at www.energy.gov on December 7, 2003.

12. White House Press Office, "President Bush, President Putin Announce New Energy Dialogue."

13. "Remarks by Energy Secretary Spencer Abraham, U.S.-Russia Commercial Energy Summit."

14. "I am pleased that this important project is under way and that the United States has actively contributed to its development," the Bush letter said. "Remarks by Energy Secretary Spencer Abraham, BTC Pipeline Groundbreaking Ceremony," September 18, 2002, electronic document accessed at www.energy.gov on December 7, 2003.

15. Ibid.

16. For background, see U.S. Department of Energy, "Remarks by Energy Secretary Spencer Abraham at the Third U.S.-Africa Energy Ministerial Meeting, Casablanca, Morocco, June 4, 2002," electronic document accessed at www.energy.gov on August 6, 2002.

17. Statement of Spencer Abraham, secretary of energy, before the House Committee on International Relations, Washington, D.C., June 20, 2002, electronic document accessed at www.energy.gov on December 7, 2003.

18. "Remarks by Energy Secretary Spencer Abraham, U.S.-Russia Commercial Energy Summit."

19. For discussion, see DoE/EIA, "Russia," country analysis brief, November 2002, electronic document accessed at www.eia.doe.gov/cabs/russia.html on November 7, 2002.

20. DoE/EIA, *IEO 2003*, tables A4 and D4, pp. 185 and 238.

21. DoE/EIA, "Mexico," February 2003.

22. DoE/EIA, "Venezuela," country analysis brief, May 2003, electronic document accessed at www.eia.doe.gov/cabs/venez.html on December 7, 2003. For discussion of Venezuela's long-term oil potential, see also Juan Forero, "Venezuela's Lifeblood Ebbs Even as It Flows," *New York Times*, February 26, 2003; "Venezuela's Oil Woes Are Long Term," *Wall Street Journal*, February 14, 2003.

23. See, for example, Edward L. Morse and James Richard, "The Battle for Energy Dominance," *Foreign Affairs* 81, no. 2 (March–April 2002): 16–31; Sabrina Tavernise, "A New Western Focus on Russia, 'Where the Oil Is,'" *New York Times*, December 5, 2001.

24. DoE/EIA, "Russia," country analysis brief, September 2003, electronic document accessed at www.eia.doe.gov/cabs/russia.html on December 7, 2003. For further analysis, see Fiona Hill and Florence Fee, "Fueling the Future: The Prospects for Russian Oil and Gas," *Demokratizatsiya*, Summer 2002, from English text available at www.brook.edu, accessed on December 8, 2003. See also David G. Victor and Nadejda M. Victor, "Axis of Oil?" *Foreign Affairs* 82, no. 2 (March–April 2003): 47–61.

25. Jeff Gerth and Stephen Labaton, "Shell Withheld Data to Nigeria on Reserves," *New York Times*, March 19, 2004.

26. See DoE/EIA, "Angola," country analysis brief, November 2002, electronic document accessed www.eia.doe.gov/cabs/angola.html on December 8, 2003; DoE/EIA, "Nigeria," country analysis brief, March 2003, electronic document accessed www.eia.doe.gov/cabs/nigeria.html on December 7, 2003.

27. See Carola Hoyos, "Caspian Oilfield Development Faces Long Delay," *Financial Times*, August 20, 2003.

28. International Energy Agency (IEA), *World Energy Investment Outlook 2003* (Paris: IEA, 2003), from the executive summary (p. 33), electronic document accessed at www.iea.org on November 5, 2003. See also Doris Leblond, "IEA: $16 Trillion in Energy Investment Needed by 2030," *Oil and Gas Journal*, November 10, 2003, pp. 35–38.

29. On impediments to foreign investment in the Russian energy sector, see David G. Victor and Nadejda M. Victor, "Axis of Oil?" *Foreign Affairs* 82, no. 32 (March–April 2003): 47–61; Gregory L. White, Jeanne Whalen, Susan Warren, and Anita Raghavan, "For West's Oil Giants, Vast Fields in Russia Prove Hard to Tap," *Wall Street Journal*, April 27, 2004. See also DoE/EIA, "Russia," November 2002.

30. See Mark Berniker, "Khodorkovsky Arrest Clouds Russia Investment Outlook," *Oil and Gas Journal*, November 3, 2003, pp. 38–39.

31. This is especially true in Angola, Azerbaijan, and Kazakhstan. See DoE/EIA, country analysis briefs for Angola (November 2002), Azerbaijan (June 2002), and Kazakhstan (July 2002), electronic documents accessed at www.eia.doe.gov on December 2, 2002, June 27, 2002, and July 16, 2002, respectively.

32. See Tim Weiner, "Corruption and Waste Bleed Mexico's Oil Lifeline," *New York Times*, January 21, 2003.

33. Quoted in Tim Weiner, "As National Oil Giant Struggles, Mexico Agonizes over Opening It to Foreign Ventures," *New York Times*, February 17, 2002.

34. See Tim Weiner, "Mexican Energy Giant Lumbers into Hazy Future," *New York Times*, February 1, 2003.

35. Quoted in Weiner, "Corruption and Waste Bleed Mexico's Oil Lifeline."

36. See DoE/EIA, "Nigeria," March 2003.

37. Ibid.

38. According to BP, Nigerian output dropped from 2.2 million barrels per day in 2001 to 2.0 million barrels in 2002—a significant development when one considers that Nigeria is viewed in Washington as a promising source of additional oil. See BP, *Statistical Review of World Energy 2003*, p. 6.

39. Cited in Henri E. Cauvin, "I.M.F. Skewers Corruption in Angola," *New York Times*, November 30, 2002.

40. Glenn Kessler, "Powell Warns of Reduction in Aid to Oil-Rich Angola," *Washington Post*, September 6, 2002.

41. See Marc Lifsher, "Strike in Venezuela Paralyzes Oil Exports," *Wall Street Journal*, December 6, 2002; T. Christian Miller, "Venezuela Strike Pushes Nation Toward Crisis," *Los Angeles Times*, December 6, 2002.

42. See "Venezuela Oil Woes Are Long Term"; Forero, "Venezuela's Lifeblood Ebbs Even as It Flows"; Marc Lifsher, "Venezuela Vows to Restart State Oil Company," *Wall Street Journal*, December 26, 2002; Scott Wilson, "Venezuela's Oil Crisis Boils Down to Power," *Washington Post*, January 17, 2003.

43. Marc Lifsher, "Oil Production in Venezuela Declines," *Wall Street Journal*, August 22, 2003.

44. For background, see Jim Nichol, *Central Asia's New States: Political Developments and Implications for U.S. Interests*, issue brief for Congress (Washington, D.C.: Library of Congress, Congressional Research Service, May 18, 2001), pp. 7–8, 9–12.

45. See "Big Oil's Dirty Secrets," *Economist*, May 10, 2003, pp. 3–54; Steve LeVine, "U.S. Bribery Probe Looks at Mobil," *Wall Street Journal*, April 23, 2003; "Swiss Launch Bribery Probe in Kazakh Case," *Wall Street Journal*, May 8, 2003; Kara Scannell and Steve LeVine, "Ex-Mobil Executive Pleads Guilty on Tax Evasion," *Wall Street Journal*, June 13, 2003; Joshua Chaffin, "ChevronTexaco Quizzed as Kazakh Bribery Probe Widens," *Financial Times*, September 11, 2003.

46. See Joshua Chaffin, "Azerbaijan Leader Implicated in Bribery Probe," *Financial Times*, September 14, 2003; Chaffin, "Bribery Case Gives Hope to Azerbaijan Opposition," *Financial Times*, September 15, 2003.

47. In Angola, for example, some of the companies that invested in offshore production have curtailed their operations because of disappointing drilling results. DoE/EIA, "Angola," November 2002.

48. In July 2003, military forces staged a coup d'état in São Tomé e Principe and imposed military rule over the small island nation, which controls a potentially rich undersea oil zone in the Gulf of Guinea. The country's president, who was out of the country at the time, was later allowed to return and resume his position under a power-sharing agreement with his political rivals. See "Military Coup Ousts Government of São Tomé in West Africa," *New York Times*, July 17, 2003; "São Tomé Agreement Reinstates President; Mutineers Pardoned," *New York Times*, July 24, 2003.

49. On March 19, 2003, ChevronTexaco suspended its oil production in the Niger Delta region, declaring force majeure on its exports following violent clashes between the Ijaw and the Itsekiri ethnic groups that have threatened the operations of the oil companies in the area. Shell, the other company with facilities in the region, removed its nonessential staff the previous weekend, and both companies then moved to shut down their operations and evacuate all personnel on March 19, 2003. DoE/EIA, "Nigeria," March 2003. For background and discussion, see Norimitsu Onishi, "As Oil Riches Flow, Poor Village Cries Out," *New York Times*, December 22, 2002; Warren Vieth, "U.S. Quest for Oil in Africa Worries Analysts, Activists," *Los Angeles Times*, January 13, 2003.

50. See Somini Sengupta and Neela Banerjee, "Nigerian Strife, Little Noticed, Is Latest Threat to Flow of Oil," *New York Times*, March 22, 2003; "ChevronTexaco Shuts Facilities in Nigeria Delta," *New York Times*, March 24, 2003; Michael Peel, "Ethnic Violence Hits Nigerian Oil Output," *Financial Times*, September 30, 2003. On the April 2004 shootings, see "2 U.S. Oil Workers Are Killed in Nigeria," *New York Times*, April 25, 2004.

51. For background and discussion, see Marc W. Chernick, "Colombia's Fault Lines," *Current History,* February 1996, pp. 76–81.

52. See Serge F. Kovaleski, "Violent Attacks by Guerrilla Undermine Colombia's Oil Boom," *Washington Post,* July 27, 1997; "Rebel Factions in Colombia Kill 23 and Cut Oil Pipeline," *New York Times,* September 8, 1996; DoE/EIA, "Colombia," country analysis brief, May 2003, electronic document accessed at www.eia.doe.gov/cabs/colombia.html on December 10, 2003.

53. Juan Forero, "Venezuelan Leader Denounces U.S. and Mocks Bush," *New York Times,* March 1, 2004; Forero, "Chávez Condemns U.S., Citing Efforts to End His Rule," *New York Times,* March 11, 2004.

54. For background and discussion, see "A Caspian Gamble," *Economist,* Central Asia survey, February 7, 1998, pp. 1–20; Ruth Daniloff, "Waiting for the Oil Boom," *Smithsonian,* January 1998, pp. 25–35; Nichol, *Central Asia's New States,* pp. 9–10; Martha Brill Olcott, "The Caspian's False Promise," *Foreign Policy,* Summer 1998, pp. 95–113.

55. Olcott, "The Caspian's False Promise," p. 96.

56. Seth Mydans, "3rd Day of Violence Claims 23 Lives in Uzbekistan," *New York Times,* March 31, 2004; Mydans, "Explosion Reported in Uzbekistan, and Police Round Up Suspects," *New York Times* April 1, 2004; Seth Mydans, "After 4 Days of Violence, Uzbekistan Wonders Whom to Blame," *New York Times,* April 3, 2004; Seth Mydans, "Uzbeks' Anger at Rulers Boils Over," *New York Times,* April 8, 2004.

57. See Steven Lee Myers, "Death Toll Rises as Bombings Escalate in Chechnya's War," *New York Times,* August 3, 2003; Myers, "Russia's View of Chechnya Clashes with Reality," *New York Times,* October 10, 2002; Sabrina Tavernese, "Chechnya Is Caught in Grip of Russia's Antiterror Wrath," *New York Times,* November 12, 2003; Patrick E. Tyler, "Chechen Civilians Are Casualties of Random Acts of War," *New York Times,* February 10, 2002; Tyler, "Chechnya Caught in Unending Limbo of War and Peace," *New York Times,* October 22, 2000; Michael Wines, "Suicide Bombers Kill at Least 46 at Chechen Government Offices," *New York Times,* December 28, 2002.

58. For discussion, see Robert D. Kaplan, "Why Russia Risks All in Dagestan," *New York Times,* August 17, 1999.

59. For background and discussion, see Richard Giragosian, "A Focus on the South Caucasus," a paper delivered at the conference on "Pipelines and Fault Lines: The Geopolitics of Energy Security in Asia," Asia-Pacific Center for Security Studies, Honolulu, Hawaii, October 21–23, 2003. See also "Black Sea Mischief," *Economist,* July 17, 1999, p. 46; Seth Mydans, "Secessionists from Georgia Hold Talks with Russia," *New York Times,* December 2, 2003.

60. Nigeria has also clashed with Cameroon over possession of the contested Bakassi Peninsula, but the two countries have agreed to abide by a decision of

the International Court of Justice awarding the area to Cameroon. See DoE/EIA, "Nigeria," March 2003.

61. For discussion, see DoE/EIA, "Caspian Sea Region," July 2002, electronic document accessed at www.eia.doe.gov on July 23, 2002. See also Gut Chazan, "Caspian Summit Fails to Resolve Energy Claims," *Wall Street Journal,* April 25, 2002; Steve LeVine, "Hunt for Caspian Oil Stokes Border Feuds and Arcane Theories," *Wall Street Journal,* August 3, 2001.

62. "Iran Is Accused of Threatening Research Vessel in Caspian Sea," *New York Times,* July 25, 2001.

63. See Douglas Frantz, "Iran and Azerbaijan Argue Over Caspian's Riches," *New York Times,* August 30, 2001.

64. Hines, "History of U.S. Central Command."

65. For background, see Klare, *Resource Wars,* pp. 1–5, 81–108.

66. White House Press Office, "Visit of President Heydar Aliyev of Azerbaijan," statement by the press secretary, August 1, 1997, electronic document accessed at library.whitehouse.gov on March 2, 1998.

67. See White House, Office of the Press Secretary, "Joint Statement on U.S.-Kazakhstan Relations," November 18, 1997, electronic document accessed at library.whitehouse.gov on November 28, 1997; White House, Office of the Press Secretary, "Joint Statement on U.S.-Turkmenistan Relations," April 23, 1998, electronic document accessed at library.whitehouse.gov on April 23, 1998.

68. President Clinton himself campaigned for adoption of this plan by leaders of the three states involved, and was present in Istanbul in November 1999 when they signed a framework document making it possible. See Stephen Kinzer, "Caspian Lands Back a Pipeline Pushed by West," *New York Times,* November 19, 1999. For background, see "By-Passing Russia," *Economist,* April 17, 1999, pp. 55–56; Kinzer, "On Piping Out Caspian Oil, U.S. Insists the Cheaper, Shorter Way Isn't Better," *New York Times,* November 8, 1998.

69. U.S. Department of State (DoS), *Congressional Presentation for Foreign Operations,* fiscal year 2000 (Washington, D.C.: DoS, 1999), pp. 656–59.

70. U.S. Department of Defense, "Joint Press Conference with Georgian President Eduard Shevardnadze, Tbilisi, Georgia," U.S. Department of Defense press briefing, August 1, 1999, electronic document accessed at www.defense link.mil on December 12, 2003.

71. The ban on U.S. aid to Azerbaijan was incorporated in section 907 of the Freedom Support Act of 1992. For background and discussion, see Thomas W. Lippman, "Oil and Iran Help Bolster U.S.-Azerbaijani Relations," *Washington Post,* July 27, 1997.

72. U.S. Department of Defense, "U.S. and the Republic of Azerbaijan Sign WMD Counterproliferation Agreement," news release, October 6, 1999, electronic document accessed at www.defenselink.mil on November 18, 1999.

73. See Svante E. Cornell, "The Unruly Caucasus," *Current History*, October 1997, p. 343.

74. For background on the U.S. military relationship with Kazakhstan, see Lieutenant Colonel William Lahue, "Security Assistance in Kazakhstan: Building a Partnership for the Future," *DISAM Journal* (Defense Institute for Security Assistance Management), Fall 2002–Winter 2003, pp. 6–18.

75. Ibid. See also Linda D. Kozaryn, "U.S., Kazakhstan Increase Military Ties," American Forces Information Services news article, November 1997, electronic document accessed at www.defenselink.mil on December 12, 2003; U.S. Department of Defense, news briefing, November 17, 1997, electronic document accessed at www.defenselink.mil on December 12, 2003.

76. U.S. Department of Defense, "Exercise Central Asian Battalion '97," news release, Washington, D.C., August 28, 1997, electronic document accessed at www.defenselink.mil on September 3, 1997. See also R. Jeffrey Smith, "U.S. Leads Peacekeeping Drill in Kazakhstan," *Washington Post*, September 15, 1997; Smith, "U.S., Russian Paratroops Join in Central Asian Jump," *Washington Post*, September 16, 1997.

77. Quoted in Smith, "U.S., Russian Paratroops Join in Central Asian Jump."

78. Quoted in Smith, "U.S. Leads Peacekeeping Drill in Kazakhstan."

79. See "Soldiers from the 10th Mountain Division March Past the Reviewing Stand in Chirchik, Uzbekistan," news photo, September 1998, electronic document accessed at www.defenselink.mil on December 13, 2003; U.S. Central Command, "Airborne Units Jump into Kazakhstan Marking Start of CENTRASBAT 2000," news release, Almaty, Kazakhstan, September 10, 2000, electronic document accessed at www.centcom.mil on February 22, 2001.

80. See Steven Lee Myers, "A Modern Caspian Model for U.S. War Games," *New York Times*, March 15, 1999.

81. See Lynn Pascoe, "The U.S. Role in Central Asia," testimony before the Subcommittee on Central Asia and the South Caucasus of the Senate Committee on Foreign Relations, Washington, D.C., June 27, 2002, electronic document accessed at www.state.gov on July 1, 2002.

82. A. Elizabeth Jones, "U.S.-Central Asian Cooperation," testimony before the Subcommittee on Central Asia and the South Caucasus of the Senate Committee on Foreign Relations, Washington, D.C., December 13, 2001, electronic document accessed at www.state.gov on July 1, 2002.

83. See, for example, Jim Garamone, "Rumsfeld Meets with Leaders of Caucasus Nations," American Forces Information Service news article, December 15,

2001, electronic document accessed at www.defenselink.mil on February 27, 2003.

84. U.S. Department of State, *Congressional Budget Justification: Foreign Operations, Fiscal Year 2004*, February 2003, electronic document accessed at www.fas.org on February 27, 2003.

85. U.S. Department of State (DoS), *Congressional Budget Justification: Foreign Operations, Fiscal Year 2005* (Washington, D.C.: DoS, 2004), pp. 345, 363.

86. See transcript of a telephone press briefing with Colonel Robert Waltemeyer, commander of the Train and Equip program in Georgia, May 30, 2002, electronic document accessed at www.defenselink.mil on May 31, 2002.

87. "Azerbaijan, Georgia Address Security Threats to BTC Pipeline," *Oil and Gas Journal Online,* January 23, 2003, electronic document accessed at www.ogj.pennnet.com on January 24, 2003.

88. U.S. Department of Defense, "Secretary Rumsfeld Press Conference with Acting Georgian President Burdzhanadze," news briefing, December 5, 2003, electronic document accessed at www.defenselink.mil on December 8, 2003. See also Thom Shanker, "Rumsfeld Visits Georgia to Bind a Partnership with an Ally," *New York Times,* December 6, 2003.

89. U.S. Department of Defense, "Background Briefing En Route to Georgia," news briefing with "senior defense official," December 5, 2003, electronic document accessed at www.defenselink.mil on December 8, 2003.

90. U.S. Department of State, *Congressional Budget Justification: Foreign Operations, Fiscal Year 2004*, p. 323.

91. U.S. Department of State, *Congressional Budget Justification: Foreign Operations Fiscal Year 2005*, p. 371. Reference to base at Atyrau is from fiscal 2004 edition.

92. "Secretary Rumsfeld and Ambassador Jon Purnell Press Conference in Uzbekistan," February 25, 2004, and "Secretary Rumsfeld Joint Availability with Kazakh Minister of Defense," February 25, 2004, electronic documents accessed at www.defenselink.gov on March 26, 2004.

93. See Robert G. Kaiser, "U.S. Plants Footprint in Shaky Central Asia," *Washington Post,* August 27, 2002; Scott Peterson, "Terror War and Oil Expand U.S. Sphere of Influence," *Christian Science Monitor,* March 19, 2002; Kurt M. Campbell and Celeste Johnson Ward, "New Battle Stations?" *Foreign Affairs* 82, no. 5 (September–October 2003): 95–103; Greg Jaffe, "In Massive Shift, U.S. Is Planning to Cut Size of Military in Germany," *Wall Street Journal,* June 10, 2003; Vernon Loeb, "New Bases Reflect Shift in Military," *Washington Post,* June 8, 2003.

94. U.S. Department of State, *Congressional Budget Justification: Foreign Operations, Fiscal Year 2004*, pp. 348–49.

95. For background, see DoE/EIA, "Colombia," May 2003.

96. BP, *Statistical Review of World Energy 2003,* p. 6.

97. For background on the conflict in Colombia, see Rafael Pardo, "Colombia's Two-Front War," *Foreign Affairs* 79, no. 4 (July–August 2000): 64–73; Michael Shifter, "Colombia at War," *Current History,* March 1999, pp. 116–21; and Julia E. Sweig, "What Kind of War for Colombia?" *Foreign Affairs* 81, no. 5 (September–October 2002): 122–41.

98. For background and discussion, see K. Larry Storrs and Nina M. Serafino, *Andean Regional Initiative (ARI): FY2002 Supplemental and FY 2003 Assistance for Colombia and Neighbors,* report to Congress (Washington, D.C.: Library of Congress, Congressional Research Service, June 12, 2002). See also U.S. Department of State, *Congressional Budget Justification: Foreign Operations, Fiscal Year 2004,* pp. 455–57.

99. See Marc Grossman, "U.S. Policy Toward Colombia," testimony before the Subcommittee for Western Hemisphere Affairs of the Senate Committee on Foreign Relations, Washington, D.C., April 24, 2002, electronic document accessed at www.state.gov on July 1, 2002. See also Juan Forero, "Administration Shifts Focus on Colombia Aid," *New York Times,* February 6, 2002.

100. U.S. Department of State, *Congressional Budget Justification: Foreign Operations, Fiscal Year 2004,* pp. 456–57. See also Juan Forero, "New Role for U.S. in Colombia: Protecting a Vital Pipeline," *New York Times,* October 4, 2002; Scott Wilson, "U.S. Moves Closer to Colombia's War," *Washington Post,* February 6, 2003.

101. U.S. Department of State, *Congressional Budget Justification: Foreign Operations, Fiscal Year 2003,* February 2002, electronic document accessed at www.fas.org on March 3, 2003.

102. DoE/EIA, "Colombia," May 2003.

103. Linda Robinson, "Warrior Class: Why Special Forces Are America's Tool of Choice in Colombia and Around the Globe," *U.S. News and World Report,* February 10, 2003.

104. For discussion, see Forero, "New Role for U.S. in Colombia: Protecting a Vital Pipeline"; James Wilson, "U.S. Goes Deeper into Colombia Conflict," *Financial Times,* January 30, 2003.

105. Quoted in Juan Forero, "Administration Shifts Focus on Colombia Aid," *New York Times,* February 6, 2002.

106. See T. Christian Miller, "Blood Spills to Keep Oil Wealth Flowing," *Los Angeles Times,* September 15, 2002.

107. Storrs and Serafino, *Andean Regional Initiative,* p. 5.

108. See Eric Schmitt, "Pentagon Seeking New Access Pacts for African Bases," *New York Times,* July 5, 2003.

109. NEPDG, *NEP 2001,* chap. 8, p. 11.

110. See Mike Crawley, "With Mideast Uncertainty, U.S. Turns to Africa for Oil," *Christian Science Monitor,* May 23, 2002; James Dao, "In Quietly Courting Africa, White House Likes Dowry," *New York Times,* September 19, 2003.

111. See James Dao, "In West African Visits, Powell Seeks to Prime Oil Pumps," *New York Times,* September 6, 2002; Dao, "In Quietly Courting Africa, White House Likes Dowry"; Richard W. Stevenson, "New Threats and Opportunities Redefine U.S. Interests in Africa," *New York Times,* July 7, 2003.

112. Quoted in Crawley, "With Mideast Uncertainty, U.S. Turns to Africa for Oil."

113. U.S. Department of State, *Congressional Budget Justification: Foreign Operations, Fiscal Year 2004.*

114. For discussion, see Campbell and Ward, "New Battle Stations?"; Loeb, "New Bases Reflect Shift in Military"; Schmitt, "Pentagon Seeking New Access Pacts for African Bases."

115. See Antony Goldman and James Lamont, "Nigeria and Angola to Discuss U.S. Plan for Regional Military Base," *Financial Times,* October 4, 2001; "U.S. Naval Base to Protect Sao Tome Oil," BBC News World Edition, August 22, 2002, electronic document accessed at news.bbc/co.uk on March 6, 2003.

116. See Jaffe, "In Massive Shift, U.S. Is Planning to Cut Size of Military in Germany"; Schmitt, "Pentagon Seeking New Access Pacts for Africa Bases."

117. Quoted in Jaffe, "In Massive Shift, U.S. Is Planning to Cut Size of Military in Germany."

118. Quoted in Charles Cobb Jr., "Larger U.S. Troop Presence May Be Needed in Africa, Says NATO Commander," posted on allAfrica.com, May 2, 2003, electronic document accessed at www.allafrica.com on May 18, 2003.

6: GEOPOLITICS REBORN

1. Zbigniew Brzezinski, *The Grand Chessboard* (New York: Basic Books, 1997), p. 37.

2. House Committee on Interior and Insular Affairs, Subcommittee on Mines and Mining, *Nonfuel Minerals Policy Review,* hearings, 96th Cong., 2nd sess., 1980, pt. 3, p. 5.

3. For discussion, see Michael Klare, "Resource Wars," *Harper's,* January 1980, pp. 20–23.

4. Brzezinski, *The Grand Chessboard,* p. xiv.

5. For background and discussion, see Fiona Venn, *Oil Diplomacy in the Twentieth Century* (New York: St. Martin's Press, 1986), pp. 35–53.

6. For background and discussion, see ibid., pp. 54–82.

7. These events are recounted in Yergin, *The Prize*, pp. 305–27.

8. For background and discussion, see Venn, *Oil Diplomacy in the Twentieth Century*, pp. 84–87; Yergin, *The Prize*, pp. 332–39.

9. William Kristol and Robert Kagan, "National Interest and Global Responsibility," in Robert Kagan and William Kristol, editors, *Present Dangers: Crisis and Opportunity in American Foreign and Defense Policy* (San Francisco: Encounter Books, 2000), p. 12. The essays in this book provide a comprehensive expression of this point of view.

10. See, for example, the much-quoted report of the Project for the New American Century (PNAC), *Rebuilding America's Defenses*, cited in chapter 3, note 32.

11. Ebel, *The Geopolitics of Energy into the 21st Century*, vol. 1, p. 7.

12. Consider, for example, U.S. success in persuading Japan and other allies to provide funds and other support for Operation Desert Storm. For background and discussion, see Lawrence Freedman and Efraim Karsh, *The Gulf Conflict 1990–1991* (Princeton: Princeton University Press, 1993), pp. 110–27.

13. Eugene B. Rummer, "Russia," in *Strategic Challenges for the Bush Administration,* perspectives from the Institute for National Strategic Studies (Washington, D.C.: National Defense University Press, 2001), p. 37.

14. For background and discussion, see Stuart D. Goldman, *Russia,* issue brief for Congress (Washington, D.C.: Library of Congress, Congressional Research Service, January 8, 2003).

15. "Putin's first and overriding priority is to synchronize his domestic and foreign agendas, which inevitably means featuring economics," Robert Legvold of Columbia University observed in 2002. "More than any recent U.S. president, his preoccupations are at home." Robert Legvold, "U.S.-Russian Relations Ten Months After September 11," in Dick Clark, editor, *U.S.-Russian Relations: A New Framework* (Washington, D.C.: Aspen Institute, 2002), p. 7.

16. For discussion, see ibid., pp. 5–15. See also Goldman, "Russia," pp. 6–9.

17. See "Smiles All Around—Till the Next Time," *Economist,* October 12, 2002, pp. 46–47; Douglas Frantz, "Russians Send a Message to Georgians: Toe the Line," *New York Times,* December 21, 2000; Frantz, "Russia's Firm Hand on Heating Gas Worries Its Neighbors," *New York Times,* January 8, 2001; Steven Kinzer, "Defiant Satellite, Georgia Finds Paternalistic Russia's Orbit Inescapable," *New York Times,* May 3, 1998.

18. See DoE/EIA, "Russia," September 2003.

19. See Carola Hoyos and Sheila McNulty, "Russia's Position Gains as U.S. Hunts for Oil," *Financial Times,* September 24, 2003.

20. See Jim Nichol, *Central Asia's New States: Political Developments and Implications for U.S. Interests,* issue brief for Congress (Washington, D.C.: Library of

Congress, Congressional Research Service, April 1, 2003), p. 6; Hugh Pope, "Moscow Lures Back Central Asia," *Wall Street Journal*, May 22, 2000.

21. For background on these developments, see Klare, *Resource Wars*, pp. 81–108.

22. As quoted in Dan Morgan and David Ottaway, "Drilling for Influence in Russia's Back Yard," *Washington Post*, September 27, 1997.

23. Andrei Y. Urnov, "Russian and Caspian Energy Export Prospects," address given at the Central Asian–Caucasus Institute of the Johns Hopkins University School of Advanced International Studies (SAIS), Washington, D.C., May 17, 2000, electronic document accessed at www.cacianalyst.org on August 7, 2000.

24. Because the Caspian Sea itself is landlocked, energy exports from the area must travel by pipeline to distant markets or to ports with access to the open seas. This means that the states on whose territory the pipelines lie are in a position to collect tariffs on the transportation of energy and also to exercise a degree of control over its rate and direction of flow. This, in turn, has led to a competitive struggle between Russia, the United States, and local powers over the routing of major pipelines. For background on these struggles, see Klare, *Resource Wars*, pp. 88–104. See also Jan H. Kalicki, "Caspian Energy at the Crossroads," *Foreign Affairs* 80, no. 5 (September–October 2001): 120–34; DoE/EIA, "Caspian Sea Region," July 2002.

25. Quoted in Kinzer, "On Piping Out Caspian Oil, U.S. Insists the Cheaper, Shorter Way Isn't Better."

26. See, for example, Legvold, "U.S.-Russian Relations Ten Months After September 11"; Fiona Hill, "The United States and Russia in Central Asia: Uzbekistan, Tajikistan, Afghanistan, Pakistan, and Iran," in Clark, *U.S.-Russian Relations*, pp. 17–22.

27. "Russia remains inescapably a major power," Peter W. Rodman wrote in *Present Dangers*. "Possessing over 20,000 nuclear weapons and a veto on the UN Security Council, exerting influence in such vital regions as Europe, the Middle East, South Asia, and East Asia, and presiding over a vast economic and technological potential that only awaits a more coherent government policy to realize it, Russia will be a preoccupation of American foreign policy now and in the decades to come." Peter W. Rodman, "The Challenge of a Failing Power," in Kagan and Kristol, *Present Dangers*, pp. 75, 83. For a similar view, see Richard Pipes, "Is Russia Still an Enemy?" *Foreign Affairs* 76, no. 5 (September–October 1997): 65–78.

28. For background and discussion, see Jim Nichol, *Central Asia's New States: Political Developments and Implications for U.S. Interests*, issue brief for Congress (Washington, D.C.: Library of Congress, Congressional Research Service, April 1, 2003), pp. 4–5. See also: Sabrina Tavernise and Birgit Brauer, "Russia Becoming an Oil Ally," *New York Times*, October 19, 2001; Andrew Higgins,

"Putin Indicates Much of U.S. Relationship to Be Rewritten," *Wall Street Journal,* November 12, 2001.

29. For background on the twists and turns in the Bush administration's stance on Russia, see Goldman, "Russia," pp. 11–15; James Goldgeier and Michael McFaul, "George W. Bush and Russia," *Current History,* October 2002, pp. 313–24; Celeste A. Wallender, "U.S.-Russian Relations: Between Realism and Reality," *Current History,* October 2003, pp. 307–12.

30. For background and discussion, see Svante E. Cornell, "America in Eurasia: One Year After," *Current History,* October 2002, pp. 330–36; Eugene B. Rumer, "Flashman's Revenge: Central Asia After September 11," *Strategic Forum,* no. 195 (National Defense University, Institute for National Security Studies, December 2002); Patrick E. Tyler, "The Morning After Dawns on Moscow," *New York Times,* December 16, 2001.

31. See Steven Lee Myers, "Powell and Putin Say Iraq Rift Is Mended, and Then Disagree," *New York Times,* May 15, 2003; Erin E. Arvedlund, "As Prices Rise, Russia Alters Oil Politics Toward U.S.," *New York Times,* May 13, 2004.

32. For discussion, see Wallender, "U.S.-Russian Relations: Between Realism and Reality."

33. When arranging for the deployment of U.S. forces in Uzbekistan, American and Uzbek leaders issued a joint statement that tied this move to the protection of Uzbekistan in the event of a spillover of the fighting in Afghanistan. "We recognize the need to work closely together in the campaign against terrorism," the statement declared. "This includes the need to consult on an urgent basis about appropriate steps to address the situation in the event of a direct threat to the security or territorial integrity of the Republic of Uzbekistan." As cited in Michael R. Gordon and Steven Lee Myers, "Uzbekistan to Let U.S. Use Bases in Return for Promise of Security," *New York Times,* October 13, 2001.

34. See "The Yankees Are Coming," *Economist,* January 19, 2002, p. 37; Jean-Christophe Peuch, "Central Asia: U.S. Military Buildup Shifts Spheres of Influence," Radio Free Europe/Radio Liberty, Prague, January 11, 2002.

35. Quoted in Thom Shanker, "Russian Official Cautions U.S. on Use of Central Asian Bases," *New York Times,* October 10, 2003.

36. See Chip Cummins, "U.S. Plans to Send Military Advisers to Georgia Republic," *Wall Street Journal,* February 27, 2002.

37. See Guy Chazan, "Russia Bristles at Possible U.S.-Georgia Plan," *Wall Street Journal,* February 28, 2002.

38. As quoted in Patrick E. Tyler, "Moscow Fears G.I.'s Role Could Deepen Conflicts," *New York Times,* February 28, 2002.

39. See Patrick E. Tyler, "Russia's Leader Says He Supports American Military Aid for Georgia," *New York Times,* March 2, 2002.

40. See David Holley, "Russia Opens a New Base," *Los Angeles Times,* October 24, 2003; Steven Lee Myers, "Russia to Deploy Air Squadron in Kyrgyzstan, Where U.S. Has Base," *New York Times,* December 4, 2002.

41. On Tajikistan, see David Holley, "Russia to Beef Up Tajikistan Presence," *Los Angeles Times,* April 28, 2003. On Russia's naval presence in the Caspian, see "Russia Moots New Caspian Share-Out," BBC World Service, London, April 26, 2002, electronic document accessed at news.bbc.co.uk on April 29, 2002.

42. See "Smiles All Around—Till the Next Time"; Michael R. Gordon, "Russia to Cut Its Military Forces in Georgia," *New York Times,* November 24, 1999; Seth Mydans, "Georgia and Its Two Big Brothers," *New York Times,* November 28, 2003.

43. Yuriy Chernogayev, "Uzbeks Will Take Up Russian Guns to Rebuff Islamist Offensive," *Kommersant* (Moscow), March 2, 2001, from translation in Foreign Broadcast Information Service.

44. See Nichol, *Central Asia's New States,* pp. 5–6.

45. See Thom Shanker, "Rumsfeld Visits Georgia to Bind a Partnership with an Ally," *New York Times,* December 6, 2003.

46. "It's completely evident that there was external pressure, interference in internal affairs by certain countries," said Foreign Minister Ivanov in an obvious reference to the American role in ousting Shevardnadze. Quoted in Mydans, "Georgia and Its Two Big Brothers." See also Mydans, "Secessionists from Georgia Hold Talks with Russia."

47. See Mydans, "Georgia and Its Two Big Brothers."

48. See Kalicki, "Caspian Energy at the Crossroads."

49. See Nichol, *Central Asia's New States,* April 1, 2003, p. 6.

50. "Russia Agrees to Discuss Debt Relief for Iraq," *New York Times,* December 19, 2003.

51. For background and discussion, see Kenneth Katzman, *Iran: Arms and Weapons of Mass Destruction Suppliers,* report for Congress (Washington, D.C.: Library of Congress, Congressional Research Service, January 3, 2003).

52. Richard F. Grimmett, *Conventional Arms Transfers to Developing Nations, 1994–2001,* report for Congress (Washington, D.C.: Library of Congress, Congressional Research Service, 2002), p. 58.

53. Katzman, *Iran: Arms and Weapons of Mass Destruction Suppliers,* pp. 5–6.

54. For background, see ibid., pp. 11–13. See also Joseph Cirincione, *Deadly Arsenals* (Washington, D.C.: Carnegie Endowment for International Peace, 2002), pp. 257–62.

55. David E. Sanger, "Russia Won't End Accord with Iran to Build Reactor," *New York Times,* September 28, 2003.

56. Katzman, *Iran: Arms and Weapons of Mass Destruction Suppliers,* p. 9.

57. Ibid., pp. 9–11.

58. This appeared to be the situation in early 2004, as mounting Chinese purchases kept the price of oil high. See Simon Romero, "Demand in China, Weak Dollar Will Support High Oil Price," *New York Times,* January 2, 2004; Bhushan Bahree and Peter McKay, "Oil Prices Near $40 a Barrel, Casting Long Shadow," *Wall Street Journal,* May 4, 2004.

59. For background and discussion, see Philip Andrews-Speed, Xuanli Liao, and Roland Dannreuther, *The Strategic Implications of China's Energy Needs,* Adelphi Paper no. 346 (Oxford: Oxford University Press and International Institute of Strategic Studies, 2002); Erica Strecker Downs, *China's Quest for Energy Security* (Santa Monica, Calif.: RAND Corporation, 2000); Bates Gill and Matthew Oresman, *China's New Journey to the West* (Washington, D.C.: Center for International and Strategic Studies, 2003).

60. For background and discussion, see Andrews-Speed et al., *The Strategic Implications of China's Energy Needs,* pp. 53–57; Gill and Oresman, *China's New Journey to the West,* pp. 15–19.

61. For discussion, see Jason D. Ellis and Todd M. Koca, "China Rising: New Challenges to the U.S. Security Posture," *Strategic Forum,* no. 175, October 2000, Institute for National Strategic Studies, National Defense University, electronic document accessed at www.ndu.edu/inss on March 11, 2003. See also Gill and Oresman, *China's New Journey to the West,* pp. 2, 13–15.

62. Characteristic of this outlook are the views of Richard Bernstein and Ross H. Munro, the authors of *The Coming Conflict with China.* "Driven by nationalistic sentiment, a yearning to redeem the humiliations of the past, and the simple urge for international power, China is seeking to replace the United States as the dominant power in Asia," they wrote in 1997. Richard Bernstein and Ross H. Munro, "The Coming Conflict with America," *Foreign Affairs* 76, no. 2 (March–April 1997): 19. For an elaboration of this view, see Ross H. Munro, "China: The Challenge of a Rising Power," in Kagan and Kristol, *Present Dangers,* pp. 47–73.

63. For discussion, see Elizabeth Economy, "Changing Course on China," *Current History,* September 2003, pp. 243–49; David E. Sanger, "Bush's New Focus Requires a Shift in His China Policy," *New York Times,* October 18, 2001.

64. For background on China's long-term energy situation, see International Energy Agency (IEA), *China's Worldwide Quest for Energy Security* (Paris: IEA, 2000).

65. DoE/EIA, *IEO 2004,* tables A4, D1, pp. 167, 213.

66. For background and discussion, see IEA, *China's Worldwide Quest for Energy Security,* pp. 22–31; DoE/EIA, "China," country analysis brief, June 2003, electronic document accessed at www.eia.doe.gov/cabs/china.html on December 29, 2003.

67. DoE/EIA, *IEA 2004,* table A1, p. 163.

68. BP, *Statistical Review of World Energy 2002,* p. 38. Data are for 2001.

69. See "Cars in China: The Great Leap Forward," *Economist,* February 1, 2003, pp. 53–54; Jane Lanhee Lee, "China Senses Need for Cleaner Fuel," *Wall Street Journal,* December 11, 2003.

70. See "Cars in China," p. 53.

71. Michael B. McElroy and Chris P. Nielson, "Energy, Agriculture, and the Environment: Prospects for Sino-American Cooperation," in Ezra F. Vogel, editor, *Living with China* (New York: Norton and the American Assembly, 1997), p. 246.

72. See Peter Wonacott, Jeanne Whalen, and Bhushan Bahree, "China's Growing Thirst for Oil Remakes World Market," *Wall Street Journal,* December 3, 2003.

73. Quoted in Keith Bradsher, "China Struggles to Cut Reliance on Mideast Oil," *New York Times,* September 3, 2002.

74. For discussion, see Andrews-Speed et al., *The Strategic Implications of China's Energy Needs.*

75. Downs, *China's Quest for Energy Security,* pp. 31–32.

76. Ibid., pp. 25, 47.

77. Andrews-Speed et al., *The Strategic Implications of China's Energy Needs,* p. 69.

78. For background on Chinese decision making in the energy field, see ibid., pp. 45–69.

79. For background and discussion, see ibid., pp. 11–44. See also IEA, *China's Worldwide Quest for Energy Security,* pp. 45–69.

80. IEA, *China's Worldwide Quest for Energy Security,* pp. 11, 74.

81. For discussion, see "Drilling for the Party," *Economist,* May 24, 2003, pp. 65–66; IEA, *China's Worldwide Quest for Energy Security,* pp. 62–69.

82. Quoted in Peter Wonacott and Gregory L. White, "China Lines Up Oil Deals Far Afield," *Wall Street Journal,* December 19, 2003.

83. For an inventory of such projects under way in 2000, see Downs, *China's Quest for Energy Security,* pp. 21–23. On more recent arrangements, see "Drilling for the Party"; Wonacott and White, "China Lines Up Oil Deals Far Afield."

84. The term *strategic orientation* is derived from Andrews-Speed et al., *The Strategic Implications of China's Energy Needs,* p. 69.

85. Ibid., pp. 15–16, 21. See also DoE/EIA, "Kazakhstan," country analysis brief, July 2003, electronic document accessed at www.eia.doe.gov/cabs/kazak.html on December 30, 2003.

86. Quoted in Lutz Kleveman, *The New Great Game* (New York: Atlantic Monthly Press, 2003), p. 114.

87. For background and discussion, see Andrews-Speed et al., *The Strategic Implications of China's Energy Needs,* pp. 58–61.

88. Quoted in Eric Watkins, "China, Kazakhstan Sign Oil Pipeline Agreement," *Oil and Gas Journal Online,* June 3, 2003, electronic document accessed at www.ogj.pennet.com on June 5, 2003.

89. DoE, EIA, "Iran," country analysis brief, May 2002, electronic document accessed at www.eia.doe.gov/cabs/iran.html on May 31, 2002.

90. The Islamist government in Khartoum has been fighting a twenty-year war against largely Christian and animist separatists in the south, led principally by the Sudan People's Liberation Movement (SPLM) and its military arm, the Sudan People's Liberation Army (SPLA); hundreds of thousands of people are believed to have perished in this conflict. For background on the fighting and human rights situation in Sudan, see Human Rights Watch (HRW), *Sudan, Oil, and Human Rights* (New York and Washington, D.C.: HRW, 2003).

91. For background, see DoE/EIA, "Sudan," country analysis brief, January 2003, electronic document accessed at www.eia.doe.gov/cabs/sudan.html on January 1, 2004. See also HRW, *Sudan, Oil, and Human Rights,* pp. 123–30, 144–49, 160–66, 182–86, 607–21; IEA, *China's Worldwide Quest for Energy Security,* pp. 17–18, 23.

92. See Bradsher, "China Struggles to Cut Reliance on Mideast Oil"; Wonacott et al., "China's Growing Thirst for Oil Remakes the Global Market."

93. See Gill and Oresman, *China's New Journey to the West,* p. 20.

94. See David Stern, "Beijing and Kyrgyzstan Hold Anti-Terror Exercise," *Financial Times,* October 15, 2003.

95. For background and discussion, see Gill and Oresman, *China's New Journey to the West,* pp. 1–9, 19–20.

96. For background on the SCO, see ibid., pp. 5–9.

97. Ibid.

98. From the foreword to Gill and Oresman, *China's New Journey to the West,* p. vi.

99. This was reported in *Jane's Terrorism and Security Monitor* for July 2001. See "Shanghai Group 'a Military Alliance,'" *Straits Times* (Singapore), July 21, 2001, electronic document accessed at web.lexis-nexis.com on October 25, 2003.

100. For background and discussion, see Katzman, *Iran: Arms and Weapons of Mass Destruction Suppliers,* pp. 15–17.

101. Ibid., pp. 15–18.

102. International Institute for Strategic Studies (IISS), *The Military Balance, 1999–2000* (Oxford: Oxford University Press and IISS, 1999), pp. 275–76.

103. On scorched-earth operations near CNPC concessions, see HRW, *Sudan, Oil, and Human Rights,* pp. 168–71, 247–59; on the role of Chinese weapons in attacks on civilian communities, see pp. 478–86, 606–7.

104. On the CSS-2 sale, see Leonard S. Spector, *The Undeclared Bomb* (Cambridge, Mass.: Ballinger and the Carnegie Endowment for International Peace, 1988), p. 29.

105. See Wonacott et al., "China's Growing Thirst for Oil Remakes the Global Market."

106. Richard F. Grimmett, *Conventional Arms Transfers to Developing Nations, 1995–2002,* report for Congress (Washington, D.C.: Library of Congress, Congressional Research Service, 2003), table 2H, p. 59.

107. Frank J. Gaffney Jr., prepared remarks before the House International Relations Committee, Washington, D.C., June 20, 2002, electronic document accessed at www.house.gov/international_relations on June 28, 2002.

108. Gill and Oresman, *China's New Journey to the West,* p. 2.

109. U.S. Department of State, Bureau of Verification and Compliance, *World Military Expenditures and Arms Transfers, 1999–2000* (Washington, D.C.: Department of State, 2001), table 3, p. 157.

110. Craig S. Smith, "Putin Visits China in Hope of Strengthening a Strategic Axis," *New York Times,* July 18, 2000.

111. See James Brooke, "The Asian Battle for Russia's Oil and Gas," *New York Times,* January 3, 2004; Erin E. Arvedlund, "Russia to Run 2,500-Mile Oil Pipleine in East Asia," *New York Times,* April 21, 2004.

112. The Sino-Russian "strategic partnership" entails no significant economic dimensions and thus is considered of little real significance by those who view trade relations as vital. "The Chinese are the ultimate realists, and they know Russia is now a third-rate country economically, technologically, and politically," observed Michel Oksenberg of Stanford University following the July 2000 summit in Beijing. Quoted in Craig S. Smith, "Russia and China Unite in Criticism of U.S. Antimissile Plan," *New York Times,* July 19, 2000.

7: ESCAPING THE DILEMMA

1. Kenneth M. Pollack, "Securing the Gulf," *Foreign Affairs* 82, no. 4 (July–August 2003): 2.

2. This assumes that operations in the greater Gulf area consume about one-third of the total Department of Defense budget of about $450 billion per

year (includes supplemental spending for Iraq). See Eric Schmitt, "Senators Assail Request for Aid for the Military," *New York Times,* May 14, 2004.

3. Based on data in DoE/EIA, *AEO 2003,* table A11, p. 136

4. Pollack, "Securing the Gulf," pp. 7–8.

5. Ebel, *The Geopolitics of Energy into the 21st Century,* vol. 1, p. 30.

6. Banerjee, "In an Oil-Rich Land, Power Shortages Defy Solutions."

7. See Paula Dittrick, "Royal Dutch/Shell Lowers Proved Reserves Estimate 20%," *Oil and Gas Journal,* January 19, 2004, pp. 20–33; Gerth, "Forecast of Rising Oil Demand Challenges Tired Saudi Fields."

8. See, for example, Deffeyes, *Hubbert's Peak;* Goodstein, *Out of Gas;* and Heinberg, *The Party's Over.*

9. Spencer Abraham, remarks at the National Press Club, Washington, D.C., July 25, 2001, electronic document accessed at www.energy.gov on July 17, 2001.

10. Spencer Abraham, remarks at the National Petroleum Council, Washington, D.C., April 10, 2002, electronic document accessed at www.energy.gov on August 6, 2002.

11. Danny Hakim, "Now, Add God to the List of Enemies of the S.U.V.," *New York Times,* November 24, 2002.

12. Among the many owners of hybrid vehicles are a group of movie celebrities who drove them to the March 2004 Academy Awards ceremony in a procession organized by Global Green USA, including Robin Williams, Tim Robbins, Jack Black, Keisha Castle-Hughes, and Sting. See Patrick Goldstein, "Celebrities Drive Cultural Issues," *Chicago Tribune,* March 24, 2004.

13. For background and discussion, see John P. Holdren, "Searching for a National Energy Policy," *Issues in Science and Technology,* Spring 2001, pp. 43–50.

14. Based on consumption and cost projections supplied by the U.S. Department of Energy. See DoE/EIA, *AEO 2003,* table A11, p. 136.

15. Based on projections supplied by the U.S. Department of Energy. See DoE/EIA, *IEO 2003,* table A11, p. 192.

16. National Academy of Sciences, National Research Council, Committee on the Effectiveness and Impact of Corporate Average Fuel Economy (CAFE) Standards, *Effectivess and Impact of Corporate Average Fuel Economy (CAFE) Standards* (Washington, D.C.: National Academy Press, 2002), p. 13. (Hereinafter cited as NAS, *Effectiveness of CAFE Standards.*)

17. See ibid., pp. 31–55, for a summary of these studies; see also the bibliography on p. 55 for additional sources.

18. For background, data, and discussion, see ibid., pp. 13–30.

19. Ibid., pp. 19–20.

20. See "A Growing Thirst for Fuel," *New York Times,* August 11, 1997; Fara Warner, "U.S. Truck Sales Reach Major Milestone," *Wall Street Journal,* December 3, 1998; Danny Hakim, "Fuel Economy Hits 22-Year Low in 2002," *New York Times,* May 3, 2003.

21. For discussion of these methods, see NAS, *Effectiveness of CAFE Standards,* pp. 31–55. See also Norihiko Shirouzu and Jeffrey Ball, "Revolution Under the Hood," *Wall Street Journal,* May 12, 2004.

22. Holdren, "Searching for a National Energy Policy," p. 46.

23. For background and discussion, see Richard G. Lugar and R. James Woolsey, "The New Petroleum," *Foreign Affairs* 78, no. 1 (January–February 1999): 88–102.

24. See ibid., pp. 94–97. See also John J. Fialka, "After Long Debate, Corn May Soon Be in More Gas Tanks," *Wall Street Journal,* August 23, 2002.

25. For background on the propulsion system of hybrids, see NAS, *Effectiveness of CAFE Standards,* pp. 51–53.

26. See Danny Hakim, "The Hybrid Car Moves Beyond Curiosity Stage," *New York Times,* January 28, 2003; Hakim, "G.M. to Offer Hybrid Power in 5 Models by 2007," *New York Times,* December 24, 2002; Norihiko Shirouzu, "When Hybrid Cars Collide," *Wall Street Journal,* February 6, 2003.

27. See Jeffrey Ball, "Global Auto Makers Are Racing to Inject Diesel into Mainstream," *Wall Street Journal,* July 28, 2003.

28. For background and discussion, see NAS, *Effectiveness of CAFE Standards,* pp. 53–55; A. John Appleby, "The Electrochemical Engine for Vehicles," *Scientific American,* July 1999, pp. 74–79; Lawrence D. Burns, J. Byron McCormick, and Christopher E. Borroni-Bird, "Vehicle of Change," *Scientific American,* October 2002, pp. 64–73.

29. "Tonight I'm proposing $1.2 billion in research funding so that America can lead the world in developing clean, hydrogen-powered automobiles," Bush declared on January 28, 2003. "A single chemical reaction between hydrogen and oxygen generates energy, which can be used to power a car—producing only water, not exhaust fumes. With a new national commitment, our scientists and engineers will overcome obstacles to taking these cars from laboratory to showroom, so that the first car driven by a child born today could be powered by hydrogen, and pollution-free."

30. For discussion of these efforts, see Vijay V. Vaitheeswaran, *Power to the People* (New York: Farrar, Straus, Giroux, 2003); Christopher Flavin and Seth Dunn, "A New Energy Paradigm for the 21st Century," *Journal of International Affairs* 53, no. 1 (Fall 1999): 167–90; Amory Lovins and Chris Lotspeich, "Energy Surprises for the 21st Century," *Journal of International Affairs* 53, no. 1 (Fall 1999): 191–208.

31. For details, see the Apollo Alliance Web site at www.apolloalliance.org.

32. For information, consult the Rocky Mountain Institute Web site at www. rmi.org.

33. "Hydrogen is the most basic and ubiquitous element in the universe," says Jeremy Rifkin, a prominent advocate of its use. "It never runs out, and produces no harmful CO_2 emissions when burned." Accordingly, "[it] has the potential to end the world's reliance on petroleum." Rifkin, "Hydrogen: Empowering the People," *Nation,* December 23, 2002, p. 20. See also Rifkin, *The Hydrogen Economy* (New York: Penguin, 2003).

34. See, for example, Scott Miller, Bhushan Bahree, and Jeffrey Ball, "Europe Launches Hydrogen Initiative," *Wall Street Journal,* October 26, 2002.

35. See U.S. Department of Energy, "FreedomCAR and Fuel Initiative," electronic document accessed at www.eere.energy.gov/hydrogenfuel/ on January 14, 2004. See also U.S. Department of Energy(DoE), *Office of Fossil Energy—Hydrogen Program Plan* (Washington, D.C.: DoE, 2003).

36. John Tierney, "Hydrogen Vans and Pumps Head for Washington," *New York Times,* March 5, 2003.

37. Peter Hoffman, *Tomorrow's Energy* (Cambridge: MIT Press, 2001), pp. 99–140; Rifkin, *The Hydrogen Economy,* pp. 192–93.

39. See Jeffrey Ball, "Hydrogen Fuel May Be Clean But Getting It Here Looks Messy," *Wall Street Journal,* March 7, 2003; Dan Roberts, "Hydrogen: Clean, Safer than in the Past and Popular with Politicians. But Will It Be the Cheap Fuel of the Future?" *Financial Times,* May 13, 2003; Rifkin, *The Hydrogen Economy,* pp. 185–86.

39. For discussion and background, see Steve Fetter, "Energy 2050," *Bulletin of the Atomic Scientists,* July–August 2000, pp. 28–38; Bob Williams, "Peak-Oil, Global Warming Concerns Opening New Window of Opportunity for Alternative Energy Sources," *Oil and Gas Journal,* August 18, 2003, pp. 18–28.

40. For discussion, see Fetter, "Energy 2050."

41. For discussion and proposals for change, see Andres Duany, Elizabeth Plater-Zyberk, and Jeff Speck, *Suburban Nation: The Rise of Sprawl and the Decline of the American Dream* (New York: North Point Press / Farrar, Straus, Giroux, 2000); Jane Holz Kay, *Asphalt Nation: How the Automobile Took Over America and How We Can Take it Back* (Berkeley: University of California Press, 1997).

ACKNOWLEDGMENTS

Planning, researching, and writing *Blood and Oil* has been a task that has consumed much of my life over the past three years. I could never have completed this demanding endeavor without the help, support, and encouragement of numerous individuals. I hope, with these few words, to convey my immense gratitude for their valued assistance.

First, I would like to thank all those at Metropolitan Books and Henry Holt who contributed in some way to the success of this effort. Most especially I want to recognize my editor, Sara Bershtel, for her hard work on this project and her continuing faith in my ability to bring it to fruition. Thank you Sara for all of your assistance and support! Many thanks also to her estimable colleagues, especially assistant editor Shara Kay.

Many other individuals played an important role by helping with research, providing documents and information, or suggesting ways of framing certain points. I am especially thankful to David Mulcahey and Craig Seligman for their superb and thoughtful assistance in editing the manuscript. Many thanks also to Edward Connelly, Tom Engelhardt, Richard Giragosian, Lincoln Mayer, Emmet O'Hanlon, David Painter, Laura Reed, Daniel Volman, and Philip Yeager for their important contributions.

Invaluable assistance was also provided by Dr. L. Fred Ayvazian, who read the entire text carefully to identify possible errors or omissions.

While working on this project, I received a grant from the William H. Donner Foundation for travel and research assistance. This grant allowed me to collect data that would otherwise have been difficult to obtain, and so I am truly grateful for the foundation's support.

Finally, and most importantly, I wish to acknowledge the loving support of my partner, Andrea Ayvazian, and my son, Sasha Klare-Ayvazian, both of whom stood by and encouraged me throughout this long process. I appreciate and cherish your comradeship and forbearance!

INDEX

Page numbers in *italics* refer to maps and tables

251

ABOUT THE AUTHOR

MICHAEL T. KLARE is the Five College Professor of Program Peace and World Security Studies at Hampshire College in Amherst. Defense correspondent for the *Nation* and a contributing editor for *Current History,* he is the author of *Resource Wars, Rogue States and Nuclear Outlaws,* and *Low Intensity Warfare.* He lives in Northampton, Massachusetts.

THE AMERICAN EMPIRE PROJECT

In an era of unprecedented military strength, leaders of the United States, the global hyperpower, have increasingly embraced imperial ambitions. How did this significant shift in purpose and policy come about? And what lies down the road?

The American Empire Project is a response to the changes that have occurred in America's strategic thinking as well as in its military and economic posture. Empire, long considered an offense against America's democratic heritage, now threatens to define the relationship between our country and the rest of the world. The American Empire Project publishes books that question this development, examine the origins of U.S. imperial aspirations, analyze their ramifications at home and abroad, and discuss alternatives to this dangerous trend.

The project was conceived by Tom Engelhardt and Steve Fraser, editors who are themselves historians and writers. Published by Metropolitan Books, an imprint of Henry Holt and Company, its debut volumes were *Hegemony or Survival* by Noam Chomsky, *The Sorrows of Empire* by Chalmers Johnson, *How to Succeed at Globalization* by El Fisgón, and *Crusade* by James Carroll.

For more information about the American Empire Project and for a list of forthcoming titles, please visit www.americanempireproject.com.